LOST RECIPES
OF PROHIBITION
MATTHEW ROWLEY

LOST RECIPES OF PROHIBITION

Notes from a Bootlegger's Manual

MATTHEW ROWLEY

The Countryman Press
A division of W. W. Norton & Company
Independent Publishers Since 1923

Page xx: Library of Congress, Prints & Photographs Division, WWI Posters, LC-USZC4-7819; xxi: *Temperance: a monthly journal of the Church Temperance Society,* April 1918; xxii: raclro/iStockphoto.com; 4: Orange County (California) Archives; 9: Charles S. Warnock, *Giggle Water.* 1928. New York Club Cocktail; 11: A Holiday Liquor Map, *The Rhinelander Daily News.* December 19, 1929; 16: LeeTorrens/iStockphoto.com; 22, 163: Judge Jr., *Here's How.* 1927. Judge Publishing Company; 22 (stamp): raclro/iStockphoto.com; 31: fotomy/iStockphoto.com; 38: Library of Congress, Prints & Photographs Division, LC-DIG-ppmsc-05880; 40: Bartender at Schiek's Restaurant serving first beer the day after Prohibition was repealed. Minneapolis: Minnesota Historical Society; 92: Everett Historical/Shutterstock.com; 111: Library of Congress, Prints & Photographs Division, LC-USZ62-12143; 119: Robert N. Dennis, from collection of stereoscopic views. Union League Club, Philadelphia; 136: Library of Congress, Prints & Photographs Division, LC-DIG-ppmsca-25463; 196: Library of Congress Prints and Photographs Division Washington, LC-DIG-npcc-00979. All botanical illustrations: *Köhler's Medizinal-Pflanzen.* Photography of journal pages by John Schulz and Daniel Fishel (StudioSchulz). Book cover photograph by Sean Hemmerle.

Copyright © 2015 by Matthew Rowley

All rights reserved
Printed in the United States of America

Book layout and design: Nick Caruso Design

For information about permission to reproduce selections from this book, write to Permissions, W. W. Norton & Company, Inc., 500 Fifth Avenue, New York, NY 10110

For information about special discounts for bulk purchases, please contact W. W. Norton Special Sales at specialsales@wwnorton.com or 800-233-4830

The Countryman Press
www.countrymanpress.com
A division of W. W. Norton & Company
500 Fifth Avenue, New York, NY 10110
www.wwnorton.com

Library of Congress Cataloging-in-Publication Data

Rowley, Matthew B., author.
Lost recipes of Prohibition : notes from a bootlegger's manual / Matthew Rowley.
pages cm
Includes bibliographical references and index.
ISBN 978-1-58157-265-0 (hardcover)
1. Alcoholic beverages. 2. Drinking of alcoholic beverages—United States—History.
I. Lyon, Victor Alfred, 1876– Works. Selections. II. Title.
TP507.R69 2015
641.2'1—dc23

2015028179

1 2 3 4 5 6 7 8 9 0

For my father, Joseph Rowley,
whose kindness and humanity shaped me
in ways I'm still discovering.

...Graduate Medical School
and Hospital

EG. 2531

℞

100M 8-27 HJL.

TABLE OF CONTENTS

WEIGHTS AND MEASURES ADOPTED BY THE UNITED STATES PHARMACEUTICAL ASSOCIATION.

534

WEIGHTS.

POUND.		OUNCES.		DRACHMS.		SCRUPLES.		GRAINS.
℔1	=	12	=	96	=	288	=	5760
		℥1	=	8	=	24	=	480
				ʒ1	=	3	=	60
						℈1	=	gr. 20

NOTE.—42½ grains added to the Avoirdupois ounce will make it equal to the above ounce.

Preface IX

Introduction XIII

CHPT. 1 | Prohibition 1

CHPT. 2 | Compounding Spirits 21

CHPT. 3 | Gin, Whiskey, and Rum 53

CHPT. 4 | Brandy, Wine, and Cider 93

CHPT. 5 | Absinthe, Cordials, and Bitters 123

CHPT. 6 | Weights and Measures 191

Resources 208

Glossary 210

Bibliography 218

Endnotes 220

Index 222

Acknowledgments 233

Preface

"Here," Fritz said. He slid a little blue book toward me across a long folding table. "This is more your area than mine."

Before he retired and decamped for a beach life in Thailand, Frederick C. "Fritz" Blank was owner and chef of the Philadelphia restaurant Deux Cheminées. Now closed, "the Doo," as he sometimes called it, sat on the corner of Locust and Camac in two Frank Furness–designed homes. For decades, it was one of the city's benchmarks of genteel dining. Some patrons addressed him as Chef Blanc. Seemed about right, Frenchifying his name like that. After all, the names of dishes on the menu were heavily Gallic—*palourdes rôties aux arômates, quenelles de brochet à la Lyonnaise, ballotine de canard, sorbet au pamplemousse, pâté aux coings,* and more.

But all that was in the dining room. Downstairs at the restaurant, past a long hall hung with copper pots and pans, it was another matter. In the basement kitchen, the French veneer peeled away and he was Chef Blank, not Blanc. His family was not Parisian or Lyonnais; they hailed from Pennsauken, New Jersey—"East Philadelphia," he liked to joke—and, before that, from Württemberg in southern Germany. Staff meals downstairs were far more likely to be something from Germany, Austria, Hungary, or other parts of Mitteleuropa than from the French menu upstairs. There might be his grandmother's *Kartoffelsalat* (a bacon-laced potato salad), for instance, slices of the simmered bread dumpling known as *Serviettenknödel,* or a Czech sauerkraut soup garnished with smoked sausage and sour cream.

Our mutual obsession with books about food and drinks brought us together, although until I met Fritz around 1997 I had been self-conscious about the sheer number of books at home. As a museum curator—I'd earned degrees in anthropology as well as museum administration—I was acquisitive by inclination and training. What started as a handful of cookbooks to get me through cooking rudimentary meals in my first apartment during undergraduate years had metastasized into a library that spread over three floors of my home. Not just cookbooks, but all sorts of related volumes: barware catalogs, corporate histories of drinks firms, pamphlets, culinary postcards, technical manuals for making ice cream and bacon, culinary histories, and more. By the time I moved to south Philadelphia, the collection was some two thousand volumes—and growing.

Blank, though, owned five times that number. In comparison, his collection made

Rye Cost to make 1-gallon

Rye whiskey	2 pints		5.00
Alcohol (95)	2 pints	1.63	3.25
Water (distilled)	4 pints		.20
Cork		.04	.01
Labels	(2.00 cost bottle)	.68	.17
Bottles		.60	.15
	\$7.95 8.05		\$7.06

With essence only

	Alcohol	4 pints	3.25
	Essence	1 ounce	1.00
	Water dist	4 pints	.10
.04	Cork	\$5.67	.01
1.42 .68	Labels		.17
.60	Bottles		.15
			\$4.69

Gallon lots	Rye	6.73
" "	Essence	4.35

= + \$2.38

Crème de Menthe

Water 5 pints

Sugar 7 pounds = syrup

Syrup - 5 pints

Alcohol - 3 pints

mine seem, well, *pedestrian*. Completely reasonable, in fact. We both claimed that these were working libraries we used every day. He had an entire wall of boxes filled with menus from restaurants around the world, and stacks upon stacks of magazines about food and beverages stretching back to the 19th century. *He* was a madman. *Me?* I was merely touched. We became good friends and, over the course of the next several years, I spent thousands of hours in his library.

Although I'd handled literally tens of thousands of cookbooks, bartenders' guides, manuals on livestock, butchery, and related material over my career as a collector, the format, color, and size of this little blue book was unfamiliar. Something unusual, then, something rare. I glanced at Fritz sitting nearby, but he looked away, pulling a folder from one of his research piles. I turned the book over in my hands. Gold letters glittered as light hit its spine. I frowned at the name they spelled and turned back to face him. "Who is Viereck?"

"I have no idea." He had already pulled his glasses down from their perch on his boxy little chef's hat and was making a show of busying himself with the folder's contents. "Look inside."

The name bothered me. George Sylvester Viereck. An author, obviously, but . . . something else. A friend of H. P. Lovecraft, maybe? One of his lesser-known colleagues? I did have a sizable collection of Lovecraft material at home. There was something to that, but when I cracked opened the book and began running my eyes and fingertips over the pages, any thoughts of weird fiction writers drained away. The wear on its cover, the brittle and slightly tanned paper, those vanilla smells of slow decomposition, and the archaic handwriting all suggested the thing was older than either of us at the table. The book's age, however, might have been one of the few true things about it. The entire thing, from cover to cover, was a deception.

Despite the spine's promise of Viereck's writing, there were no printed pages at all. Instead: hundreds of handwritten notes about, and formulas for, booze. Recipes for gin and other juniper spirits cropped up again and again; so did a dozen or so for absinthe. Cordials. Whiskeys, both real and artificial. Brandies. Not brandies for connoisseurs, but there they were along with notes on how alcohol reacts under certain conditions and how Cognac might be colored with oak extract and adjusted with syrups to get ready for market. Loose slips of paper tucked in its pages tied it to Prohibition-era New York; here was a prescription form from a Manhattan hospital, there a business card from Harlem. Flipping between the pages, I realized most of the recipes were in English, but dozens were in German, a language I hadn't spoken since I was an adolescent. There was *Kümmel, Doppel Kümmel,* and *Eiskümmel.* Latin, too, crept in as later entries veered into pharmaceutical preparations. Lotion for head lice. Salves for chilblains and cures for freckles. I looked up at Fritz. "Freckles need cures?"

He smiled and waved away my question with an avuncular shoo. "It's yours. Have it."

And so that little blue book came to me, its temporary custodian. One day it will end up with someone else, maybe in a library or museum. But first, I'm sharing it with you. I hope you enjoy it as much as I have.

s

in impalpable
ster 1-dram
ate. Apply
ne in thickness
strips of
r 5-days
tion will
ays leave
ly a very

sh

times day

℥ ss
ʒ ii
℥ ss
ʒ i
℥ vi

ful water
d p.c.

Removal of Tattoo Marks

Salicylic acid massed with glycerin to consistence of dough. This is applied over the marks with a compress and strips of adhesive plaster and allowed to remain in contact for a week. After the first dressing the epidermis over the marks is removed and a fresh application of the salicylic paste is applied. Usually it is said the second application removes the marks, but sometimes it is necessary to make a third.

Tattooing in a strong solution of tannin and rubbing a silver nitrate pencil over the spot until it is blackened by the formation of silver tannate.

Marks are tattooed with solution of zinc chloride 30 in water 40. A slight crust forms after these applications the spontaneous removal of which after 2 weeks is followed by a pink cicatrix which gradually becomes of normal color

Tool Etching

Salt one ounce
Copper Sulfate two ounces
Vinegar one quart

Spread thin layer of soap on surface to be etched. With sharp stick cut letters in soap exposing metal drip solution into cuts sufficient to start action on metal. Leave on until full etch complete & wipe with cloth

Introduction

Since I was a toddler, I have plished and plashed in pools and puddles of illicit liquor. Oh, it's not my family's fault particularly. All things considered, I imagine my mother would prefer not to have introduced me to distilling before kindergarten. We're not a moonshining or bootlegging family, mind you, but it was she who brought me to my first moonshine still in 1971 when she toted me along on a hunt for antiques in the wooded and remote New Jersey Pine Barrens. These trips—to estate sales, yard sales, antique shops, wherever old and neglected treasures might have lurked—were the bane of my childhood existence and left me numb with boredom. On this one, she was admiring the enormous copper "water heater" sequestered in the basement of an abandoned and dilapidated old house when a stranger with a shotgun appeared at the top of the steps. The rough-looking fellow didn't point the gun at us, but did suggest that we move along. Mom's bold, not foolhardy; we moseyed. That night, she described the big copper rig to my father. "It's a wonder," he said, shaking his head, "you two are still alive." Of course, that was no water heater, but quite literally an underground distillery.

Once old enough to read, I plunked down in front of my parents' fireplace with the Foxfire books about Appalachian folkways, poring over descriptions of backwoods stills and wildcat whiskey. While my peers wanted to grow up to play football or fight fires, I yearned to explore hidden hollers and secret caves where scofflaw distillers tried to evade meddlesome revenuers. My version of cops and robbers, I suppose.

Eventually I did get to explore those secret and hidden places: the woods, warehouses, basements, and garages where unlicensed distillers made their homemade hooch. In fact, I have spent more than half my life researching clandestine booze and those who make it. There have been death threats and more shotguns, sure, but those are rare. Overwhelmingly, the men and women who have shared with me their liquor, their time, and their trust since my college days have treated me as a peer and, here and there, a friend. A few years back, I turned some of their stories and recipes into a book called *Moonshine!* People seem to like it.

That moonshine reputation is how this secret formulary ended up in my hands. When Chef Blank gave me the notebook, he knew that a book about suspect alcohol would give me more joy than it would him. He was right. I suspect that the old chef, who died in

2014, also knew that the old museum curator wouldn't keep it to himself, but share it. Once again, he was right.

What Is This?

Physically, the book Blank had given me is a duodecimo (5" x 7.75") with a dark blue hard cover. It is old but not ancient. In faded gold typeface, the spine reads *The Works of George Sylvester Viereck*: under that *The Candle and the Flame*. Inside, though, it's something else. Once I began thumbing through it, I realized that the notebook was a compounder's formulary, a collection of recipes for making alcoholic beverages, disguised as a rather dreary book of poetry from 1912. Although it's rare to find handwritten formularies, they do surface now and then. The more I pored over it, though, the more I wondered who would have made this one—and why.

Before someone filled them with handwriting, the book's pages had been blank. It was possibly a salesman's dummy or a printer's mock-up. Some pages have been cut out and a few remain blank, but the others are jammed with recipes (in English, German, and occasional Latin) for spirits, cordials, oils, bitters, tinctures, and notes on alcohol production and analysis. Several pages detail treatments for freckles, coughs, and chilblains; abortifacients; fly paper; "lotion for children's heads"; label glue; tattoo removal; "non poisonous straw hat cleaner"; the sort of preparations one would expect from a Prohibition-era pharmacy. In fact, several bits of ephemera tucked in the pages date the book to 1920s and early '30s New York.

Was it someone's attempt to cram for Prohibition? A bootlegger's recipe book? A pharmacist's collection of profitable recipes? After all, the formulas are disorganized, but they aren't random; of the tens of thousands of such booze recipes floating around a century ago, the compiler selected many with supposed health-giving properties. And what was the connection to Viereck? After my years of moonshine fieldwork, many methods and ingredients were familiar. As I flipped through, some recipes were as well. Stomach bitters "equal to Hostetter's for one quarter cost," for instance, used specific phrasing I'd seen elsewhere. Despite penciled adjustments here and there, further research revealed that almost none of these alcohol formulas were original, but were instead culled from English and German language druggists' handbooks, journal articles, farming books, distillers' treatises, and cordial-makers' manuals dating back to the middle of the 19th century—earlier than Prohibition, earlier even than Bram Stoker's *Dracula*.

How It's Organized

The original notebook is neatly penned but disorganized, the formulas, notes, and recipes haphazard. Some recipes show up repeatedly. Others are broken into parts scattered over multiple pages. Here and there, clusters of similar wording and format suggest a common source. It includes several iterations of beading oil, also known as The Doctor, an ancient cheat of unscrupulous 18th-century rum merchants and 1920s moonshiners alike. Rather than present annotations of every single page—believe me, as an historian, the temptation is strong—I've rearranged the entries and grouped them in broad categories. Whether they are real or faked, most of the whiskeys, for instance, are lumped together here rather than scattered higgledy-piggledy as in the original. Same with the wines, cordials, rums, and so forth. Repeats are mostly omitted. Mostly.

Each section about spirits or cordials in this book has descriptions of relevant ingredients or techniques. It also includes recipes. Some are transcribed directly from the notebook, some scaled down or adapted for modern ingredients. Others still are riffs on the handwritten recipes or use their ingredients in contemporary mixed drinks and cordials.

But before we dive into recipes, we'll take a look at Prohibition in America, see where formularies such as this fit into the world of drinks, and review some of the gear and techniques for making at least some of the recipes from that old handwritten notebook.

Doctor Lyon Has a Secret

Despite worn corners and minor tears, the old blue notebook has stood up well since Prohibition. Over time, acids have turned its pages tan and brittle. A tear mars the spine, but there are no spills or stains inside, no smudging, and the ink remains dark. Loose sheets from prescription pads, newspaper clippings, pages from other books, an urgent note signed "Lucy," and various notes give the book a New York City provenance. The

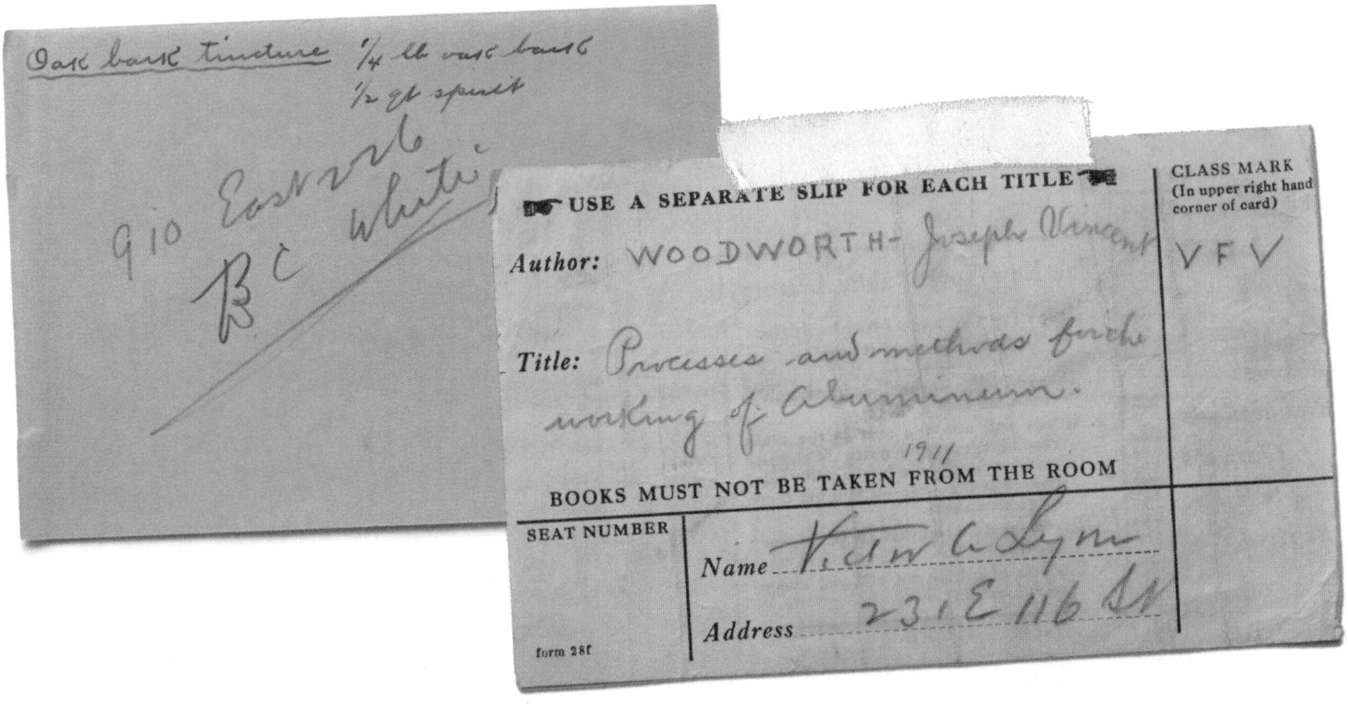

Alcohol Fabrication

Traubenzucker } $C_6 H_{12} O_6$
Fruchtzucker } Geistige Gährung

$$C_6 H_{12} O_6 = \begin{matrix} C_2 H_6 O \\ C_2 H_6 O \end{matrix} \begin{matrix} + CO_2 \\ + CO_2 \end{matrix}$$

1 Traubenzucker 2 alcohol 2 Kohlensaüre

Ethyl alcohol		$C_2 H_6 O$
Propyl	"	$C_3 H_8 O$
Butyl	"	$C_4 H_{10} O$
Amyl	"	$C_5 H_{12} O$

Mässig verdünnte Zuckerlösung bei Temperatur 20-36 C mit Hefe. In 12-14 Stunden tritt gasentwickelung ein. Die passende Temperatur ist 20-30 C. Sehr grosse Koncentration der Flüssigkeit beschränkt die geistige Gährung und eine aus 1 Teil Zucker und 4 Teilen Wasser also 25% lösung ist am günstigsten. Das Ferment ist die Hefe Eine sehr kleine Menge Hefe genügt. "Zymase" ferment der Hefe.- erzeugt durch zerreiben mit Kieselgur und Abpressen. Erregt Zellenfreie Gährung.

92 parts Alcohol 8 parts Water boils 61 R
1 " " 99 " " " 79 R

Fuselöl entfernt durch digestion mit gut ausgeglühter Holzkohle welche die Riechstoffe fixiert.

Lucy note and a prescription slip from J. F. Lyon helped zero in on the compiler's identity, but a New York Public Library call slip with distinctive handwriting yielded a name: Victor A. Lyon.

Victor Alfred Lyon was born in Germany in 1876 to Louise and Jonathan Fish Lyon. His mother was German, but J. F. hailed from an old New England family and earned his medical degree from the University of Heidelberg. In time, Victor and his younger brother became physicians as well. ZaZa (as young Berlin-born Walter was called by his classmates) earned his MD from Yale while Victor got his from Bellevue Hospital Medical School (later absorbed into NYU's School of Medicine) in 1898. Although ZaZa left medicine, by 1908 the elder Lyon brother was practicing as a surgeon at St. Elizabeth's and Philanthropin Hospitals in New York City.

At the onset of national Prohibition, Victor and his sister Lucy lived with their parents in Harlem at 231 East 116th Street, an area once heavily populated by German immigrants. Their father kept office hours in the building and saw patients at nearby hospitals. Victor did as well, but Victor had a secret tucked away in a nondescript little book of poetry.

Now, Victor Lyon was a master at the low profile. No photo of him—not even from a

DR. J. F. LYON
OFFICE HOURS:
8 TO 10 A. M.
2 TO 3 P. M.
7 TO 8 P. M.
231 EAST 116TH STREET
TELEPHONE 2951 HARLEM
NEW YORK
℞

The Handwriting

Although Victor Lyon surely wrote most of the entries, the notebook's handwriting shifts over time. Whether his writing changed as he aged (certainly mine has) or someone else penned later entries, I don't know. I briefly considered that the man who wrote the formulary was Hohenzollern cousin (and later-disgraced American Nazi apologist) George Sylvester Viereck. Samples from University of Delaware Library, though, demonstrated that the writing in the formulary was nothing like Viereck's. Of the handwriting samples I collected for Victor, Walter, Lucy, and Jonathan Lyon, only Victor's matched the notes and formulas.

passport application—has surfaced. After his mother died in 1921 and his father four years later, federal and state census workers noted him living at the Harlem address for decades with his unmarried sister (a "spinster," the records call her). He pops up in some medical directories, alumni lists, and served on an exemption board for conscripts in the First World War. In that war, he had registered as a physician working for General Electric. Other than that, the man's a ghost. His registration form for the war notes that he is tall with grey eyes and grey hair. He claims, writing in that familiar script we see in the notebook, to be native-born American, but that is a lie; rampant anti-German hysteria in the United States led many so-called hyphenated Americans to hide or outright reject their Germanic heritage (see "Hoch der Kaiser! A German America," page XX).

By the Eisenhower years, Lyon had stopped practicing but lived at the same old address. In 1961, he's listed (albeit with "address unknown") in the *American Medical Directory*. Two years later, the directory drops him entirely. He is presumably dead, though missing from death records of the time. He would have been 87 years old by then, unmarried, childless, a man who left nothing for posterity.

Well. Maybe one thing. There was, after all, that little blue book bearing the name George Sylvester Viereck.

George Sylvester Viereck
A Venom-Bloated Toad of Treason

Before his name was stricken from the rolls of esteemed authors, before the *New York Tribune* suggested that he be kicked up the stairs and down again,[1] and before Colonel Henry Watterson of the *Louisville Courier-Journal* summed a popular sentiment of the day by calling the man a "venom-bloated toad of treason,"[2] Munich-born New Yorker George Sylvester Viereck (1884–1962) was a darling of the American literary scene. He had been, it was said, America's Oscar Wilde, a wunderkind fluent in English and German who, as a youngster, wrote for *Die New Yorker Staats-Zeitung*, Baltimore's *Der deutsche Correspondent*, and his father's American paper *Der deutsche Vorkämpfer* (The German Pioneer) which later became the bilingual *Rundschau Zweier Welten* (Review of Two Worlds). He was an American correspondent for the popular *Berliner Tageblatt* and served on the editorial boards of *Current Literature* and the *International*. Viereck's books received acclaim in both Germany and the United States, where the young man was compared to poets such as Shelley, Keats, Swinburne, Baudelaire, and Heine. He was precocious, prolific, and had no small opinion of himself. Viereck's burgeoning arrogance is hinted at in a 1907 *New York Times* interview in which the 23-year-old poet declaimed, "I sometimes feel . . . as if I were a sort of Colossus of Rhodes, with one foot in Europe and with one foot here."[3]

His literary stature, however, was not the article's main thrust. Rather, Viereck used the interview to confirm a decades-old rumor that tied him to the imperial throne of

Germany by what a later author delicately termed "a pedigree of human frailty."[4] It was widely assumed, in fact, that Viereck's father was the illegitimate son of the bewhiskered old emperor himself, Wilhelm I. Which is to say that this would-be Colossus was a direct descendant of Frederick the Great and first cousin to Wilhelm II, the bellicose kaiser who was soon to wage war against Britain and her allies in the Great War. Although he made certain to confirm his Hohenzollern family connections in the *New York Times* article, they were entirely beside the point. Young Viereck was a poet! A genius! "I, George Sylvester Viereck," he insisted, "would rather have written 'Nineveh, and Other Poems' than be the German Emperor." It probably didn't strike readers as true then, either.

The family connections aren't mere court gossip. Viereck's ultimate disgrace was grounded in the kinship he felt with his cousin the kaiser and with his deep identification with the Fatherland. Within a dozen years of that interview, the ground had shifted. War had come and gone. Sylvester, as he was known to friends and family, was on the outs. His strident and bombastic pro-German writings leading up to, and during, World War I were almost entirely to blame. That he was alleged to be involved in more sinister plots of espionage and sabotage against the United States did the rest.

By 1919, he was drummed out of the Poetry Society of America, a group he had help found, and expelled from the Author's League of America.[5] Even the New York Athletic Club gave him the boot.[6] By the time Victor Lyon got his hands on the blank book that would become his formulary, the name George Sylvester Viereck was anathema. Few, even in German American families, would have thought to pluck *The Candle and the Flame* from the shelf, much less poke through it.

It was one of the best hiding places Lyon could have devised.

Hoch der Kaiser!
A German America

A decade before Prohibition, some 2.3 million German-born immigrants lived in the United States,[7] including most of the Lyon family. Yet by the time the Volstead Act (the National Prohibition Act) took hold, many strove to downplay, hide, or outright repudiate their "hyphenated" status as German Americans.

Those who did so didn't just stop speaking German in brewers' meetings or in churches; they shed their German identity, even down to their names. Herr Müller became Mr. Miller; Frau Schmidt transformed into Mrs. Smith. Spurred on by the sinking of the British ship *Lusitania* and America's subsequent entry into World War I, anti-German hysteria rose to fevered pitch. The people of Cincinnati changed the names of German, Berlin, and Hanover Streets to English, Woodward, and Yukon Streets.[8] Chicago's German Hospital morphed into Grant Hospital as "alien" Germans were fired from their jobs across the nation. In St. Louis, Kaiser Street became Gresham Avenue and the Berlin Hotel polished its image with a new name: the Bonair.[9] Sauerkraut was out; "victory cabbage" was in.

The University of Michigan all but shut down its German program when it dismissed six of its professors for their perceived lack of support for the Allies.[10] In 1917, the Nebraska State Council of Defense—a virulent investigator of patriotism, loyalty, and "anti-American" activity—voted unanimously to have all German books removed from the public libraries. For the council, it seemed, merely reading German was sufficient grounds to question someone's loyalty.

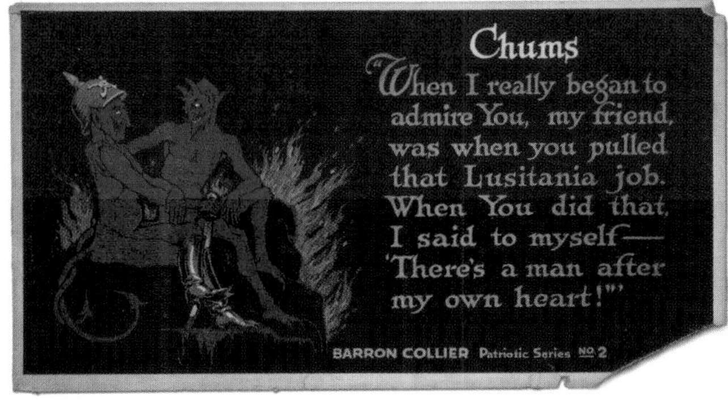

Germany's sinking of the *Lusitania* shocked Americans, helping to galvanize them against "the Hun" both abroad and at home. That *Fatherland* editor George Sylvester Viereck warned Americans to stay off British ships beforehand only confirmed his perfidy in the eyes of Americans.

ROOSEVELT BARS THE HYPHENATED

No Room in This Country for Dual Nationality, He Tells Knights of Columbus.

TREASON TO VOTE AS SUCH

In the twisted logic of the time, speaking German was prima facie evidence of sedition. Prohibitionists leveraged that general animosity to target German American brewers and beer not merely as unpatriotic but downright anti-American. Cartoons of stout American flag–waving Germans drinking from steins and exclaiming "*Hoch der Kaiser*!" ("Up with the kaiser!") were among the propaganda images meant to highlight the divided loyalties of beer-swilling "hyphenated Americans." During World War I, who stood with Kaiser Bill and the Hun to menace America? Why, John Barleycorn, of course, who diverted grains from the war effort and weakened America's troops fighting in Europe. Prohibitionists had already gotten absinthe banned before the war; peeling off beer by manipulating Americans' anti-German sentiment was just the next step in their campaign to eradicate alcohol entirely.

The Mint Julep

HIS drink proves conclusively
at the South isn't so solid!

Dampen a small bunch of mint, dust with powdered sugar, bruise and pour over it a little boiling water;
strain into a tall, thin glass;
fill the glass with finely cracked ice;
fill with brandy;
add sprigs of mint and serve with straws.

AST: *Here's to our bills—and*
ve some day meet 'em.

ACTS MADE UNLAWFUL UNDER CONSTITUTIONAL PROHIBITION

Under constitutional prohibition it is unlawful:

To buy or sell a drink anywhere except for sacramental or medicinal purposes.

To give or take a drink anywhere except in the house of the man who owns the liquor.

To keep any liquor in storage anywhere but in your own home.

To try to get such reserves out of storage.

To have more than two drinking residences—one in the country and one in the city.

To restock your home supply when it runs out.

To move your home supply from one house to another without obtaining a permit. To get this you must prove that you came by the supply before July 1, 1919.

To display any liquor signs or advertisements on your premises.

To buy, or sell, or use a home still or any other device for making liquor in the home.

To buy or sell any formulas or recipes for home-made liquor.

To make a present of a bottle of liquor to a friend.

To receive such a present from a friend.

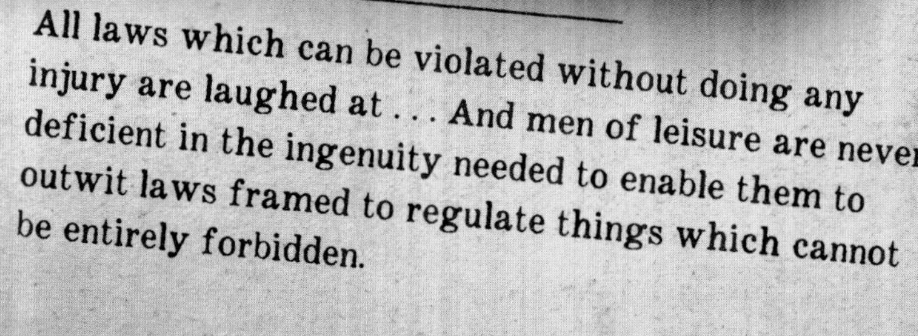

All laws which can be violated without doing any injury are laughed at . . . And men of leisure are never deficient in the ingenuity needed to enable them to outwit laws framed to regulate things which cannot be entirely forbidden.

—Baruch Spinoza, *Tractatus Politicus* (1677)

Chapter one

Prohibition

New laws forbade publishing recipes

If Doctor Lyon had published the formulas and recipes he recorded during America's Prohibition years rather than keep them hidden in a secret notebook, he likely would have been tossed in jail. They were not strictly secret, but were not what we'd call common knowledge. Prohibitionists aimed to keep it that way. Pharmacists, physicians, and some journalists knew about blending and compounding colors, aromas, and flavors with spirits and syrups, as did blenders, liquor wholesalers, distillers, saloon owners, and others who handled liquor in their profession.

Starting in 1920, though, new laws forbade publishing recipes, formulas, and directions for making alcoholic beverages. American publishers released a smattering of cocktail guides during Prohibition—after all, cocktails per se were not illegal. Instructions for *producing* alcohol, however, were. Publishers could be, and were, arrested and fined if they provided formulas for making liquor. Just days into the "noble experiment" in 1920, for instance, revenue agents nabbed John Mitchell, editor of the *Richmond Planet*, for publishing a liquor recipe collection.[11] American libraries pulled books that dealt with manufacturing cordials, wines, liquor, and other intoxicating beverages. To their credit, many librarians did not destroy the books, but shifted them to reference shelves. At the New York Public Library, librarian Edwin P. Anderson announced, "We would no more think of forbidding readers to consult such books in our reference department than we would books on flying. After the prohibition amendment goes into effect there will be additional reasons for them, as they will be histories."[12]

What refreshing irony that Prohibition itself is history. Mostly.

Cocktails per se were not illegal

A History of Doctored Drinks

Some argue that scabrous, degraded spirits of Prohibition, such as bathtub gin, fake brandy, and synthetic whiskey, stood in sad contrast to the glories of pre-Prohibition bartending. Hogwash. Doctored drinks go back millennia. Counterfeit whiskey didn't just come into existence ex nihilo in 1920; synthetic, fraudulent, and adulterated—even merely spiced and seasoned—wines, spirits, and cordials were well established by the time Prohibition descended over the United States. Pre-Prohibition distillers knew what they were making; wholesalers who bought from them generally did as well. Beyond that, though, things got iffy. Joseph Fleischman set the scene in his 1885 manual on blending liquor:

> The moment a barrel of liquor leaves the bonded warehouse, the first thing thought of, and done, is to reduce its cost. The blender knows how to make the bonded liquor produce a profit of 25 to 50 per cent on the amount he paid for it, and frequently a great deal more.
>
> For the changes made by these cheapening processes neither the saloon-keeper nor his bartender is responsible; they can only offer for sale what they are able to purchase. The purchaser accepts the liquors he buys for what they are represented to be. [*The Art of Blending and Compounding Liquors and Wines.* New York: Dick and Fitzgerald, (1885)]

Of course, Fleischman was trying to appeal to blenders, distillers, bartenders, and others who would buy his manual, so his claim that everybody makes highly profitable blends should be taken with a grain of salt. But the thing is, books like his were immensely popular among those in the liquor business and did describe widespread practice. Bootleggers treasured them.

What Was Prohibition?

When we talk about Prohibition, most people think of the years in the early 20th century when alcohol was forbidden across the United States. For almost 14 years, the nation tried a new approach to drinking. In the eyes of those who strove earnestly to eliminate saloon culture and Demon Rum, these were real, palpable evils that destroyed lives, wrecked families, and threatened the ruination of civil society. Images spring to mind of a nation in which alcohol was made suddenly illegal across the board and everyone who drank it was a law-breaker.

Close, as carnival barkers of the era cried, but no cigar. The actual situation was more nuanced. This *noble experiment*, as some later called it, would forbid nearly every iteration of alcohol its forgers could manage to squeeze into law. Those laws, as so many before and since, were built on concessions, compromises, and loopholes.

> No person shall . . . manufacture, sell, barter, transport, import, export, deliver, furnish or possess any intoxicating liquor except as authorized in this Act, and all the provisions of this Act shall be liberally construed to the end that the use of intoxicating liquor as a beverage may be prevented.
>
> —National Prohibition Act, Title II, Section 3

What we call Prohibition was an accretion of shifting laws and regulations—bookended by two constitutional amendments—that controlled production of and access to industrial, medicinal, and beverage alcohol in the United States from 1920 until 1933. Propelled by a mix of idealism, naïveté, browbeating, and regional successes of "local options" to go dry, prohibitionists had been pushing language that would become the 18th Amendment through Congress since 1917. After a year of political wrangling that saw Democrats, Republicans, and a few independents pitted against one another, dry forces had enough votes to present the proposed amendment to the states. Mississippi ratified the document first, then Virginia, Kentucky, and North Dakota. By the end of 1918, 15 states had ratified the document. Of the 48 then in the Union, 36 states needed to accept its terms for the amendment to pass. On January 16, 1919, Nebraska became that 36th. After that, the remaining states, except for Connecticut and Rhode Island, ratified the document. Bully for them.

The National Prohibition Act, a federal law that spelled out

A Second Fourth of July

On the sixth anniversary of Nebraska voting for the 18th Amendment, evangelical and resolutely dry Georgia congressman William Upshaw hailed the date as a great national holiday comparable to the day commemorating the 1776 adoption of the Declaration of Independence. "The 16th of January will evermore be a second fourth of July," he declared, "not only for America but, through America's example, for humanity everywhere. It marks the day of our independence from the legal right of the liquor traffic to corrupt and debauch humanity. The fight is not yet ended, but America is grandly on its way to victory."[13]

Who today bothers to remember the sixteenth of January? Rather, every December 5, let's raise our glasses, coupes, bottles, and cups to mark that day in 1933 when the 18th Amendment was repealed: Repeal Day.

Dumping seized beer, wine, and spirits into gutters and drains was a routine PR move for Prohibition agents. Here the Orange County (California) sheriff and his staff dispatch a load of contraband to the ocean.

enforcement details of the 18th Amendment, overcame a veto from President Woodrow Wilson on October 28, 1919, and took effect at the stroke of midnight on January 17, 1920. Its full title was "An Act to prohibit intoxicating beverages, and to regulate the manufacture, production, use, and sale of high-proof spirits for other than beverage purposes, and to ensure an ample supply of alcohol and promote its use in scientific research and in the development of fuel, dye, and other lawful industries."

Most folks called it simply the Volstead Act after Andrew Volstead, a Republican representative from Minnesota who sponsored the legislation. But we should be clear; despite assurances from some historians who insist that alcohol was forbidden across the board, that every brewery and distillery was shuttered, and that every permit to handle liquor was revoked, many legal loopholes and exemptions existed—as the act's long title hints. Between legally produced sacramental wine being consumed by suddenly religious families, medicinal whiskey for those stubborn coughs, and various high-proof products such as vanilla extract that manufacturers successfully lobbied to have defined as something other than "beverages," getting alcohol to the masses wasn't just possible, it was profitable.

The kinds and quality of available alcohol shifted between 1920 and 1933, but drinking didn't stop. Especially in New Orleans, Chicago, Kansas City, Philadelphia, New York, and other cities, the flow of booze continued not just unabated, but seemed to gush. Home distilling went on (as it ever has and does today) and great volumes of illicit spirits came from smuggled booze, cutting plants, moonshine syndicates, and alcohol diverted from legal industry, such as cosmetics and perfumery. Breaking the law, unthinkable for some, became something of a national pastime when it came to alcohol.

At its very best, Prohibition-era alcohol was exactly what it had always been. Smugglers routinely slipped high quality spirits past government agents. Genuine Champagne, Scotch and Canadian whisky, European aperitifs, proper wine, and monastic liqueurs, such as Chartreuse and Benedictine, could, for a price, be had. Yet it's worth keeping in mind a saying about American drinking habits that was an old joke among distillers even before Prohibition struck: in any given year (and it varies: 1854, 1867, 1902, take your pick) Americans consumed more French brandy than had been distilled in all of France. The same could be said of most imported spirits; American boosters had argued since the 18th century that domestic spirits every bit as good as imported could be made with native ingredients. The implication, of course, is that, whether they knew it or not, American bartenders very often poured spirits that bore only superficial resemblance to whatever the bottle and kegs were within indicated.

The 18th Amendment finally was repealed in 1933 with passage of the 21st Amendment, but small-*p* prohibition didn't disappear. Pre-Prohibition bans on absinthe and home distilling endured even after repeal. Some areas of the United States still exercise "local options" and forbid alcohol sales entirely. Others restrict them to certain days.

Whiskey-Made Criminals

Of all the claims temperance unionists and anti-saloon legionnaires made in their clamor for nationwide prohibition, perhaps the most naive—aside from the conviction the policy would actually work—was that, once whiskey, rum, gin, and other spirits were driven from the American landscape, the nation's asylums, jails, and prisons would be emptied. They would be relics, vestiges of an older world, no longer of any use in the Arcadia of boozeless

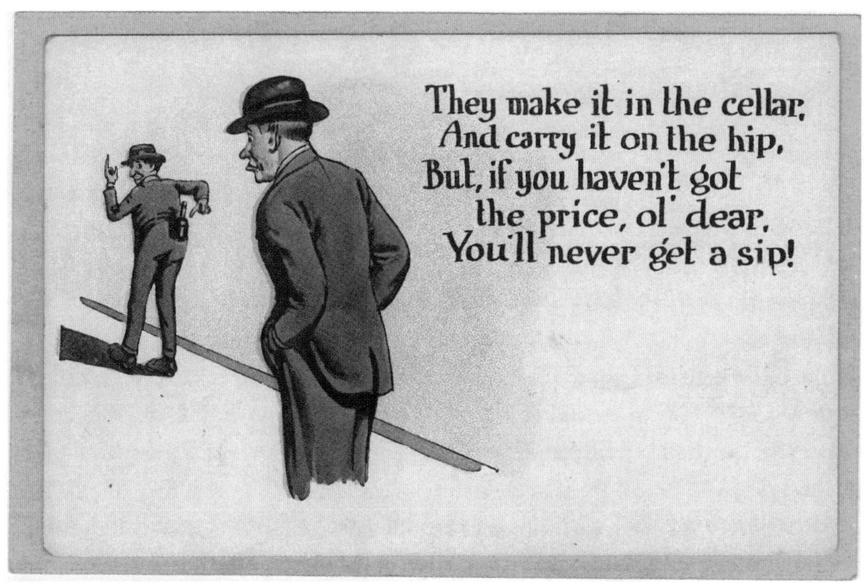

America. For these would-be reformers, alcohol truly was the root of *all* evil. As many of them saw it, eliminating alcohol and the saloons in which it was served was essential for physical, mental and moral health. Few captured that special flavor of fervor better than baseball player turned evangelist William "Billy" Sunday. Sunday railed against sin in his popular sermons, but took particular affront to liquor. In 1916, he thundered to a Boston audience of 55,000,[14] "Listen! Seventy-five per cent of our idiots come from intemperate parents, 80 per cent of the paupers, 82 per cent of the crime is committed by men under the influence of liquor, 90 per cent of the adult criminals are whiskey made . . . Whiskey and beer are all right in their place, but their place is in hell."[15]

Without alcohol degrading the very souls of America's citizens, their minds would clear, families would stay together, and an altogether wholesome way of life would take hold. Ice-cream parlors and buttermilk dens would hang shingles where once saloons blighted neighborhoods. And crime? Crime would be history. Prisons would take in fewer and fewer inmates until one day they simply could be shuttered as the last offenders cycled back into the general population. State and federal governments would be relieved of the financial burden of housing, supporting, and guarding prisoners.

Of course, after a few years of living under the Volstead Act and its attendant laws and regulations, the folly in that line of thinking became manifest. Prisons didn't empty; they were fuller than ever. Between 1914 and 1919, the federal prisoner population hovered between 4,000 and 4,800. By 1929, that number was over 12,000, not counting those farmed out to state, county, and city jails because federal prisons were at capacity. In Atlanta's federal penitentiary, about half of the prisoners were moonshiners who, generally after short sentences, went home armed with new advice about distilling from fellow prisoners. Rather than dissuading illegal distilling, prison for some was a clearinghouse for moonshine tips and techniques.

Victor Lyon's Formulas

As a rare peek into the secretive beverage arts of Prohibition-era America, Victor Lyon's notebook is fascinating in and of itself. The formulas in it, though, didn't just spring up like mushrooms when the nation—ostensibly—went dry. Some of his formulas and recipes come from German distilling manuals, some from farmhouse books published in England, and others still from books and magazines printed in the country that had just outlawed exactly these sorts of things. Many come from medical texts. Most date from the middle of the 19th century to the 1920s, making them older than L. Frank Baum's *The Wonderful Wizard of Oz,* older than the first American football game, older even, in some cases, than the American Civil War and the stories of Mark Twain. These aren't formulas that originated in the Jazz Age; in most cases, they preceded it.

No matter how extensive his notes on manufacturing liquors and cordials are, though, they're only a fraction of the thousands upon thousands of recipes and formulae

Alcohol

To deodorize whiskey or alcohol and free it from Fusel oil

To the barrel of liquor add about a gallon or more of water saturated with chlorine Stir up thoroughly and let it rest 12 hours. Then saturate with chalk. Add another gallon of water and distill.

Fusel oil can be removed from small quantities by adding a few drops of olive oil to spirit agitating thoroughly in a bottle and after settling decanting. The olive oil dissolves and retains the fusel oil.

Test for fusel oil

10 grains nitrate of silver in 1 ounce pure distilled water. Take tumblerful of suspected liquor and drop into it 25 drops of solution. If it contains grain oil it will assume form of black powder and float on surface. Must wait sometimes 1-30 hours especially if well rectified alcohol and even then it is necessary to expose the glass to strong light to discover the powder.

waiting to be rediscovered in old manuals for tinctures, bitters, spirits, and cordials. Here and there, he's got outliers, but for the most part, Lyon wrote formulas for unpretentious beverages: gins, whiskeys, mostly simple cordials, rums, and absinthes.

Something else to note about Lyon's formulas: many of them have more or less overt connections to medicine. Yeah, sure, there's hardly an ingredient under the sun that someone doesn't regard as a remedy for this or that complaint, and spirits themselves are medicine for many, but the frou-frou fancy concoctions from the 1860s on are entirely omitted. There is, for example, no violet-scented purple Parfait Amour, essential to an Aviation cocktail, but probably not a fast seller in a 1920s Harlem doctor's office. He passes on such suggestive, deluxe, and frivolous concoctions as Crème de Nymphe (cinnamon, mace, and rose), Culotte de Pape ("Pope's Britches," a blend of Ceylon cinnamon, cloves, and vanilla), or a cordial the color of old moss made with caraway seeds, orange skins, anise, and carrot flowers. Nineteenth-century saloonkeepers might have kept that last one in the storeroom in small kegs labeled "Oil of Venus"—but sold it as Huile de Venus. Those were the recipes of a baroque Gilded Age when gold seemed to flow in the streets, not of Prohibition when Americans died in the gutters for wont of good liquor.

> Purchasers of bootleg liquor are running enormous risks, for labels are not only counterfeited, but bottles of recognized brands are refilled over and over again, the contents consisting of diluted alcohol and coloring matter and flavoring extracts. The reason so much gin is being peddled is because the concoction consists mostly of alcohol, flavored with oil of juniper. With bottles fra[u]dulently labeled, purchasers are deceived.
>
> —J. M. Doran, head of the Industrial Alcohol and Chemical Division of the Prohibition Unit, as quoted in "Bootleg Liquor," *Journal of the National Medical Association* 14, no. 1 (1922)

Gin blossomed as a Prohibition staple in part because nearly anybody could make simple versions with nothing more than juniper oil, alcohol, and a jug, but since its earliest days, the juniper-flavored spirit has been touted as sovereign against urinary tract complaints. Peppermint oil, essential to so many crème de menthe formulas, has been used to settled disruptive bellies since colonial days. Still is. Ginger wine? Official pharmacy manuals prescribed it for stomach complaints for centuries. Brandy comforts colds and, like whiskey, is still used as a solvent for medicinal herbs. Absinthe, banned even before national Prohibition, gained traction in part because Swiss and French doctors prescribed it as an antimalarial.

Unlike Lyon, however, I am not a physician. I may throw in a comment here and there, but explicating medicinal applications of these old recipes is a task for someone else.

LISTEN FRIENDS!
Try a few drops of Our Highly Concentrated (Imported) Extracts in an ounce glass of water and Presto you will have your favorite; Anisette, Bourbon, Holland Gin, Rye, Slivowitz, French Vermouth; exclusively for Culinary use. Two Dollars for one kind. make one gallon or any six bottles for Ten Dollars. We Guarantee Them. Send your order today, and be convinced. Our new U. S. Custom House Proof Tester will test from 0 to 200 proof; Most accurate and Practical Tester Made: Price $3.00. We ship same day order is received. Circular gladly sent on request. Oakland Importing Company, Oakland Station, Pittsburgh, Pennsylvania.

How Did Americans Get Alcohol During Prohibition?

Although total prohibition in America was the utopian dream of some of temperance crusaders and anti-saloon zealots, what the 18th Amendment actually forbade was not alcohol but *intoxicating beverages*. Smart business owners and interest groups understood that the loopholes inherent in that phrase were so big that they could sail boats through them and lobbied to get their products labeled as something other than *intoxicating* or *beverages*. Americans who wanted to drink alcohol during the Volstead years had several options for getting their giggle water. From conning their ways into congregations to distilling at home, here are some of the sources of alcohol.

Giggle water was an example of "Volstead's English"—slang that emerged in the 1920s to joke about, mock, and speak softly about drinking. This 1928 cocktail guide of the same name contained many 19th-century drink recipes: fixes, cobblers, fizzes, juleps, and more.

Legal Booze

Pre-Prohibition Hoards

The Volstead Act did not prevent Americans from drinking alcohol they already owned before Prohibition took effect. As the onset of Prohibition approached in 1920, many drinkers bought as much liquor as they could afford, hoarding the bottles for their own use or sometimes as investments for the coming dryness. Citizens could store as much alcohol as they liked in their homes, where they could shake, stir, and drink it at their leisure. They were even allowed two homes; one in the city and one in the country, though booze could not be shifted from one to the other without proper permits. Countless millions of bottles of gin, whiskey, kümmel, rum, and other spirits and cordials were tucked away in basements, cabinets, and throughout homes and farms across the country. Every now and again during a renovation or estate sale, some of those hoards are uncovered, much to the delight of vintage spirits collectors and bartenders.

Medicinal Alcohol

Physicians were specifically allowed to write prescriptions for medicinal alcohol during Prohibition. With scrips in hand, their patients could purchase "medicinal" whiskey, brandy, or fortified wines (22% abv [alcohol by volume] compared to the usual 12%–14%) from druggists who paid for an annual permit to handle such wet goods. You never saw a nation of such sickly people.

Hard Cider

Appeasing rural districts was key to passing the 18th Amendment. Early on, one of the bones tossed to their representatives was permission to ferment sweet apple cider. The resulting hard cider, perfectly legal to drink at home, could pack a serious punch.

Sacramental Wine

If you were Catholic or Jewish during Prohibition (or could pass as such, anyway), you were in luck. Both Jews and Catholics were permitted sacramental wine under the new laws. To the sputtering indignation of Wets, congregations swelled as newly religious citizens took full advantage of the loophole while Irish and African American "rabbis" purchased bulk wine for nonexistent congregants (but very real customers).

Travel

For those who could afford it, international travel was the most straightforward opportunity to drink without fear of legal repercussions. A trip to Canada, Cuba, Mexico, Panama, or Europe was the perfect setting to indulge in spirits, cordials, and cocktails, sometimes made by bartenders who relocated rather than become soda jerks or waiters in New York, Boston, and other US cities where their professions were now forbidden.

Such liquid souvenirs were forbidden back in the States, but they did make it back, sometimes by the steamer trunkful.

Having spent years among felons and criminals of many stripes, one thing always struck me as discordant about the idea that the alcohol Americans drank constituted genuine goods when they traveled during Prohibition. It's this: whenever counterfeit booze is in the local market, everything—and I do mean *everything*—about drinking becomes suspect. Grifters, opportunists, and outright criminals simply cannot resist an easy mark. And, man, were Americans easy marks. Look at it like this: if you're running a bar in Canada or Mexico along the US border or in the Caribbean during the Volstead years, yeah, sure, you can sell hordes of unruly Yanks genuine spirits. Many did just that and made good money doing it. But . . . but . . . if you're amenable to a little extra on the side and pretty sure you'll never see that mook again (or he's too drunk to notice), what's to stop you from pouring cut liquor and pocketing the difference?

A stretch? Not at all. Consider the case of Boston distiller J. F. McCarthy. Before Prohibition, McCarthy made Sheridan Rye, a well-regarded whiskey. But he shuttered the firm and sold his lead bottle caps—emblazoned with his name—as scrap to junk dealer in nearby Chelsea, Massachusetts. Fast-forward to 1924. McCarthy is cooling his heels in one of Havana's better saloons. He asks the waiter for American whiskey. But of course, sir. A few moments later, the bottle is delivered. "There you are, sir! One of the best brands of American whiskey!" It's McCarthy's own Sheridan Rye. Except . . . not. The label had been counterfeited, the contents wholly factitious, but the lead caps? The very ones the distiller had sold as scrap years earlier.

Before I was old enough to buy beer, I could buy the ingredients for brewing beer in my college apartment. This poster, which hung next to my mother's stove since I was a child, may have helped nudge me into that particular epiphany.

Low-Alcohol Near Beer

Few cared for it, but beer under 0.5% alcohol content was permitted under Volstead as "non-intoxicating." Until they realized the greater profit in selling malt syrup for people to brew beer illegally at home, some breweries eked through Prohibition making near beer by heating regular beer in open containers to drive off ethanol. Enterprising bootleggers reintroduced alcohol (usually neutral spirits) to make "needled" beer. People did not love it.

Illegal Sources

Home Brewing and Home Distilling

Countless Americans took to brewing their own beers at home during Prohibition. Their suds may not have been exemplars of the brewing art, but what they were quaffing was probably better than crude needled stuff. At the same time, many immigrants and native-born Americans alike knew how to build and operate small stills to make various sorts of moonshines in their homes. While their owners may not have been selling their makings, by 1926 millions of stills churned out a lot of homemade liquor.[16]

Denatured Industrial Alcohol

Many in industry and the arts, from manufacturers to painters, insisted there simply was no reasonable substitute for ethanol as a solvent. The problem for temperance types is that pure industrial ethanol is chemically identical to the ethanol in whiskey, gin, wine, and cider. By government diktat, then, producers of industrial alcohol were required to "denature" it by using one of several approved formulas that would render it unfit to drink. Bootlegger chemists devised ways to "*re*nature" such tainted spirits while government chemists revised official formulas to stay ahead of them. Plain alcohol like this needled beers, bumped the proof of watered whiskey, and formed the base of compounded gins and other spirits. Results were mixed. Oftentimes, counterfeit booze made from incompletely processed industrial alcohol carried the off tastes and smells of denaturing chemicals.

Bootleggers

Moonshining and bootlegging, two related activities, are often conflated. Although the same person may do both, they are, in fact, separate undertakings. Moonshiners distill spirits illicitly; bootleggers sell spirits (and other contraband) illicitly, whether or not they were made legally. Swarms of Americans became opportunistic bootleggers during Prohibition, selling pints and quarts here and there. They were cab drivers, elevator operators, bellboys, doctors, cigar store owners, milkmen . . . even kindly matrons in the "fruit jar trade" delivering high-proof preserves to neighbors in gingham-lined baskets. Selling booze on the side

Formula 39-B

In 1928, New York City medical examiner Charles Norris called out Alcohol Formula 39-B as a favorite among bootleggers.[17] The particular denatured alcohol had been used in toiletries, cosmetics, lotions, and perfumes since 1921, when C. P. Smith, acting commissioner of Internal Revenue, issued instructions for mixing 2 1/2 gallons of slightly unpleasant-smelling diethyl phthalate to every 100 gallons of pure ethyl alcohol.[18] Bootleggers preferred it over 39-A, which contained skin-irritating quinine, because their chemists would remove the diethyl phthalate with relative ease, leaving mostly pure ethanol that could then be used to make other ersatz spirits from gin to whiskey.

made money, but it wasn't generally their primary income. Other bootleggers worked more or less full-time for or in cahoots with criminal syndicates, distributing liquor that they or they colleagues distilled, diverted, hijacked, compounded, or smuggled.

Nanosmuggling

Big-time smugglers hauled truck- and boatloads of liquor into the United States, but not everyone was big-time. Despite the likelihood of getting caught, Americans returning from abroad routinely squeaked in a souvenir bottle or two. Sometimes, hauls were more substantial. American government officials on official missions, for example, could be granted free entry; on their return, their luggage, like modern diplomatic pouches, would not be searched.

In 1928, Congressman M. Alfred Michaelson was busted following such a trip to Panama after a railway baggage man in Florida traced leaking liquor to one of his six trunks. The ostensibly dry Michaelson had brought back 6 quarts of John Haig whiskey, two quarts of crème de menthe, one quart each of "taffel Akavait" (a caraway-flavored Scandinavian spirit), crème de cacao, and cherry brandy. Oh, and a keg of Barbancourt rum. A year later, his prohibitionist colleague William M. Morgan of Ohio was likewise busted with four bottles of whiskey. "I never," later explained the honorable representative, "took a drink in my life."[19]

As part of a series of raids on moonshine operations feeding New York, Philadelphia, and Atlantic City, New Jersey troopers pose with several 5,000-gallon fermentation vats discovered outside Fort Dix.

Bootleg Booze Quotations.

New York, Oct. 28—Price quotations on liquor in the New York booze market today included:

Scotch whiskey $12 per quart.

Rye whiskey $6 to $10 per quart.

Gin $5 to $7 per quart.

Baycardi rum $5 per quart.

Cognac and brandy $8 per quart.

Sherry wine $2 per quart.

Beer (3 and 4 percent) 50 cents to $1 per bottle.

Individual drinks were being sold from 50 cents to $1.50.

Drugstore Whiskey

Although the United States did not issue a license to a pharmacist until 1816, druggists, whether they were called apothecaries, pharmacists, or some other name, had been dispensing alcohol to their patients for centuries, a practice that stretched back to Europe and was older than America itself. Medicinal alcohol was such an ingrained part of American culture by the 1920s that even moderate temperance advocates whose lips, they insisted, would never touch alcohol regarded whiskey, brandy, and rum as important medicines in and of themselves; they relieved coughs, kept the cold at bay, and helped revive flagging spirits. Beyond plain bottles of whiskey, though, druggists made heavy use of nearly pure, practically flavorless "rectified" alcohol that typically ran 90%–95% ethanol. It was part and parcel of their trade, a vital ingredient used in the legitimate medicines many made in their back rooms and basement workshops.

> We are demanding a clean profession, with the highest ideals. The illegal whiskey prescriptionist, the abortionist, and the unlawful dispenser of narcotics have no place in the fellowship of the National Medical Association. We relegate these three classes of practitioners to the dump heap of society.
>
> —John Turner, MD,
> Annual Address of the President of the
> National Medical Association, 1921

National Prohibition was meant to eradicate alcohol from public life, but in truth, the laws and regulations were never watertight; for those who wanted it, supplies of one sort of alcohol or another could always be found. Drugstore whiskey was one of the alternates to which people flocked, since physicians operated under an exemption that allowed them to write their patients prescriptions for medicinal whiskey. Whether patients presented those scripts in all sincerity with a straight face, or with a broad wink, retail druggists were those who filled them.

There was grousing in Brooklyn and booze was to blame.

In May 1922, members of the Kings County Pharmaceutical Society gathered at the Brooklyn College of Pharmacy for their monthly sit-down. The meeting began with good news; over two hundred seniors had passed their qualifying exams, making it the largest graduating class in the college's history. One can imagine self-pleased harrumphs around the room. Afterward, there was a brief, relatively mundane discussion of tariffs and duties on glassware. Then things turned sour.[20]

Like their colleagues in other cities, New York druggists chafed under new rules meant to control alcohol. Most were adamant that, whether they were consumed as is or used in bitters, tonics, tinctures, and other compounds, spirits helped their patients maintain good health. What they didn't mention, but everyone in the room understood, was that spirits also contributed mightily to their profits. While Prohibition laws allowed them to continue their trade in alcohol, the obstacles thrown in their way were infuriating.

Members railed against local Prohibition directors who disparaged them in newspaper interviews as criminals and tangled their work with red tape. There were bitter complaints that officials intentionally dragged their feet when druggists applied for permits to sell alcohol. Although pharmacists were permitted to dispense alcohol and use it in various preparations, the law demanded that such spirits were strictly for medicinal purposes; whiskey for a cough was allowed. Whiskey for a julep, though? No dice. But so-called medicinal whiskey—*spiritus frumenti* or *spiritus fermenti* in apothecary Latin—was meant to be a hassle to obtain. People weren't supposed to be able to just walk into a drugstore and buy a pint of bourbon or rye as they could in many places before Prohibition (or since, for that matter). Instead, anyone who wanted to buy a bottle of otherwise outlawed spirits needed a prescription.

The problem was, prescription slips were easy to fake. The market was flooded with counterfeits. This was one of the reasons Prohibition directors didn't simply rubber-stamp applications for liquor permits. There was a growing and well-founded sense that staunching the flow of alcohol was not going to be as straightforward as Prohibition's advocates had hoped. Furthermore, drug-

> I will fill the jail so full of doctors and druggists that their feet will stick out the windows.
>
> —Major Alfred V. Dalrymple, as quoted in the *Chicago Defender*, April 17, 1920

gists and physicians were part of the problem.

Medicinal Wine and Spirits

When the Volstead Act went effect in 1920, Major Alfred Vernon Dalrymple was appointed chief prohibition officer in Chicago. There he oversaw a twenty-one man crew who sought to crush the trade in alcohol, wine, and beer. Strict enforcement of the law was absolutely necessary, he argued, to maintain the "morale" of the newly arrived immigrants—never mind that they might have come from Germany, Italy, Ireland, China, or other parts of the world where drinking was regarded a comfort. In a speech at Chicago's City Club,[21] the major drew clear distinctions between law-abiding citizens and the treasonous behavior of those who continued to trade in intoxicating beverages.

"Benedict Arnold," he thundered, "was no greater traitor than any citizen who opposes the enforcement prohibition while it remains a law." The issue was not temperance, or prohibition, but law enforcement. Dalrymple singled out two groups involved for particular excoriation: druggists and doctors.

Major Dalrymple comes across as a bit of a blowhard, especially as we look back with almost a century of hindsight. But here's the thing: he wasn't wrong.

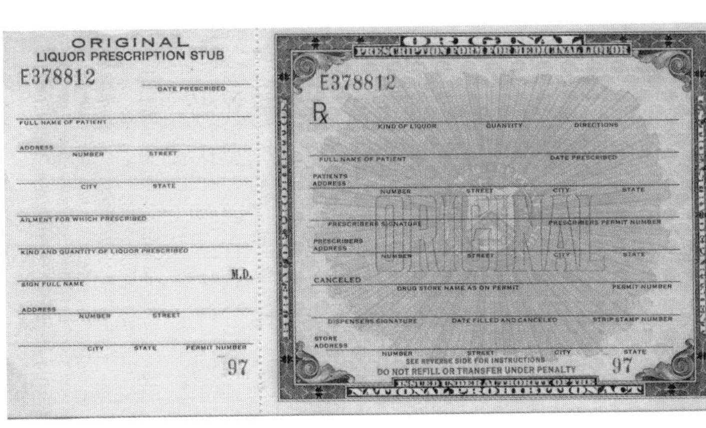
ORIGINAL
LIQUOR PRESCRIPTION STUB
E378812
DATE PRESCRIBED
FULL NAME OF PATIENT
ADDRESS NUMBER STREET
CITY STATE
AILMENT FOR WHICH PRESCRIBED
KIND AND QUANTITY OF LIQUOR PRESCRIBED
M.D.
SIGN FULL NAME
ADDRESS NUMBER STREET
CITY STATE PERMIT NUMBER
97

ORIGINAL
PRESCRIPTION FORM FOR MEDICINAL LIQUOR
E378812
℞
KIND OF LIQUOR QUANTITY DIRECTIONS
FULL NAME OF PATIENT DATE PRESCRIBED
PATIENTS ADDRESS NUMBER STREET CITY STATE
PRESCRIBERS SIGNATURE PRESCRIBERS PERMIT NUMBER
PRESCRIBERS ADDRESS NUMBER STREET CITY STATE
CANCELED
DRUG STORE NAME AS ON PERMIT PERMIT NUMBER
DISPENSERS SIGNATURE DATE FILLED AND CANCELED STRIP STAMP NUMBER
STORE ADDRESS NUMBER STREET CITY STATE
SEE REVERSE SIDE FOR INSTRUCTIONS
DO NOT REFILL OR TRANSFER UNDER PENALTY
97
ISSUED UNDER AUTHORITY OF THE
NATIONAL PROHIBITION ACT

Under the Volstead Act, physicians were permitted to write liquor prescriptions for "medicinal purposes." It wasn't supposed to be a free-for-all; physicians were required to keep records indicating what liquor for what ailment, how much, in what dose, and for whom they wrote prescriptions. Druggists who filled those prescriptions had to buy annual licenses and keep records as well. But for patients with legitimate medical complaints (as well as thirsty souls who knew an obliging doctor), a supply of bonded whiskey, brandy, New England rum, or fortified wines was as close as the nearest drugstore. Druggists were inundated with prescriptions both because prescription blanks were easy to counterfeit and because plenty of doctors would, for a small fee of course, dash off *spiritus frumenti* prescriptions for patients with imaginary ailments.

The medicinal spirits exemption was a particular bother for Prohibition agents. Dalrymple told members of the City Club that a single druggist had sold 800 gallons of whiskey in nine days. Bartenders selling that much whiskey these days might get a visit from brand ambassadors wanting to know how they could help them sell even more. Those are *great* numbers. Eight *hundred* gallons! Even so, he was trumped by the physician who issued 7,534 prescriptions for alcohol in about four weeks—some 250 every day, including weekends. Assuming each of those were for a pint to quart (the maximum allowed to any one patient per month), that's about 940 to 1,880 gallons of whiskey, brandy, and other spirits. The poor guy must've been doing nothing but writing prescriptions for alcohol. Here's hoping he had the sense to hire some assistants to give his wrist a break.

Potus Inebrians

No, no, no. It's not that the president is drunk. Well, possibly. But that's not what's going on here. *Potus,* before it became an acronym for the President of the United States, was a medical Latin term for "drink." *Potion, potable,* and *potation* come from the word. Although plenty of beverages we wouldn't necessarily call wines today paraded under the name of *vinum, potus inebrians* referred to a strong drink more broadly. *Potiones ardentes* could mean either wines or more ardent waters, the cordials and distillates of the pharmaceutical trade.

It is the ancient custom of compounders to call wines, beers, and spirits by their Latin names. We don't need to concern ourselves with every last one, but it's worth taking a look at a few that appear as common names in old recipes for compounded cordials, wines, and spirits. *Spiritus* referred to distilled alcohol and crops up often.

Spiritus vini gallici ....French brandy
Spiritus sacchari ....rum
Spiritus oryzae ....arrack
Spiritus juniperi..................gin, Holland gin, genever
Spiritus lactis equini ....koumiss, fermented mare's milk

Wine was extensively called for in older recipes, often by its Latin name, *vinum*, followed by some modifier. There was, for example *vinum album* and *vinum rubrum* (white and red wine, respectively), but also *vinum Gallicum, Burgundicum, Burdigalense*, or *Germanicum* (French, Burgundy, Bordeaux, or German wine). When wine was pure and unmixed, not watered or flavored, it might be referred to as *merum*. Others that show up in compounding manuals include:

Vinum Lusitanicum . . . . port wine
Vinum Toccaviense ....Tokay
Vinum Hispanicum album ....Spanish white wine
Vinum Xeres......................sherry
Vinum Maderaicum ....Madeira

Cerevisia/cervisia/zythum........beer or ale
Cerevisia Londinensis ....porter
Cerevisia tenuis ....strong beer
Vinum pomaceum ....apple cider
Vinum pyraceum ....perry (that is, cider made of pears; quite delicious)

Pumpenheimer

The termination *heimer* (*Heim*, home) is in German given to many wines, as *Laubenheimer, Rudesheimer* &c—Pump water is sometimes jocosely called at table *Pumpenheimer.*[22]

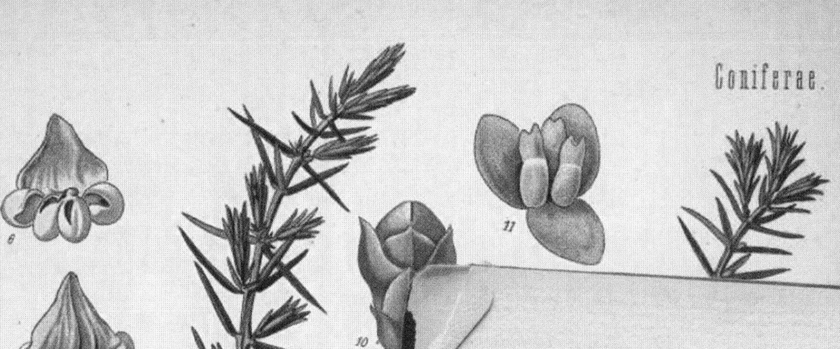

SUGAR WHISKY, NOTED FOR ITS "AUTHORITY," FOUND IN KENDALL CO.

Special to The News

San Antonio, Tex., Oct. 10.—Sugar moonshine was the new brand of whisky found by federal prohibition agents Saturday in raiding a still in operation at a house near Boerne, Kendall County.

The liquor is said to be similar to the famous cane whisky of North Texas, which is noted for its "authority."

In the raid the officers found five barrels of mash that contained no grain. The two men arrested explained that the mash was made of sugar, yeast and water. Ten gallons of the liquor seized tested 90 proof.

THE

PRACTICAL DISTILLER:

OR

AN INTRODUCTION TO MAKING

WHISKEY, GIN, BRANDY, SPIRITS, &c. &c. OF BETTER QUALITY, AND IN LARGER QUANTITIES, THAN PRODUCED BY THE PRESENT MODE OF DISTILLING, FROM THE PRODUCE OF THE UNITED STATES:

SUCH AS

RYE, CORN, BUCK-WHEAT, APPLES, PEACHES, POTATOES, PUMPIONS AND TURNIPS.

WITH DIRECTIONS

HOW TO CONDUCT AND IMPROVE THE PRACTICAL PART OF DISTILLING IN ALL ITS BRANCHES.

It is a generally well understood fact that the thirsty individual who takes his glass of whiskey at any of even the first-class public bars, saloons or parlors, does not know what he drinks. The proprietor who purchases, and the bartender who dispenses, the liquors are probably also in the same blissful state of ignorance. Very few persons, outside of those engaged in the wholesale trade, understand what is meant by blending and compounding liquors.

—Joseph Fleischman,
The Art of Blending and Compounding Liquors and Wines (1885)

Juniperus

SCOTCH WHISKEY

Chapter Two

Compounding Spirits

ways to use spirits and essential oils in beverages

The alcohol entries in Victor Lyon's notebook, regardless of the language in which they're written, fall into two broad categories. The first concerns alcohol production and analysis—how ethanol behaves when mixed with water, for instance, or price lists for raw supplies. Notably, there is little information about operating a still, that essential piece of equipment needed to extract high-proof spirits from low-alcohol beers, wines, and washes. The assumption with almost all of these formulas is that the spirits, cider, or wine used to make them are purchased just like any other ingredient or supply. The second type of entry follows from that assumption: it covers formulas and recipes for making cordials, syrups, tinctures, and high-proof spirits. Some use botanicals, such as orange peels or juniper berries, which we're used to seeing in modern cocktail bars. Others rely on essential oils and aromatic compounds to provide flavor and aroma to the finished product.

In this chapter, we'll do three things. First, we'll set up historical context for these sorts of recipes and formulas by looking at early medical texts. Second, we'll review gear for making compounded beverages, from must-have kit, such as bottles and spoons, to more specialized equipment. Last, we'll examine ways to use spirits and essential oils in beverages.

Not Your Grandmother's Recipes (Unless Gran Was a Bootlegger)

Doctor Lyon's notes, by and large, are not homestyle recipes. Sure, some of them can be scaled down and made in kitchens and bars by using pitchers, jugs, and measuring cups. We'll take a look at some of those. Except for examples with a bit of a British farmstead vibe, though, there's very little domestic about his writing. Unlike cookbooks of the era,

Formula vs. Recipe: What's the Diff?

In casual conversation, the terms *formula* and *recipe* tend to be interchangeable. They are not, however, quite the same. Cookbooks and drinks guides generally present recipes; exact amounts (or ranges) of ingredients with instructions for preparing them. Formulas, more often written for professional audiences, may also have instructions but they denote ratios rather than exact amounts. A Manhattan recipe calls for two ounces of bourbon or rye, one of sweet vermouth, and perhaps a sour cherry or an orange twist. A Manhattan formula, on the other hand, might call for two parts whiskey to one of vermouth (a 2:1 ratio) with appropriate garnish and embellishment per drink. Consider that popular Prohibition-era drink, the Mary Pickford cocktail, named after the silent-film actress:

MARY PICKFORD RECIPE

- 2 oz white rum
- 1 oz pineapple juice
- 1 bar spoon (5 ml) grenadine
- 1 bar spoon (5 ml) maraschino liqueur

MARY PICKFORD FORMULA

- 12 parts white rum
- 6 parts pineapple juice
- 1 part grenadine
- 1 part maraschino liqueur

Combine the ingredients in a shaker and shake with ice. Strain into a chilled glass and garnish with a brandied cherry.

Lyon's formulas and notes were not intended for home cooks. Nowhere do we see teacups, dessertspoons, or hands used to measure ingredients. There are no dimensions, such as "the size of a walnut" or "as big as a pea," as we might expect from someone writing about preparing meals for a household. The scale of these recipes is commercial; even the most ardent DIY bitters enthusiasts and home cocktail fiends tend not to work with 40 or 100 gallons of whiskey at a time.

A few entries concern genuine spirits, but the most of the 300-plus entries are recipes and formulas for compounded wine and spirits—making whiskey, brandy, rum, absinthe, gin and genever, kümmel, port wine, cordials, and so forth, from neutral spirits, essences, flavorings, various botanicals, and, from time to time, genuine spirits. Such wholesale compounding was commonplace among liquor brokers and saloonkeepers at the turn of the 20th century, but is largely forgotten now and little known outside professional or hobbyist distilling circles and curious bartenders.

Rather, these recipes and formulas fall into the domain of chemistry, of rules and laws. One senses an orderly, if occasionally disorganized, mind at work. The metric measurements throughout the notebook were commonplace by the end of the 19th century in professional European manuals, whether they dealt with liquor or charcuterie. Herbs and spices seem not to have been harvested from a nearby garden—there is no information about seasons, pests, ideal harvest times, seed saving, and so forth—but bought from merchants. Several recipes deal with making extracts and essences, but there's nothing about distilling essential oils. As the purview of specialists, these, too, must be purchased.

Nov 8-1920 **Prices**

Ol Juniper ℥ .50 2^{75} lb 2 rect 4^{50}

" Anise ℥ .12½ - Russ lb 4^{50} - 5^{00}

" Corn Pint .55

" Coriander ℥ 3.35 10^{00} lb

" Bitter Almond ℥ .15 ART sine Acid \$12 - \$13 pound

Vanillin ℥ 1.40 - .60 - .65

Tr Cochineal ℥ .25

Tr red Saunders ℥ .11¼

Sugar Color Pint .45

Orange flower Water lb .60

Benzaldehyde lb 2^{25} - 2^{65}

Oil Lemon Terpeneless - 10^{75} lb

Oil Cloves lb 3^{40} - 3^{65}

Carrot oz 1^{50} 4^{50} ½ pd.

Oil Angelica oz 3^{50}

Terpeneless Juniper lb 8 - 8^{50}

Oil Caraway lb 6 - 6^{50}

Butyric Ether (Absolute) lb 3^{25}

Amyl Valerianate lb 8^{50} (Pure)

Oil Cinnamon 2^{50} - 2^{75}

Ol Aurantii 7^{40} - 7^{50} pound

% **Terpene Content**

Angelica	95
Cinnamon Cas.	35
" Ceylon	30
Clove	30
Coriander	35
Juniper	96
Lemon	96.5
Orange - bitter	98.4
" sweet	98.4
Tangerine	98.4

The Doctor Is In

An Ancient Cheat of Acid and Oil

Modern craft bartenders achieve a rich, frothy head on cocktails a few ways, including shaking drinks with cream, egg whites, or pineapple juice. Tech-forward types may even dispense stabilized aromatic foams from nitrogen-charged whipping siphons. Withal, 18th-century rum merchants and 1920s moonshiners alike made spirits foam ever, ever so lightly with a bit of liquid prestidigitation. Their trick—and almost always it was an underhanded trick meant to fool customers—was an ancient cheat known as The Doctor, false-proof, beading oil, or simply beading. They are usually equal parts of sweet almond oil and sulfuric acid dissolved in high-proof spirits. Lyon includes a lot of such recipes. Despite minor variation in wording or directions, they are practically unchanged from such recipes over the last three centuries. Consider William Smyth's directions for publicans from 1781:

THE DOCTOR

Two drams of oil of almonds
Two ditto of oil of vitriol
One jill of spirit of wine [i.e., gill, or one-fourth of an imperial pint or 142 ml]

Shake well, and use occasionally.[23]

The Doctor is a cheat because it affects how spirits behave when they're agitated. Shaking a sample of spirits is a crude, seat-of-the-pants test for determining its proof. Try it with whiskey, vodka, or whatever you have lying around. Regular-strength spirits (that is, 40% abv) will produce many small bubbles that quickly dissipate on the liquid's surface. Higher-proof spirits yield slightly larger and longer-lasting bubbles that some call *goose eggs* or *frog's eyes*. They don't last more than a few seconds, but some customers looked on those bubbles or beads as proof positive that the spirit they were about to buy were, in fact, proof spirits. Beading oil allowed dealers to water down the product and still get that slight head. It was also handy when saloonkeepers who bought gin in bulk might water it down too much (for some cutting was always expected). Beading oil with a little tincture of cassia and chiles—and syrup, of course—would seem to bring that proof right back up. Occasionally, as in William Loftus's 1869 recipe that follows, the foaming seems to have surpassed mere beads and produced proper foamy heads in doctored spirits.

RECEIPT FOR SPIRIT BEADING

Oil of sweet almonds 1 ounce   Oil of vitriol [sulfuric acid] ditto.

Rub together in a mortar, and add by degrees about two ounces of lump sugar, rubbing well with the pestle until it becomes a paste. Then add small quantities of spirits of wine until a thin liquid is formed. This quantity of beading is sufficient for 100 gallons of gin, and will cause the spirits to carry a fine pearly bead, when drawn from a little height into a glass.[24]

These oils are curiosities. Please don't make them. If you have one, please don't use it. Sulfuric acid can be dangerous for those who aren't versed in its safe handling. Unlike syrups and caramels, which may be deployed occasionally in quality spirits, beading oils really have no wholesome purpose in spirits.

Sliwowitz

Persiköl	10	dkg
Zimtöl	1	"
Amylalcohol	1	"
Essig aether	1	"
Annanasaether	1	"
Rosinenaether	1	"

Man mischt und destilliert aus einer tubulierten Glasretorte mit etwas gebrannter Magnesia.

Brandy Essence

Oil Prunes	2 ounces
Butyric ether	1 dram
Oil Cognac	4 drams
Wine Ether	1 ounce
Alcohol	4 ounces

Kognac Essence

Hochgradigen Spiritus 5 liter
Feinstes Weinbeer oder Cognacöl 5 dkg
dazu geschüttet und geschüttelt bis alles aufgelöst ist und setzt dann
Feinsten Essigether 50 dkg
und Feinsten Weinenether 50 dkg dazu

Läßt alles 48 Stunden stehen und rectificiert alsdann in einer Glasretorte über gebrannter Magnesia

What Is a Flavor?

What is a flavor? Pfft. Come on, now. Who makes drinks and doesn't know what a flavor is? Put a glass to your lips, take a sip, *boom*, there it is: elderflower, or mint, or whiskey. Orange. Juniper. Cinnamon. Rum. Whatever. We can parse those broad strokes into even more nuanced detail, but we know on a gut level what tastes are. Our understanding of how taste buds function has evolved over the last century, but the basic premise holds. Little structures called papillae in your mouth and throat detect qualities such as sweet, sour, bitter, salty, and—now that we can put a name to it—umami, that satisfying "savory" flavor we can pull from such foods as aged beef, certain cheeses, and some seafood. Ditch the outdated idea that tongues can be sectioned into areas that detect only sour or only sweet or some other taste. We know now that *all* areas of the tongue, not just certain sections, can detect different tastes.

But taste buds are only one part of the picture. Most scientists who look at this sort of thing, in fact, report that smell accounts for the lion's share of what we call taste. What else? How about pain? You bet. Flavor, wrote R. L. Hall in 1968,

> is the sum of those characteristics of any material taken in the mouth, perceived principally by the senses of taste and smell, and also the general pain and tactile receptors in the mouth, as received and interpreted by the brain. (R. L. Hall, "Food Flavors: Benefits and Problems," *Food Technology* 22 [1968]: 1388)

With this definition, we are reminded that part of the taste of a Bloody Mary is the pain of horseradish, that back-of-the-throat itch from good black pepper, and the irritation caused by hot sauce if that's in there, too. Tannins in oak and tea can contribute astringent, drying sensations to drinks. We can talk about menthol in mint juleps and grasshoppers, which is hardly any kind of taste at all . . . not until you inhale, drawing air across your moist tongue, and suddenly your mouth comes alive with a bracing, spiky, cool *mintiness*.

Flavor in spirits and cordials is rarely so simple as single notes, such as "lemon" or "anise," because of the immense variability in the composition of raw ingredients, the chemical transformations that happen while aging, and how they are handled. That chemical complexity was the subject of much curiosity in the middle of the 19th century. Analyzing spirits and cordials to uncover their constituent parts allowed liquor producers to understand, on a chemical level, the compounds and substances that imbued whiskeys, brandies, wines, and other beverages with their distinctive aromas and flavors. Putting that knowledge to practice laid the groundwork for much of the bootleg liquor that changed hands during Prohibition.

Justus von Liebig, Father of Organic Chemistry

Innkeepers, cellar masters, importers, blenders, and distillers—not to mention makers of wine, cider, beer, mead, and just about anything else you'd care to pour down your throat—had been adding herbs, spices, minerals, even animals and insects to their drinks since time immemorial. When Jesus was offered a mix of vinegar and, depending on whose Gospel you favor, gall (Matthew 27:34) or myrrh (Mark 15:23) to drink on the cross, it was hardly a new idea. When 12th-century French cleric Peter of Blois entered the service of the Plantagenet king Edward II, he began a long career as a diplomat and sort of propagandist for the monarch. While Peter's loyalty seemed unshakable, his reports of English wine were harrowing. Even at the court of the king, the wine was

> sour or musty; muddy, greasy, rancid, reeking of pitch and quite flat. I have witnessed occasions when such dregs were served to noblemen, they had to sift it through clenched teeth and with their eyes shut, with trembling and grimacing, rather than just drink it. (Quoted in Jack Turner, *Spice: The History of a Temptation* [New York: Alfred A. Knopf, 2004], 114–15)

In the days of Solomon adulterated liquors were in use, and from that time to the present men have made, and bought and sold, adulterated liquors; but it remained for the Germans of the nineteenth century to discover a process by which all kinds of intoxicating liquors could be made without one single drop of the pure article in any one of them.

When first this new process was mentioned to me, I said, "Oh, that is all right; I am glad of it. I wish they would make it so poisonous that it would kill every man who drank it, in twenty-four hours. Then perhaps we could induce men to let it alone."

—Eli Johnson,
***Drinks from Drugs* (1881)**

Combinations of wine, say, or beer and medicines or flavorings were not necessarily haphazard, but they were not *analytical*. Enter German chemist Justus von Liebig (1803–1873). Distillers know his name because a distillery condenser that he popularized almost 200 years ago remains popular today. Water-cooled Liebig condensers convert hot, ethanol-rich vapors coming off stills back into liquids that become gin, whiskey, brandy, absinthe, and so on. Other ways of condensing ethanol vapors exist, but over the last quarter-century, I've seen more elegant little Liebig condensers mounted to homemade stills than any other, from Seattle to rural Ireland.

By his late twenties, von Liebig had become deeply engaged in teasing apart various substances, learning how they interact with one another, and what roles they had in determining the characteristics of, say, essential oil of bitter almond.[25] In "*Untersuchungen über das Radikal der Benzoesäure*," an 1832 article von Liebig wrote with colleague Friedrich Wöhler, he made a bold assertion.

> The production of all organic substances no longer belongs just to living organisms. It must be seen as not only probable, but as certain, that we shall be able to produce them in our laboratories. Sugar, salicin, and morphine will be artificially produced. Of course, we do not yet know how to do this, because we do not yet know the precursors from which these compounds arise. But we shall come to know them. (Quoted in William H. Brock, *Justus von Liebig: The Chemical Gatekeeper*, 1st ed. [Cambridge, UK: Cambridge University Press, 1997])

Nineteenth-century temperance crusader Eli Johnson made a handsome living decrying liquor in the United States and Europe. His "Magic Box"—painted black and gussied up with a skull and crossbones—held essential oils and other aromatic compounds from which he might concoct his "drinks from drugs."

But we shall come to know them. Freiherr von Liebig's acolytes took those words to heart. By 1840, a wave of new texts were flooding scientific circles in Europe as von Liebig's writings were translated into multiple languages and colleagues did experiments of their own to determine the constituent parts of such substances as Cognac, gins, whiskeys, arrack, and more. It wasn't long before liquor merchants, distillers, and compounders took notice and began to change their formulas to include vastly more essential oils and other aromatic compounds. New language crept into the manuals. There was much talk of the "poisonous" liquors of the old days (that is, 10 or 20 years back) and how, even if the directions on offer were for imitation gins and bogus brandies, such formulas only included compounds found in the original, genuine spirits, so they could not possibly be harmful.

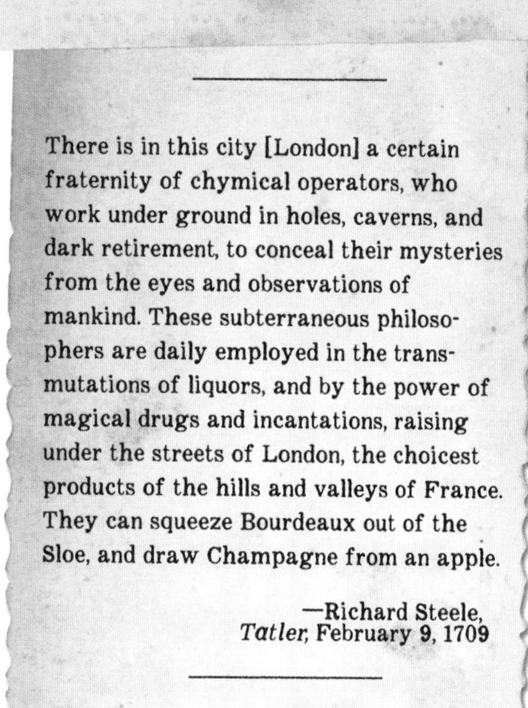

There is in this city [London] a certain fraternity of chymical operators, who work under ground in holes, caverns, and dark retirement, to conceal their mysteries from the eyes and observations of mankind. These subterraneous philosophers are daily employed in the transmutations of liquors, and by the power of magical drugs and incantations, raising under the streets of London, the choicest products of the hills and valleys of France. They can squeeze Bourdeaux out of the Sloe, and draw Champagne from an apple.

—Richard Steele,
Tatler, February 9, 1709

Compounding

What Victor Lyon put together in the first decade of Prohibition wasn't a distiller's manual, nor was it a bartender's guide. Despite some overlap with each, it was something altogether different. Not a single cocktail recipe appears in the book and, despite notes on purifying caramel, whiskey mash bills, and small-scale distillation, anyone reading those parts would have to know how to operate a still already to make sense of them. Rather, his manuscript falls into an old tradition of compounding formularies.

Historically, compounding formularies were books, collections of notes on analyzing materials and formulas for using them. Some physicians kept such notebooks with their personal favorite preparations, but they were more commonly used by druggists who made (or, rather, compounded) medicinal preparations on site: ointments, pills, skin creams, freckle cures, spirituous waters, and other medicaments. They were also used by those in the beverage trade to keep track of their favorite (and often secret) preparations.

Because adulteration was rife in the botanicals and drugs trade, a good liquor manufacturer needed to know how to test his supplies for purity—whether the juniper oil, for instance, was cut with turpentine or whether the "French Cognac" was German beetroot spirits laced with Cognac oil, rounded out with syrup of raisins, and goosed with caramel to simulate age. Keeping notes about successful processes and useful preparations was an important part of the job.

The sources of these sorts of recipes could be anything from herbals to cookery manuals and medical journals. Many were culled from more substantial, comprehensive tomes called pharmacopoeias or dispensatories. Pharmacopoeias stretch back centuries before the earliest cocktail books, yet that's exactly the font from which they spring. If, like me, you love poring over modern cocktail guides, such as the fat little *PDT Cocktail Book* or Death & Co.'s gorgeous thick tome, you'll see them on an entirely different level after reading old pharmacopoeias.

1.1 mol UREA
U
0.15 mol NaCl
1.1 mol UREA
U
0.15 mol NaCl
1.1 mol UREA
U
0.15 mol NaCl
1.1 mol UREA
U
0.15 mol NaCl
Ol. Ricini
Glycerin
Glycerin
Tinct.Chinae comp.

Origins of Pharmacopoeias

It may seem a stretch at first blush, but the lineage of modern cocktail guides and recipe books goes back a lot further back than Jerry Thomas and his 1862 *Bar-Tender's Guide*. In fact, we can trace their line at least to the time when Romans ruled Britain. Without losing sight of the fact that the manuscript at the heart of the book in your hands was written during American Prohibition, it's worth looking at a few of the older texts that paved the way for later books on alcohols, syrups, tinctures, and the other preparations that lie at the heart of modern bartending.

Ancient Romans, Greeks, Chinese, Indians, Mesopotamians, Egyptians, and others developed more or less sophisticated knowledge about the healing arts that included how to prepare treatments from animal, mineral, and plant sources. For nearly 2,000 years, that collective knowledge has gone by a shorthand name in the West: *materia medica*. You still hear it used today, though we're more likely to call the field *pharmacy*. A book that gathers those directions for identifying, analyzing, and preparing compounded medicines is called a pharmacopoeia (also pharmacopeia, pharmacopœia, pharmacopoea, and related spellings, all of which are taken from the ancient Greek, meaning "drug-making"). Such books dictate ingredients, proportions, and processes for making the official compounded medicines of this or that city or nation. Invariably, these included medicated wines, bitters, and various alcoholic preparations.

Hippocrates, Theophrastus, Celsus, Galen, Pliny the Elder, and others contributed to a growing understanding of medicine from the fifth century BC to the second century AD. The term *materia medica*, though, comes from Dioscorides, a military physician in Nero's army, who traveled widely with the army and penned a treatise around AD 77 called *De Materia Medica* (Latin for "Concerning Medical Material"). His five-volume work described roots, seeds, vines, oils, herbs, and animals used in, and as, medicine. Over the next 1,500 years, through the Dark Ages and into the medieval era and the Renaissance, the text was translated into many languages; despite local favorites here and there, it became a basic treatise on medicinal preparations throughout Europe.[26]

In the 7th through 13th centuries, Dioscorides's book and other Graeco-Roman medical texts made their way to Arab physicians, such as Avicenna, Yuhanna ibn Masawaih (known as John Mesue in English), and Ibn Baitar, who wrote their own texts, adding new spices, herbs, and oils to the earlier works. In the 13th century the ambitious and powerful Holy Roman Emperor Frederick II had many of these works translated from Arabic to Latin. From there, they entered the broader European *materia medica*.

The First Pharmacopoeia

Okay, so maybe you don't fully buy into the argument that Harry Craddock's 1930 *The Savoy Cocktail Book* or Paul Clarke's 2015 *The Cocktail Chronicles* are direct descendants of works that were knocking around when Roman legions got their asses handed to them by German tribesmen at the Battle of Teutoberg Forest. You'd be wrong, but let's let it slide.

Skip ahead to the 16th century. Using those old texts that had been circulating for more than a millennium, physicians and apothecaries in cities across Europe were developing rudimentary pharmacopoeias of official medical preparations. Beyond the walls of their own cities, such works had little reach. That changed when a German physician named Valerius Cordus presented *Dispensatorium Pharmacopolarum* to the Nuremberg senate in 1542. *Dispensatorium* was based on earlier works, but Cordus organized the entries alphabetically and included descriptions of preparations made from essential oils, including juniper and lavender. The senate was taken with his contribution and published it posthumously in 1546. As its use spread beyond the city, *Dispensatorium* became arguably the first proper pharmacopoeia with wide reach, known across Europe as the *Nuremberg Pharmacopoeia*.

By 1618, physicians in London had adopted their own official pharmacopoeia. Dublin, Edinburgh, Amsterdam, and others followed. Published in Latin, these were scholarly books written in a language the unlettered were neither apt nor meant to understand. The first *British Pharmacopoeia*—a national, rather than city-based—version was published in English in 1864 and revised in 1867 to supersede those of Dublin, London, and Edinburgh. By then, an American version, *The United States Dispensatory*, already ran over 1,300 pages. Time and again, my own worn, leather-bound sixth edition from 1845 has proved invaluable when researching 19th-century alcohol and botanicals.

Why Latin?

Understanding the oldest pharmacopoeia formulas for tinctures, syrups, cordials, and distilled spirits is slow-going without some Latin under your belt. But it's not impossible. Modern physicians and pharmacists regularly write and understand abbreviations and shorthand terms in a language most of them don't speak. But why Latin? Why not use English? Or German or French or whatever the local language is, a language that everyday people would understand? Surely the local language would have eliminated a lot of confusion. "This," opined one pre-Prohibition pharmacist, "is a popular delusion." He continued:

> To a qualified dispenser a Latin prescription is more familiar and readily understood than an English one. The language is concise and the abbreviations convenient and perfectly well understood. The chief or only difficulty in reading prescriptions consists in deciphering bad writing; and when words are illegible it matters little, whether they are in

> English, Latin, or Arabic . . . A knowledge of Latin may be taken to some extent as a guarantee of a liberal education, without which a young man would be more safely employed in measuring tape or ribbon, than in weighing morphia. ("Fatal Accidents," *Pharmaceutical Journal and Transactions* [1855], 393)

So, snarky comments about ribbons aside, the writer points out one of two good reasons to use Latin. Regardless of whether a pharmacist was in New York, Munich, Marseille, Turin, Stockholm, or Edinburgh, if he were an educated man—and in those early days, nearly all druggists were men—he could read the formulas of his colleagues from any of those places. With a knowledge of Latin, he could read not just a compounding formula here and there from a foreign source, but entire formularies and pharmacopoeias, cross-checking ingredients, amounts, and preparation methods with those of other traditions. For much the same reason, biologists, botanists, and others who study living organisms use Latin for nomenclature; local names are all over the board, but if there's general agreement on the Latin, they can better understand one another.

The other reason Latin remained popular with druggists is hinted at in that last word in the quote above: *morphia*. Morphine, as we'd call it now, is an important medicine. The potent painkiller derived from opium poppies is highly addictive and can be dangerous if used improperly. An apothecary's shop could have hundreds of such problematic substances on hand—or they would be problematic if they fell into the wrong hands. Uneducated people who didn't understand Latin could do some real harm if they were to get their hands on narcotics, opiates, and other potent drugs. But if everything is in Latin? All the bottle and drawer labels, the prescriptions, the formula books? It might as well be gibberish and, like Victor Lyon's notebook, could be hidden in plain sight. Latin wasn't just a way to communicate with international colleagues; it was a way to encrypt those communications.

The Emergence of Compounding Formularies and Rectifiers' Manuals

By the 18th century, distilling and blending had emerged as serious commercial concerns. As distilling technology advanced, distillers were able to produce spirits faster and with greater purity, compounding formularies had evolved into a genre distinct from their predecessors and cousins, the pharmacopoeias and cookbooks. They came to bear a lot of resemblance to perfumers' manuals and, in fact, called for many of the same exotic ingredients from the same faraway lands. Manuals for the ice-cream and soda fountain trade arose slightly later but from the same sources.

Gone for the most part were formulas that were meant to be taken as remedies for such maladies as scrofula and venereal diseases. In the place of alcohol as a solvent and carrier for medicine were liqueurs and spirits meant to surprise and delight drinkers (and turn a profit for rectifiers who blended and sold such concoctions). The formulas in these liquor manuals are chockablock with calls for chemicals, compounds, balsams, and extracts to flavor—or to craft facsimiles of—spirits.

Chiefest among these aromatic compounds were essential oils. Essential oils are aroma incarnate. They are highly concentrated isolates of the chemicals that give each plant its characteristic smell. An older name, *quintessential oils,* reinforces the point they are the most perfect, pure expression of the flowers, seeds, roots, rhizomes, barks, and other plant parts used to make them.

Although truly bad, even dangerous, beverages stemmed from misuse of such formulas, they weren't *necessarily* meant to be cheats. Even today, rectifiers generally make crème de menthe with peppermint oil because fresh leaves don't provide enough taste and aroma to make a strong, stable, long-lasting mint cordial.

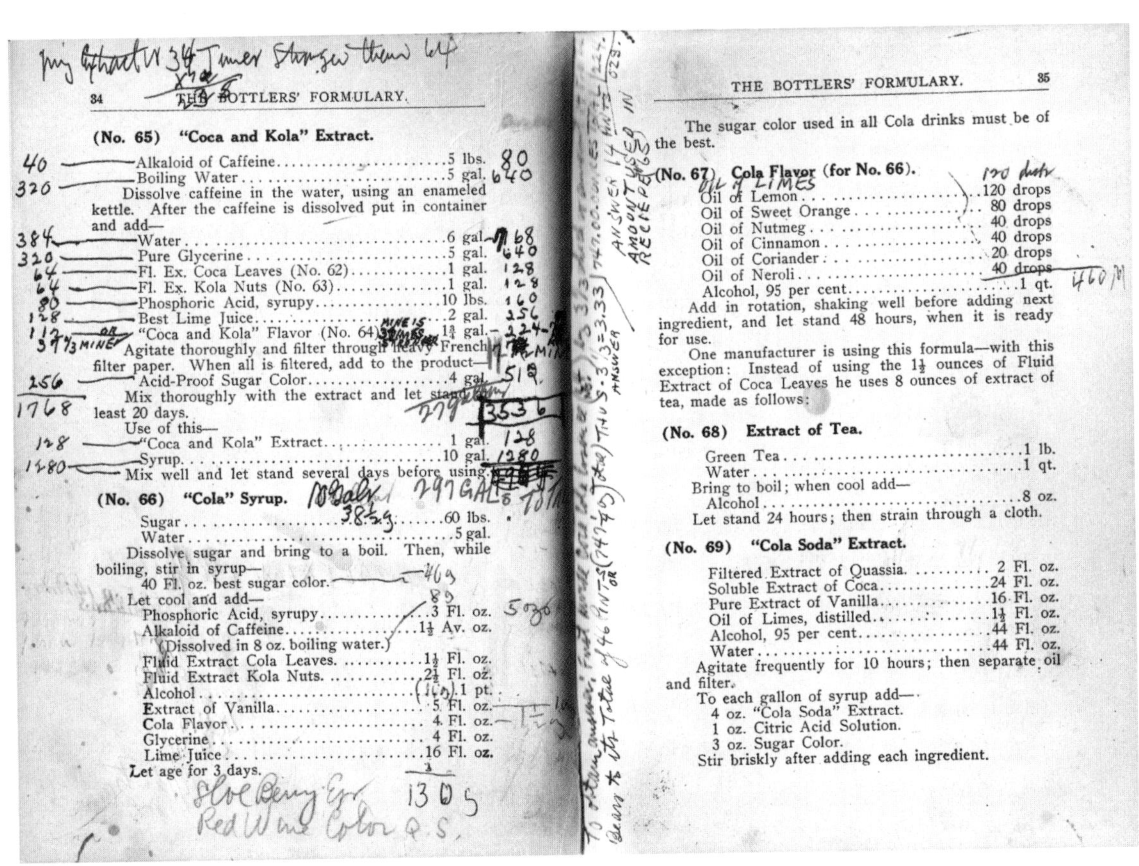

34 THE BOTTLERS' FORMULARY.

(No. 65) "Coca and Kola" Extract.

Alkaloid of Caffeine .... 5 lbs.
Boiling Water .... 5 gal.

Dissolve caffeine in the water, using an enameled kettle. After the caffeine is dissolved put in container and add—

Water .... 6 gal.
Pure Glycerine .... 5 gal.
Fl. Ex. Coca Leaves (No. 62) .... 1 gal.
Fl. Ex. Kola Nuts (No. 63) .... 1 gal.
Phosphoric Acid, syrupy .... 10 lbs.
Best Lime Juice .... 2 gal.
"Coca and Kola" Flavor (No. 64) .... $1\frac{3}{4}$ gal.

Agitate thoroughly and filter through heavy French filter paper. When all is filtered, add to the product—

Acid-Proof Sugar Color .... 4 gal.

Mix thoroughly with the extract and let stand at least 20 days.

Use of this—

"Coca and Kola" Extract .... 1 gal.
Syrup .... 10 gal.

Mix well and let stand several days before using.

(No. 66) "Cola" Syrup.

Sugar .... 60 lbs.
Water .... 5 gal.

Dissolve sugar and bring to a boil. Then, while boiling, stir in syrup—

40 Fl. oz. best sugar color.

Let cool and add—

Phosphoric Acid, syrupy .... 3 Fl. oz.
Alkaloid of Caffeine .... $1\frac{1}{2}$ Av. oz.
(Dissolved in 8 oz. boiling water.)
Fluid Extract Cola Leaves .... $1\frac{1}{2}$ Fl. oz.
Fluid Extract Kola Nuts .... $2\frac{1}{2}$ Fl. oz.
Alcohol .... 1 pt.
Extract of Vanilla .... 5 Fl. oz.
Cola Flavor .... 4 Fl. oz.
Glycerine .... 4 Fl. oz.
Lime Juice .... 16 Fl. oz.

Let age for 3 days.

THE BOTTLERS' FORMULARY. 35

The sugar color used in all Cola drinks must be of the best.

(No. 67) Cola Flavor (for No. 66).

Oil of Lemon .... 120 drops
Oil of Sweet Orange .... 80 drops
Oil of Nutmeg .... 40 drops
Oil of Cinnamon .... 40 drops
Oil of Coriander .... 20 drops
Oil of Neroli .... 40 drops
Alcohol, 95 per cent .... 1 qt.

Add in rotation, shaking well before adding next ingredient, and let stand 48 hours, when it is ready for use.

One manufacturer is using this formula—with this exception: Instead of using the $1\frac{1}{2}$ ounces of Fluid Extract of Coca Leaves he uses 8 ounces of extract of tea, made as follows:

(No. 68) Extract of Tea.

Green Tea .... 1 lb.
Water .... 1 qt.

Bring to boil; when cool add—

Alcohol .... 8 oz.

Let stand 24 hours; then strain through a cloth.

(No. 69) "Cola Soda" Extract.

Filtered Extract of Quassia .... 2 Fl. oz.
Soluble Extract of Coca .... 24 Fl. oz.
Pure Extract of Vanilla .... 16 Fl. oz.
Oil of Limes, distilled .... $1\frac{1}{2}$ Fl. oz.
Alcohol, 95 per cent .... 44 Fl. oz.
Water .... 44 Fl. oz.

Agitate frequently for 10 hours; then separate oil and filter.

To each gallon of syrup add—

4 oz. "Cola Soda" Extract.
1 oz. Citric Acid Solution.
3 oz. Sugar Color.

Stir briskly after adding each ingredient.

Printed drinks formularies were once commonplace. As users altered or improved formulas to suit local tastes and available ingredients, such books as this 1910 *The Bottlers' Formulary* could become heavily annotated. From the collection of the University of California, Davis.

Gear

For centuries, compounded spirits and cordials have been made using little more complicated than buckets and spoons. Some gear, though, does make the process easier, cleaner, and faster. From blenders to bottles, here are some pieces of kit to consider. What follows is just gear for making, flavoring, and storing alcohol, bitters, syrups, and tinctures. You better believe I put a still on the list. If you're looking for dashers, shakers, jiggers, and things like that, check out a good bartending manual, such as Jeffrey Morgenthaler's *The Bar Book* (2014).

Glass Bottles or Mason Jars

Glass, not plastic, bottles are indispensable for storing finished wet goods.

Blender

A blender is useful for making some cordials and syrups. For 1:1 or 50% simple syrup (see page 143 for more about syrups), add equal weights of sugar and water to the blender, fire it up to high speed, and stop when the sugar is dissolved; the air bubbles will dissipate. Several commercial essences that mimic popular brands of spirits and liqueurs call for pouring about an ounce of essence into a blender. Add a bottle of vodka and sugar, then blend until the sugar dissolves. Follow the manufacturer's instructions on those, but, as always, beware the fragrant taint (see page 47) and use glass blender pitchers; plastic can absorb the strong aromas of essential oils and contaminate everything you ever make in that blender again.

Spice or Coffee Grinder

Spoons

Bottle Brush

Pipettes or Micropipettes

Many people who work with essential oils advise using eyedroppers to dole out precise doses of these concentrated compounds. In fact, lots of brands include droppers in the bottle design so users don't accidentally pour out too much of the bottle's precious contents. The trouble is that a "drop" is a squirrelly measurement. The size of a drop can vary depending on the viscosity of the liquid being dispensed, the width of a dropper's aperture, the force used to squeeze the bulb, and other factors. A glass or plastic pipette, on the other hand, measures absolute volume, usually in milliliters.

Measuring Cups and Spoons

Go with stainless steel or damage-resistant borosilicate (such as Pyrex). Plastic can be okay; just make sure it doesn't come into contact with undiluted essential oils or other strong-smelling compounds. Measuring cups sold for homes and commercial kitchens are super handy for measuring volumes. The thing is, some are off the mark. In a set I bought recently, 1,000 grams of water (which should take up 1,000 ml) measured 890 ml, 1,050 ml, and 960 ml in the variously sized cups *made by the same manufacturer*. "Close enough for government work," my father might joke, but not when you want precise measures. Either verify with a graduated cylinder or scale or invest in proper, calibrated flasks from a lab supply firm.

Funnel

Strainers

Filtering Medium

Peeler

Microplane

Kitchen Scale

It's the 21st century. Get a kitchen scale already. You won't need it for everything, but there's no substitute when you need 42 grams of this or 12 ounces of that. I have two. One is for measuring 5-gram intervals that I use for baking and making big batches of syrups. The other registers tenths of a gram and is perfect for weighing spices, herbs, and small amounts of other ingredients.

Nice to Have

Once you have the basic tools for compounding, a few others can make the job easier. These are not strictly necessary, but you'll be glad to have them.

Flasks

One- or 2-liter flat-bottomed Erlenmeyer flasks are useful for blending small amounts of alcohol. Some recipes that call for oils and essences instruct readers to put them into a bottle and shake . . . and shake . . . and *shake* until the oils finally dissolve from all the agitation. Ain't nobody got time for that. Dissolve the oils with high-proof alcohol in an Erlenmeyer flask, drop in a mag bar (see below), and top off with the amount of alcohol the recipe calls for. Set it on a stirrer (see following item) and let the magnets do all the agitation. Spend the extra buck or two to get a ground glass stopper that fits the flask to help contain the compounds you're agitating.

Electromagnetic Stirrer

Like the Erlenmeyer flask, an electromagnetic stirrer isn't absolutely necessary, but, man, it makes light work of blending liquids. Toggle the switch, set the speed, and a small motor sets magnets rotating under the metal plate at hundreds or even thousands of rpm. On some models, that plate heats as well, but don't use it; heat degrades essential oils. The concave bottoms on most wine, beer, and spirits bottles will throw the magnet to one side, where it will impotently spaz and bang against the glass; they are worthless here. Use only flat-bottomed flasks and bottles on a stirrer.

Mag Bar

If you do use a stirrer, you will need a short, coated magnetic bar that spins inside the flask and gets the liquids moving. Fish it out afterward either with a fridge magnet (my method) or a coated magnetic stick (the preferred method).

Mortar and Pestle

Bigger versions exist made of hollowed tree stumps and tree limbs rounded at one end for pounding manioc and whatnot, but the size you want is a countertop model: heavy stone or ceramic bowl (the mortar) with a shillelagh-looking little club that fits in one hand. Use that pestle to crush spices in the mortar or, as old-timers did, to grind essential oils with sugar and mix in high-proof alcohol to dissolve the mass.

Graduated Cylinder

A footed glass cylinder with marks up the side noting volume. Get one from a lab supply firm such as Cynmar.

Büchner Funnel

This fancy little two-part contraption attaches by tubing to a water faucet; the resulting vacuum draws liquids through a filter paper, leaving behind the solids. Pricier than coffee filters or cheesecloth stuck in a funnel, but if you want crystal clear tinctures and bitters, they're the way to go.

Spirit Hydrometer

Useful for determining the alcoholic strength of your spirits if you make your own or cut high-proof spirits with water to drinking strength.

Brix Refractometer

A countertop Brix refractometer measures the sugar concentration in aqueous solutions, such as bar syrups.

Separatory Funnel

This allows separation of materials such as fruit pulp and juice or, if you're distilling essential oils, hydrosol and oil.

A Still

Prohibition, so we're told, was repealed in 1933. That's true as far as it goes, but the federal prohibition on home distilling remains ironclad. If you intend to make whiskey, rum, brandy, and other genuine spirits, then a still is essential. If, however, you plan to make cordials, liqueurs, and cocktails, you can get along just fine without one. Making intoxicating beverages without the use of a still was, in fact, the major selling point of most of those old compounders' manuals.

Arthur Burdett Frost's 1921 sketch, "He made some hooch and tried it on the dog," poked fun at homemade liquor and a nation of scofflaws, many of whom were trying their hands at distilling and compounding for the first time.

Alcohol

When buying $400 worth of liquor from the grocery store in the morning, as I do from time to time, I've learned the easiest answer to the inevitable question is "Yes, I *am* having a party." The truth is, a whole bunch of 80-, 100-, and 192-proof spirits went into testing recipes from Victor Lyon's notebook.

Distilled spirits, whether brandy, whiskey, "alcohol," or some other type are at the core of old recipes and formulas for cordials, bitters, tinctures, and compounded spirits. The reasons are threefold. First, we like the taste of intoxicating beverages and the effect of drinking them. Second, spirits are especially good at extracting and retaining flavors and aromas. Third, spirits—but only high-proof ones—can thoroughly dissolve (or "kill" in old recipes) essential oils. Lower-proof spirits, such as everyday vodka or whiskey, incompletely dissolve essential oils, leaving the resulting mix cloudy. For a review of "proof" and different ways to measure it, see page 201.

High-proof, relatively neutral-tasting alcohol in old texts is sometimes as low 83% ethanol, but 90%–95% is more common (the rest is water and trace amounts of other compounds). It may also be called Köln or Cologne; silent, neutral, or velvet spirit; or simply plain, deodorized, or absolute alcohol. That last one more properly refers to 100% ethanol, also called anhydrous or dehydrated alcohol (not because it's a dry powder, but because its water has been removed). Outside labs, it's uncommon because 100% alcohol is unstable; open a bottle and the proof starts dropping immediately as the liquid absorbs moisture from the very air. During Prohibition, this 90% to 95% spirit is the type of alcohol that bootleggers would have used to cut smuggled spirits or simply to fabricate factitious spirits using essential oils, ethers, and other aromatic compounds.

> The introduction of grain or neutral spirit was never demanded by public taste; it was dictated solely and simply by economical motives. The time required for maturing genuine whisky is thus saved, and the practice of blending is carried to an enormous, if not appalling, extent, with handsome profits to the blenders.
>
> —S. Archibald Vasey, *Guide to the Analysis of Potable Spirits*
> (London: Bailliere, Tindall & Cox, 1904)

Essential Oils: The Fifth Element

Essential oils, ubiquitous in old manuals and starting to creep into modern cocktail recipes, are aroma incarnate. Old texts sometimes call them *quintessential* oils after *quintessence*, a term derived from medieval Latin. Because they were something altogether different from Aristotle's four elements of earth, air, fire, and water, they were *quinta*

Spank it

For an especially good mai tai or mint julep, grab a small bundle of mint by the stems and smack it against your other hand (a technique many bartenders refer to as "spanking" the mint), then tuck it into the drink so the leaves stick out. Spanking the mint breaks cell walls and releases mint oil, thereby making the drink smell mintier than just tucking in the sprig.

Squeeze That Lemon

I'm not a coffee drinker, but I make up for it in spades with tea. Hot, iced, spiced, plain breakfast teas, or the subtle blends I pick up at Dallmayr, one of my favorite Munich provisioners, I guzzle the stuff year-round. One of the more disheartening ways to have it served, however, is with a slice of lemon. Yeah, I know, lemon complements many teas. But to just slide a wedge into a cup or glass fails to take advantage of its potential. Rather, squeeze that wedge, expressing juice and fresh oil alike into your drink. Is it indelicate? Look, any place fancy enough to frown on such behavior will have napkins. Use one if your fingers get all sticky.

By the same token, when you want an extra last-moment burst of aroma in your drinks, squeeze slices, wedges, twists, or even just sections of citrus peel into the glass before pouring or over the finished drink just before drinking it. Lemon, orange, blood orange, grapefruit—a spritz of oil from citrus that is already in the drink can make a good final push of aroma.

essentia, a fifth element, the very life force of plants. In less prosaic language, they are complex mixtures of volatile compounds isolated from whole plants or parts of them. Just about all plants are capable of producing essential oils, even if only in trace amounts, but not all of them are commercially useful. They are immensely popular today and widely available to consumers, partly because proponents of aromatherapy have driven retail demand.

But before we go any further, a bit of clarification; essential oils are not actual oils in the way that the fatty, heavier, so-called fixed oils, like those of olives, almonds, or avocados are. Essential oils are lighter, more ethereal, more fugitive, dissolve readily in alcohol, and are not at all greasy. An alternate name, *volatile oils,* reminds us that they tend to evaporate, dissipating quickly at room temperature in the air. In general, essential oils smell pleasant, though a few are so strong and penetrating that they block out nearly every other smell. Clove, cassia, and rosemary come to mind. I particularly like cade oil for this reason; its intense, smoky, phenolic smell reminds me of a campfire still smoldering from the previous night. To keep its aroma from contaminating my entire office, though, I keep its bottle inside a somewhat larger jar. Oils or not, the old name has stuck, so that's what we'll use.

Scrape a sweet orange with your fingernail or squeeze a piece of peel. Its smell, unmistakable for any other in your kitchen or bar, will fill the space in front of you. That's because breaking the cell walls of its skin releases tiny watery geysers rich with orange oil into the air or, if you aim it that way, over the surface of your cocktail. That is one of the simplest essential oils, one that anybody who has ever peeled an orange will recognize. These oils are not uniform. Instead, they are mixes of compounds, often hundreds of them. The bulk of orange oil's weight, for instance, is a molecule called d-limonene; the rest is a blend of acids, aldehydes, and diesters[27] that can vary by the type of orange as well as its origin. The result: essential oils culled from the orange trees in my California garden won't smell or taste the same as those harvested in Florida, south Louisiana, Sicily, Algeria, Tunisia, Morocco, Spain, Israel, Italy, or just about anywhere else oranges grow. Those who use essential oils for perfume, food, or beverages pay particular attention not just to how they were made, but to their place of origin.

Terpeneless Oils

Relatively flavorless compounds called terpenes comprise a large proportion of the bulk of essential oils. Because they are poorly soluble in weak alcohol, mixing them with lower-proof spirits results in cloudiness. Since the 19th century, so-called terpeneless oils, made by distilling essential oils with alcohol, have been available. Their advantage lies in readily dissolving in regular, everyday 40% abv vodka. Unfortunately, far fewer varieties of terpeneless oils are available to the public than regular essential oils. No matter: use high-proof alcohol to dissolve your oils whether they have their terpenes or not.

Emulsion of Terpenless Oils

Tragacanth gum whole 1 ounce
Water 32 ounces
Terpineless oil ½ ounce

Mix tragacanth with 16 ounces of water let stand 24 hours; then add balance of the water and allow to stand 12 hours longer; then strain and beat the mixture with an egg beater. Then incorporate the oil. This "emulsion" need not be colored.

Gin

How Essential Oils Are Made

Historically, producers have used two primary methods to extract essential oils. In **expression** or **cold pressing** citrus oils, producers squeeze citrus peels (or sponges that had been rubbed over them) in presses, then collect the oils, water, and other heavy liquids that ran off. Once these liquids settle, the portion that floats on top can be skimmed and may undergo further treatment such as filtering, rectification, or blending to become "essential" oils. Modern producers are more likely to use centrifuges which are less work and give higher yields.

The other method, today's standard approach, would have been familiar to importers and dealers in essential oils. It involves a device producers sometimes call an extractor, which any distiller would recognize immediately as a still. In a thumbnail, here's how **distillation** works for essential oils. A load of a single botanical—anise seeds, cinnamon bark, ginger, juniper berries, whatever—is loaded into a still which is then sealed and heated. The botanicals may be in direct contact with water inside the still's boiler, as mint leaves, pine needles, and rose petals often are; subjected to a mix of water and steam; or undergo the most common treatment, **steam distillation**, in which steam is injected directly into the still, creating vapors that are drawn off and condensed. From those, the essential oils are extracted. Essential oil yields and quality can be affected by variables that include the weather, growing conditions, time of harvest, still temperature, and skill of the operators. Yields range from a fraction of a percent for something like orange flowers to perhaps 7 percent for eucalyptus or caraway.

Hydrosols and Flower Waters

After extracting as much essential oil as feasible from botanicals, distillers don't necessarily throw away water left in the still. Whether they are byproducts of distillation or the end result, **hydrosols**, as such fragrant waters are known, retain many of the characteristics of whatever had been distilled. Orange flower and rose waters are "leftovers" from making neroli and attar (or otto) of rose. While hydrosols aren't central to modern drinking, I've had lovely Champagne cocktails with rose water and any Ramos Gin Fizz made around here gets a splash of orange flower water.

Less frequently used procedures include a modern innovation called **hyper** (or **super) critical carbon dioxide extraction**. In this process, pressurized carbon dioxide pulls desirable compounds from botanicals at a lower temperature than steam distillation. Without such high heat, fewer chemical reactions take place. Fans of **CO_2-extracted** oils find them to have a fuller spectrum of aromatic compounds. Some bartenders insist on these whenever possible. Last, in **enfleurage** repeated batches of flowers are either pressed with cold fat or mixed with warmed fat until the fat is saturated. That scented fat is then washed with high-proof ethanol which evaporates and leaves behind a highly concentrated absolute. But now we're wandering into the perfumers' pantry, so let's leave off and get back to drinks.

To Dissolve Essential Oils with Alcohol

Overproof spirits, such as 50% abv vodka or whiskey, are more effective at dissolving essential oils than are the everyday 40% varieties that leave such mixtures cloudy. Still, it can be done better. To dissolve essential oils with alcohol thoroughly, pour at least twice the volume of neutral spirits (90%–95% abv) as the volume of oils into a glass bottle or flask. Add the oil(s). Either close the top and shake or spin the liquids on a magnetic stirrer. Stop when the mix is clear and limpid. If it remains clouded, add more spirits and repeat until it clears.

A Bit of a Disclaimer

To hear some in homeopathic medicine and aromatherapy crowds, essential oils can cure everything from stretch marks to Ebola. They have the power to calm and soothe anxieties or, alternately, to excite you and push you to the very limit of sexual stamina. They will, I have been assured, protect one from measles, eradicate acne, eliminate eczema, assuage chest and belly complaints, rid children of intestinal worms, and "promote healing." How do we untangle bogus assertions and dangerous practices from those that have varying degrees of support among different schools of healing? Simple: we don't. Not here. Look, here's the deal. I'm not a physician. I'm not a homeopath, allopath, osteopath, or any other kind of healer. I'm an historian. When I write about medicine, it's as an historian, not a practitioner. This book doesn't promote the healing properties of anything, much less essential oils.

Recently, an Ebola outbreak that began in Africa jumped the ocean. When the deadly virus turned up in American cities, people freaked right the hell out. For a while, a claim that cinnamon oil would cure the disease was going around. The Food and Drug Administration shut down that nonsense, but the fact remains that people ascribe to essential oils all sorts of near-miraculous powers. This is not the book to explore those possibilities. It doesn't matter that, in my personal experience, ginger seems to settle a rebellious belly or that I find the aromas of certain mint oils relaxing. I'm not a doctor, so I make no health claims at all in this book about essential oils, herbs, spices, or any of that lot. Zero. They can smell good, they can be relaxing, they can help make some tasty beverages, but will essential oils cure gout and revive faded hair follicles? It's not for me to say. If you want to learn more about that sort of thing, look elsewhere.

In fact, if you look at websites devoted to understanding or selling essential oils, you're likely to see some language along the lines that humans should never, ever, in any circumstances consume essential oils.

Given the changing landscape and understanding of what is safe and what is not, I would refer readers to the International Fragrance Association, which has evolving standards on its website that explains which essential oils are **GRAS (generally recognized as safe**, see page 45), which should be avoided, and which fall into some middle space—perhaps safe to consume, but may cause photosensitivity or they are safe for most people, but not in those who are allergic to the substance. Use common sense, but also tap the resources in this book to research on your own the current understanding of what is safe.

That having been said, allow me a few basic words of safety when using essential oils.

- Read and follow all label cautions and warnings.
- Keep away from babies, children, and pets.
- Do not allow undiluted essential oils to contact skin or eyes.
- Never taste or consume undiluted essential oils or put them on your tongue.
- If ingested, call the American Association of Poison Control Centers (800-222-1222) immediately.
- Essential oils are flammable; do not use them near open flames.
- If you have any serious medical condition or are pregnant, consult your physician before using essential oils.
- For characteristics, warnings, contraindications, or other considerations of any essential oil, ask the vendor or look online for its Material Safety Data Sheet (MSDS).

On the Toxicity of Old-School Ingredients

Many of the ingredients in Lyon's notebook and other old recipes are more or less safe for use at home. Some fall into the category generally recognized as safe (GRAS) used by the United States Food and Drug Administration (FDA) to designate food additives that, after decades or even centuries of regular use, show no particular harm to users. Yes, nutmeg may cause intense cramps and hallucinations, but not in the small quantities you're likely to use in a cake or dusted on the top of a drink. It is, as they say, generally recognized as safe.

Anyone who considers re-creating or tweaking old recipes, whether they're from this book or other sources, needs to understand that physicians, botanists, chemists, and others in the know have realized that more than a few ingredients in those recipes should be used with caution or not at all. Whether because of its carcinogenic properties or because of its role as a precursor for making the festival drug ecstasy, for instance, sassafras oil is tightly restricted in the United States. If you want it for root beers or syrups, a safrole-free extract is available that sidesteps both of those concerns. Likewise, the traditional botanicals Virginia snakeroot and calamus root are banned.

Nostalgia aside, not everything in the old days was wholesome. Some old-timey ingredients are more trouble than they're worth while others are downright deadly. Methanol, for instance, has gone under a variety of names since the 19th century, but no matter what you call it, the clear, vodkalike alcohol is a potent toxin that can sicken, blind, and kill humans; it should *never* be consumed as a beverage or served to anyone. A professional distiller, on the other hand, or a food chemist might have a reason to use sulfuric acid safely in the making of drinks, but you at home or in your bar? Unless you have the training, know *exactly* what you're doing, and take appropriate caution, skip it. Read those formulas the way you might a letter from your great-great-grandmother trying to maintain her dignity on a cross-ocean steamer—and maybe there's a serial killer on board: a revealing peek into the past, but it's not necessary, or even wise, to relive her travails.

GRAS: Generally Recognized as Safe

Just because it's natural doesn't mean it's good to put in your mouth. Arsenic, belladonna, and cyanide are as natural as they come. Do you really want them in your cocktail? Others—say, caffeine—are relatively innocuous up to a point. Then there are food additives that have been around so long and used by so many with little ill effect that the FDA regards as them as GRAS. Some are granted GRAS status after scientific review. Rather than rely strictly on printed books (even this one) that become obsolete, for the last word on which oils or compounds are safe to put in food and drinks, check the latest information from the FDA as well as GRAS lists from the Flavor & Extract Manufacturers Association and the International Organization of the Flavor Industry's Global Reference List. See "Organizations and Useful Websites," page 206.

Even the Adulterants Were Adulterated

Because essential oils are both expensive and liquid, they have been easy to adulterate and a target for adulteration since the earliest days of their production. Just after Prohibition, E. W. Bovill quipped in a British journal that "a large proportion of the oil sold as American Peppermint Oil has never seen either America or the true peppermint plant, and the world consumes vastly more Otto of Rose then is ever distilled from rose petals."[28]

Adulteration, in fact, seems to have been the rule rather than the exception in the 19th and early 20th centuries. Pharmacopoeias of the time are rife with the exact characteristics (or at least their normal range) of essential oils and how to detect fraud, often with specific adulterants. Oils labeled "commercial grade," "second grade," and "imitation" hint at this, but even "pure" oils were not always . . . well, pure. Oil of turpentine and alcohol itself were frequently added to bulk up essential oils, sometimes to make up as much as 90 percent of the volume of oils they purported to be.

A handwritten notebook at the University of Wisconsin offers a rare look into how the sorts of essential oils used in cordials and spirits were adulterated at the retail level in the early 20th century. Its oil of wormwood was half turpentine. Neroli, supposedly distilled from orange flowers, was half petit grain, a less costly oil distilled from immature fruit or leaves and stems of orange trees. Oil of cumin was one-third alcohol. Oil of juniper berries? One part oil of juniper berries, two parts turpentine. "Pure" oil of wintergreen was entirely synthetic and boosted with camphor, turpentine, and iron. Sweet almond oil was only two-thirds that; the rest was sesame oil. Oil of spearmint? One-quarter turpentine.[29] You'd be excused for cocking an eyebrow at the claim when packages arrived at the pharmacy from wholesalers that they were at all pure in the first place.

The adulterated oils of the past are, thankfully, largely past. The takeaway from this, though, is that cordial and compounded spirits recipes from old books may work with modern oils—or they may not. It's not that the *recipes* are necessarily bad, but that the *ingredients* may have been; users developed formulas based on what was available. When reading old recipes, then, don't take their measurements at face value. Rather, gauge their relative amounts and work up new formulas using them as guides, not diktats.

50

BERLINER KUMMEL ESSENCE.

Oil of Caraway Seed,	2 ounces
Oil of Anise,	½ ounce
Oil of Dill,	½ ounce
Cologne Spirits,	14 ounces

Mix them.

BLACKBERRY ESSENCE.

Acetic Ether,	1½ ounces
Formic Ether,	½ ounce
Butyrate of Amyl,	2 drachms
Acetate of Amyl,	1 drachm
Glycerine,	2 ounces
Cologne Spirits,	12 ounces

Mix and filter.

BOKER BITTER ESSENCE.

Fluid Extract Quassia,	4 ounces
" " Calamus,	4 ounces
" " Orange Peel, bitter,	6 ounces
" " Catschu,	2 ounces
" " Cardamon,	1½ ounces

Mix them.

BOONEKAMP BITTER ESSENCE.

Oil of Angelica,	½ ounce
Oil of Bitter Orange,	½ ounce

51

Oil of Anise,	½ ounce
Oil of Lemon,	3 drachms
Oil of Coriander,	3 drachms
Oil of Galanga,	2 drachms
Oil of Marjoram,	2 drachms
Oil of wormwood,	2 drachms
Oil of Peppermint,	1½ drachms
Fluid Extract White Agaric	1 ounce
Cologne Spirits,	12 ounces

Dissolve the Oils in the Spirits, then add the Fluid Extract of White Agaric.

BOURBON OIL.

Fusel Oil,	16 ounces
Sulphuric Acid,	1 ounce
Acetate of Potassium,	1 ounce
Dissolve Sulphate of Copper,	½ ounce
and Oxalate of Ammonium,	½ ounce
each in Water,	1 ounce
add Black Oxide of Manganese,	½ ounce

Place them all in a glass percolator and let them rest for 12 hours; then percolate and put into a glass still and distill 16 ounces of Bourbon Oil. Bourbon whiskey is made from this Oil by taking 1 to 1½ ounces of Oil, cut it well in a pint of alcohol; mix into 40 gallons of proof spirits and add one quart of sugar syrup: color with sugar coloring (use 4 ounces). Dissolve the coloring first thoroughly in a quart of liquor before putting in the barrel. Mix all well.

Turpentine was a once common whiskey, gin, and essential oil adulterant. Nasty on its own, in small amounts and perhaps mixed with tea and a bit of barrel char, says cocktail historian Ted "Dr. Cocktail" Haigh, "It's closer than you would ever, ever want to admit to yourself to the flavor of whiskey."

Beware the Fragrant Taint

Alcohol's ability to extract and retain flavors and aromas makes it a fantastic base for drinks. The downside is that alcohol, like butter, milk, and eggs, can suck up ambient smells you'd rather it didn't. A constant refrain from dry Prohibition agents was that much of the illicit hooch of the 1920s and '30s was made in filthy settings. How could it be wholesome liquor when hogs were slopped nearby, when discarded tins and sugar sacks were strewn about the distillery floor, when stills were so unclean that they were dubbed "black" pots?

When you're compounding beverages, work in a clean, well-organized space. Avoid doing anything that raises a stink. I'd even argue not to use perfume, cologne, or scented soap that day, but others might think I'm being a tightass. In any event, don't slice onions, cook cabbage soup, mix tuna salad, snack on kimchi, or whip up a batch of aioli. Likewise, don't clean on days you mix. Hot water is fine, but just the ambient smell of cleaning compounds can taint a batch of spirits. Once your anisette or ginger brandy smells of fish sauce or scrubbing powder, you're going to have to get a whole lot more creative in figuring out what to do with it (other than dumping it).

Just as alcohol absorbs aromas, essential oils can leave them where they're not wanted. Wooden spoons and plastic utensils, bottles, container liners, and blenders are particularly prone to picking up odors after direct contact with essential oils. Unless the tool is disposable, such a pipette, use glass, porcelain, or stainless-steel gear instead for mixing and blending. Don't use bottles or other containers that smell even slightly of what they used to hold.

Essence

Essence is a slippery word when it comes to beverages. Because its meaning shifts with users, it may refer to essential oils, extracts of botanicals in alcohol, or essential oils or other aromatic compounds dissolved in alcohol. In his 1910 *Manual for the Essence Industry*, Eric Walter explains the confusion:

> The medium for transferring flavors is called in general "essence." This word is derived from the Latin "esse," to be, i.e., it is, or will be, the essential part of something. In the former case the term "essence" refers to the source; in the latter, the purpose for which it is used. Sometimes both interpretations agree, as for instance a raspberry essence will be made from raspberry fruit and is to be employed for imparting a raspberry taste or flavor to any substance. However, many essences bear the name only of the product which is to be made, and the essence, which may be synthetically made, bears no relation whatever to the natural fruit product, as for instance in the ease of artificial raspberry essence; then again, rum essence is not made from rum, although it is employed for making rum-like substitutes. [New York: John Wiley and Sons (1910)]

Some home distillers, and those who distill neutral spirits in particular, rely on commercial essences to emulate a huge array of spirits. I've never had good whiskeys, brandies, or rums from such essences, but passable cordials and some decent gins can be made from little more than a bottle of vodka, an ounce or so of essence, and perhaps some sugar.

Buying Essential Oils

Always buy essential oils from reputable suppliers. Research them online and ask friends and colleagues for recommendations for vendors. A few things to keep in mind when shopping for oils to be used in beverages:

- Look for essential oils designated "food safe."
- Local and common names for plants vary considerably; buy from reputable vendors who can provide the Latin denomination of their oils to assure you're getting the product you intend.
- Avoid products labeled "fragrance oil" or "perfume oil" which are likely made from something other than the supposed fragrance. Instead look for "pure essential oil" or "100% essential oil."

Essences

Brandy: (see page 3')

Oil of Cognac	1 ounce
Oenanthic Ether	1 "
Ol. Bitter Almonds	2 drams
Orris root powder	16 ounces
Tannin	2 ounces
Alcohol q.s. to make	1 gallon

Macerate the orris root in the alcohol for a week and percolate until one gallon is obtained. To this add the tannin, dissolve and filter and then dissolve the oils and ether in the filtrate. Half pint of this essence is sufficient for 40 gallons of the brandy.

Rum Essence (Fleischmann) (see page 3')

	Alcohol	32 ounces
C.P.	Sulfuric Acid	4 ounces
	Manganese Dioxid	2 ounces
	Pyroligneous Acid	4 ounces

Distil and add to 32 ounces of distillate

Acetic ester	32 ounces
Butyric ester	8 ounces
Saffron extract	16 ounces
Oil of Birch	1/8 ounce

- Buy oils in dark glass (darkness protects against sunlight damage and undiluted oils can dissolve rubber and plastic) or lined aluminum bottles.
- Compare prices. The most expensive may not be the best, but reputable vendors do have different suppliers, so prices vary. If you have questions, call: most suppliers are happy to answer questions.

Storing Essential Oils

- Store all essential oils in a cool, dark place. The fridge is fine, but do not freeze them. At the least, keep them out of direct sunlight. Keep them away from areas with variable temperatures, such as next to appliances, outer walls, or windows.
- Citrus oils in particular tend to degrade after six months or so. Buy them in the quantities you need and store them in the refrigerator to extend their usefulness.
- The shelf lives of volatile oils vary. Check with the vendor for expiry information.
- If the oils arrive in bottles with rubber droppers, switch the lids; oils may dissolve rubber over time.
- Store oil in dark bottles (amber or cobalt). Even better, use bottles with UV protective coating or lined aluminum.
- A few oils may cloud or solidify when cold. If this happens, hold the bottle in your hands for a few minutes; your body warmth should liquefy the mass.
- Always return the cap as soon as you've extracted the amount of oil you need and make sure it's screwed on tightly.

The Pearson Square and Cider Oil

Spend enough time around hobbyist distillers, winemakers, and certain bartenders and you are bound to hear talk of the Pearson Square. No, it's not some disreputable plaza where they all hang out and swap their homemade wares (though that does sound like the kind of place I'd like to whittle away an afternoon). The Pearson Square is a simple mathematical model used to determine the ratio of ingredients to combine in order to reach a particular final concentration. People who make wine and cordials use it to determine how much of one low-proof liquid should be combined with a higher-proof liquid to reach some point between the two strengths. There are no complicated algorithms to figure; it's basic arithmetic.

So, how's it work? Well, picture the Pearson Square as a great big circle. Nah, I'm jerking your chain; it's a square. Make it as big or small as you like. It measures proportions, so the units can be anything that holds liquid: pints, liters, gallons, buckets, jars, whatever. Its four corners are indicated by the letters A (upper left), B (lower left), D (upper right), and E (lower right). The center, where lines drawn from A to E and from B to D, is labeled C. Disregard any negative numbers obtained so that -13, for instance, is merely 13.

A = the alcohol content of the stronger spirit

B = the alcohol content of the lower-proof or nonalcoholic liquid

C = your target alcoholic content, the final proof you want

D = (B minus C), the proportion of stronger spirit you need

E = (A minus C), the proportion of lower-proof liquid you need

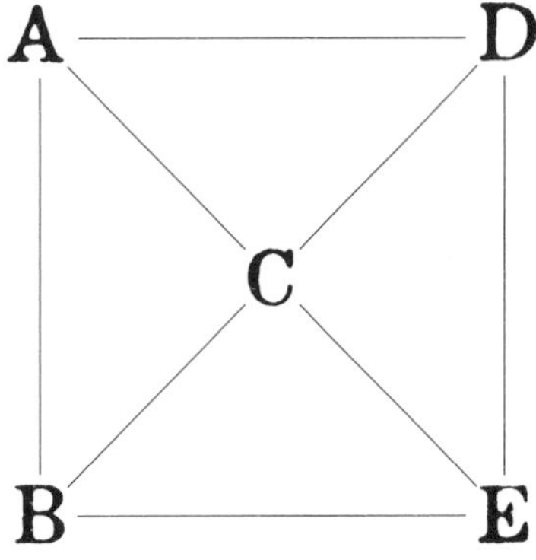

For instance, you want to mingle a batch of hard, low-proof apple cider with apple brandy to make a homemade Cider Oil (page 107). How much of each do you use if you want a specific final proof? The Pearson Square lays it out.

Say you want your cider oil to be 18% alcohol (C). Your brandy is 50% alcohol (A) and your cider is 5% (B). The proportion or parts of brandy you need (D) is (5 minus 18) = –13 (disregard negative values, so this is 13) and the proportion of cider you need (E) is (50 minus 18) = 32. If you add 13 parts of 50% abv apple brandy to 32 parts of 5% hard cider, you'll end up with 45 parts of 18% cider. Remember: "Parts" can be milliliters, ounces, yogurt containers (clean ones, please), or other measures you find convenient. A 750 ml bottle of bonded apple brandy will yield a little over 2.5 liters of cider oil, plenty enough to get your wiggle on.

See pages 105–111 for Victor Lyon's cider-based recipes.

Scotch Whiskey

Proof whiskey 20 gallons
Acetic acid 1 ounce
Loaf sugar ½ pound
30 drops creosote dissolved in one pint alcohol.

Let it stand 48 hours

Rye Whiskey

Proof spirit 40 gallons
Peach flavoring 2 gallons
White vinegar 1 pint
Oil cognac 12 drops

(192 gtt) (48 gtt to qt)

Gin-making and gin-drinking have erected themselves a tradition. When prohibition struck the country and bathtub gin came into being, men drank it reluctantly, as though it were a mixture of iodine, stove polish and spinach juice. But in 13 years they have become accustomed to it. It's the cheapest of all drinks, considering the wallop it carries. And many a person will tell you that gin, whether in cocktail or highball, will remain the national potation in spite of repeal.

—"Repeal of Prohibition in Practical Effect in N.Y.,"
San Bernardino County Sun,
October 14, 1933

Chapter Three

Gin, Whiskey, and Rum

These are the acts of someone calculating the logistics

Victor Lyon's notebook doesn't contain obvious recipes or formulas for moonshine, but that's hardly unusual. Few written recipes for making moonshine survive from those years. Such recipes were part of oral traditions and tended not to be written anyway. What we tend to see instead in historic collections—when there's anything written at all—are ledgers and penciled calculations of profit and loss for making alcohol: grains, yeast, sugar, sorghum, or molasses, supplies such as bottles and corks. We can infer recipes and yields from those. Occasionally, such files list customers by name, address, and how much liquor they bought and their debts. If Lyon kept such explicit records, they are lost to us. In fact, it's not clear from the notebook that the Harlem physician sold liquor at all. No mug shots, no arrest reports, and no articles have surfaced to link him to bootlegging.

But there are hints that suggest perhaps he both made and sold contraband liquor. In the back of the notebook are price lists for essential oils and contact information for firms that sold supplies for making and bottling alcohol. Here and there, he makes adjustments to formulas, and figures the cost of each bottle of various compounded spirits. Idle curiosity? Perhaps. At the very least, though, these are the acts of someone calculating the logistics of clandestine liquor for sale.

In this chapter, we'll look at some of the notebook's entries on gin, whiskey, and rum, along with others such as arrack, that would have been available on the black market in Prohibition-era New York.

Caramel Color
Thomas Henderson & Co 14 Cliff St.
D.D. Williamson 86 Fulton St.

Bottles
T. C. Wheaton Co. 165 B'way.
Millville N.J.

American Perfumer - Journal 14 Cliff St.
2nd year

Synfleur Scientific Laboratories
Alois von Isakovics - Monticello N.Y.

Westman Press Ltd.
72 Queen St. West Toronto Canada
(Technical Publications)

Emil Greiner Co. N.Y.C instruments

Meyer-Cameron Co. 13 St. 3 Ave. "Tins" building

B. L. Patterson 304 East 27 St. N.Y.C.

Analyses whisky of all types - Papers by Schidrowitz & Kaye J. Soc Chem. Indust
1902-1905

Vasey - Analysis of Potable spirits

Ortho .06 per lb 6.00
Cal Prep .20 " 4.00
10.00

1.20 .10 for 1½

Nov 8-19
Ol Juniper
" Anise
" Corn
" Coriander
" Bitter Alm
Vanillin
T. Cochineal
T. red Saunde
Sugar Color
Orange flower
Benzaldehyde
Oil Lemon Terp
Oil Cloves
Carrot
Oil Angelica
Terpeneless Junip
Oil Caraway
Butyric Ether (
Amyl Valerian
Oil Cinnamon
Ol Aurantii
%
Angelica
Cinnamon
" Cu
Clove
Coriander
Juniper
Lemon
Orange - bitter
" sweet
Tangerine

Gin

One should always age homemade gin, goes a bit of Prohibition-era snark, until it cools to at least room temperature.

One of the reasons gin was so popular during Prohibition is that it was relatively easy to make with home-distilled spirits or, more commonly, redistilled and scrubbed denatured industrial alcohol. With a formula and good ingredients in hand, drinkers could make what we call a compounded gin now: a blend of high-proof spirits, essential oils or extracts, and water, maybe with a touch of syrup or glycerin to smooth out rough edges.

On repeal, most drinkers ditched counterfeit whiskeys and other ersatz spirits as soon as they could get genuine wet goods. Not homemade gin. In fact, New York dealers said that after the 21st Amendment ended Prohibition, sales of neutral spirits showed no decline at all.[30] Today, so-called bathtub gin stands as shorthand for the horrors of Prohibition-era drinking, the nadir of beverage arts in America, the lowest point in our collective drinking shame. But what was that stuff? Bartenders' folklore abounds with anecdotes about old-timers using oil of juniper berries to make bathtub gin, named supposedly for the unsanitary conditions in which its detractors claimed it was made.

I suspect we've been calling it bathtub gin for the wrong reason. The common assumption is that such gins were actually mixed in bathtubs, the alcohol commingling with soap scum, loose hairs, rusty fixtures, and sloughed dead skin—which would be super nasty. I'm not saying that *never* happened, but old-timers I interviewed who mixed alcohol and flavorings with their parents described using large glass demijohns and jugs called carboys to mix gin. When they added water to the mixture to bring its 90% abv or so down to drinking proof,

Geneva Liqueur Oil (see page 28 Complete Formula) 1/4 dram
Oil of Lemon (terpenless) 6 3/4 "
" " Cognac 7 "
" " Wormwood 10 "
" " Cardamom 1 ounce
" " Juniper (terpenless) 2 ounces
" " Mace 2 1/2 ounces
" " Cloves 9 ounces
Absolute alcohol 1 pound.

Artificial Steinhager
Carvol 1/4 ounce
Oil of Angelica 1 ounce
" " Juniper (terpenless) 1 ounce
Absolute Alcohol 13 3/4 ounces
1 pound

Gin

Corn spirits	80 gallons
Oil of turpentine	1 pint
Oil of Juniper	8 ounces
Salt	21 pounds
Water	35 gallons
Oil of caraway	1/2 ounce
Oil of sweet fennel	1/4 ounce
Cardamons	8 ounces

Distil over 100 gallons.

Ageing and improving taste
For dark colored liquors

Tincture Kremaria 1/4 pound to one gallon is to be recommended

---

Terpenes cause liquor cloudiness
Terpeneless oils dissolve better in low proof alcohol.

Silent Spirit is pure diluted alcohol.

Tannin hastens ageing and improves taste hence oak casks are best adapted for liquors.

those oversized jugs did not fit under a kitchen sink faucet. Tilted to one side, though, the jugs could be topped off readily using the bathtub's tap. As someone who has fermented, distilled, blended, and shifted a lot of alcohol, that seems a much more reasonable explanation for the term.

Either way, we rarely get the opportunity to examine what such concoctions actually, truly were.

Here is our chance.

Types of Gin

The US Alcohol and Tobacco Tax and Trade Bureau (TTB for short) recognizes three distinct types of spirits within the broader class of gin: distilled, redistilled, and compounded. All of them are at least 40% alcohol and flavored primarily by juniper berries.

Distilled gin

Gin produced by original distillation from mash with or over juniper berries and other aromatics or their extracts, essences, or flavors

Redistilled gin

Gin produced by redistillation of distilled spirits with or over juniper berries and other aromatics or their extracts, essences, or flavors

Compounded gin

Gin produced by mixing neutral spirits with juniper berries and other aromatics or their extracts, essences, or flavors

Lyon's gin recipes don't encompass all the official modern permutations. There is, for instance, none that start with a low-alcohol mash run through a still. Rather, most are compounded. A few are redistilled. One British recipe is something of a hybrid, combining corn (i.e., grain) spirits with essential oils and whole cardamom, a gin botanical enjoying some vogue with newer American distilleries now.

The notebook also includes genever and cordial gins. **Cordial gins** are sweetened and sometimes made with additional flavors. **Sloe gin**, made by infusing purplish-black sloes, is one example. Its dominant flavor comes from an infusion of small, astringent, plum-like fruits of *Prunus spinosa*, a thorny hedgerow plant also called blackthorn. Plymouth and the Bitter Truth sloe gins are available in the United States. Venerable **Old Tom** is more nebulous. When it was sweetened, Old Tom was cordial gin, but even distillers who make it now disagree on just how sweet it was and whether it should be aged. In practice and over time, variation in the style made it as diverse as modern gins.

And **genever**? Why, that gets a section of its own.

To give new brandy all the qualities of old.

Aqua Ammonia 30 drops

Add to one gallon new brandy shaking it well that it may combine with the acid on which the taste and other qualities of the new liquor depend.

Gin Heading

Oil of Vitriol	one dessertspoonful
Oil of almonds	" "

mix with a portion of spirits of wine and add the whole to 100 gallons of made up gin. (see page 30)

To make up 30 gallons of raw spirit into cordial Gin

Oil of turpentine	2 penny weight
Oil of juniper berries	3 penny weight
Oil of vitriol	2 penny weight
Oil of almonds	2 penny weight
Elder flower water	1 pint

Mix the oils with a pint of spirits of wine, and add about 8 pounds of loaf sugar 25 gallons of spirits, one in five, which will bear five gallons of water. Rouse it well and in order to fine it take 2 ounces of alum and one of salt of tartar, boil it till it be quite white, then throw it into your cask continually stirring it for 10 minutes, bung it up and when fine it will be fit for use.

(192 gtt
48 gtt to gt)

Gin Cocktails

Black market gins were especially easy to source during Prohibition because they were so easily made. When the blender wasn't particularly skilled or the base alcohol imperfectly redistilled to remove denaturants, mixing sweet and bitter ingredients in gin cocktails helped—more or less—to buff out rough edges. If re-creating the notebook's gin recipes somehow doesn't make it to your to-do list, you can still satisfy a taste for Volstead-era gin cocktails with some of these using modern gins.

DUBONNET COCKTAIL

Gin shows up again and again in Prohibition-era cocktails because it was an easy spirit to make for nonchemists; just add juniper oil to a batch of high-proof spirit, water it down, and as soon as you can say, "Bob's your uncle," you've got a batch of basic gin. Mixing it with Dubonnet, a mildly bitter aperitif, rounds its rough edges.

Combine equal parts gin and Dubonnet (with a dash of orange bitters if you like) in a mixing glass with ice. Stir until chilled, then strain into a cocktail glass.

THE LAST WORD COCKTAIL

The word is that the Last Word cocktail was invented by bartender Frank Fogarty at the Detroit Athletic Club in 1922. It fell between the cracks of history, however, until Seattle bartender Murray Stenson rediscovered it about a decade ago in Ted Saucier's 1951 bartenders' guide *Bottoms Up!* and became something of an evangelist for this exquisite drink. We have been guilty, on particularly boisterous evenings, of mixing them by the quart.

- 0.75 oz gin
- 0.75 oz green Chartreuse
- 0.75 oz maraschino liqueur
- 0.75 oz fresh lime juice

Shake the ingredients with ice and strain into a chilled cocktail glass. Garnish with a lemon twist.

LUCIEN GAUDIN

Fencing is my all-time, hands-down, favorite sport. And I've scars to show for my love of it. Seriously, kids: wear a mask and glove when you take up a saber. These days, I'm more likely to take up a shaker, though, and mix this bittersweet cocktail named after a 1920s Olympic fencer. The Lucien Gaudin is kissing cousin to that darling of the American cocktail scene, the Negroni. Gaudin brought home two silvers and two gold medals. I'll settle for just one of these.

1 oz gin
0.5 oz Campari
0.5 oz Cointreau
0.5 oz dry vermouth

Stir well in a cocktail shaker with ice. Strain into a cocktail glass or a coupe. Garnish, if you like, with a flamed orange peel.

SOUTHSIDE

A Prohibition keeper that doesn't get enough play in modern bars, the Southside blends gin with lemon juice and mint for a drink that's kissing cousin to the more familiar mojito. It's like a minty gin lemonade. And who doesn't like lemonade? Give it a splash of soda to lighten the drink, if you like, and a dash or two of aromatic bitters, but really, it's fine as is.

2 oz gin
6 to 8 fresh mint leaves
1 oz fresh lemon juice
0.75 oz simple syrup (page 145)
Splash of soda (optional)

Shake the ingredients with ice in a shaker. Strain into a cocktail glass or coupe.

BEE'S KNEES

Another recipe sweetened to take that bathtub edge off Prohibition-era gins. Because honey syrup blends especially well with many rums, consider swapping out the gin with a white *rhum agricole* here.

- 2 oz dry gin
- 1 oz honey syrup (half honey, half water, heated briefly until uniform, then cooled)
- 1 oz fresh lemon juice

Shake the ingredients with ice and strain into a chilled old-fashioned glass with fresh ice.

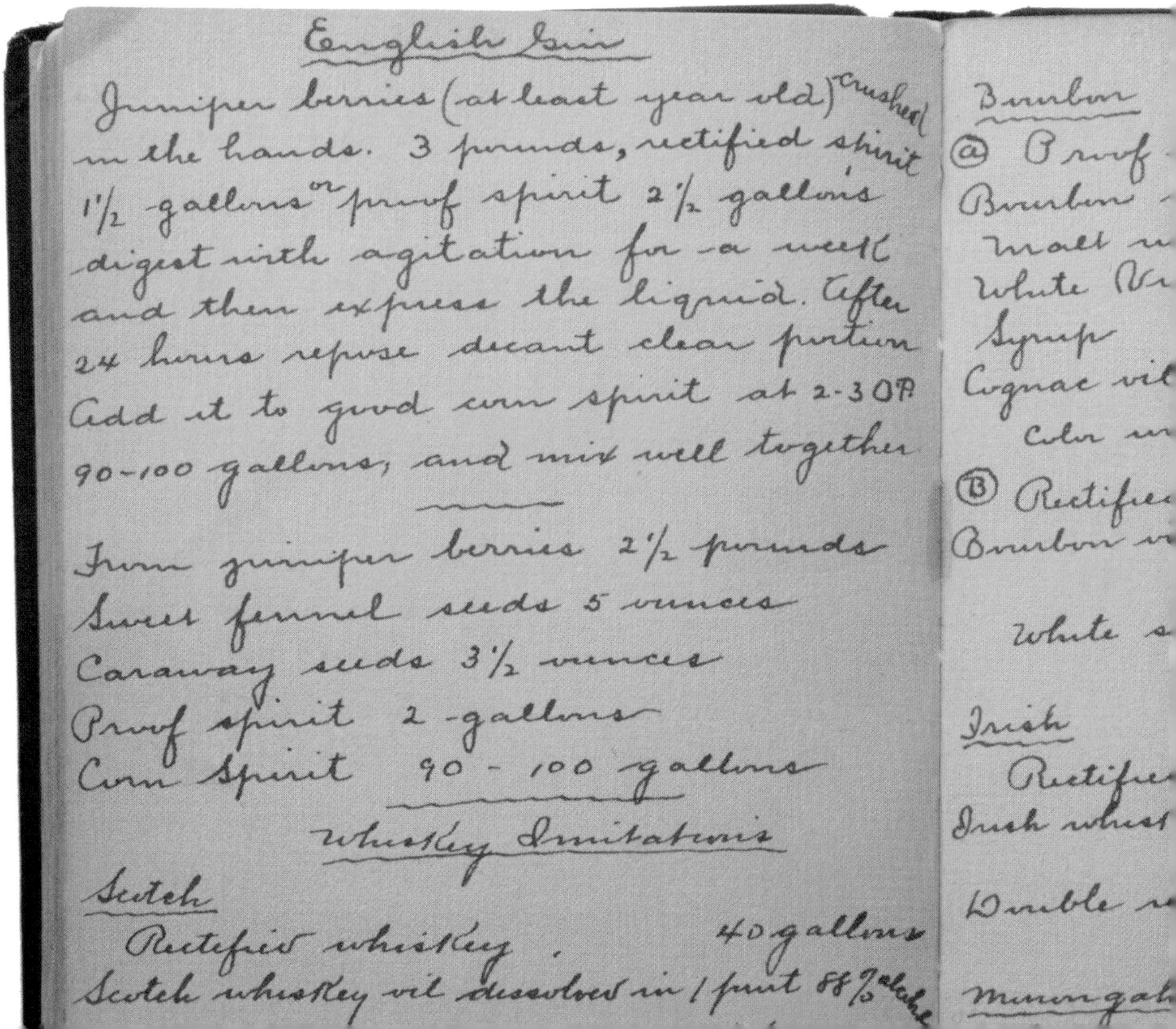

English Gin

Juniper berries (at least year old) crushed in the hands. 3 pounds, rectified spirit 1½ gallons or proof spirit 2½ gallons digest with agitation for a week and then express the liquid. After 24 hours repose decant clear portion Add it to good corn spirit at 2-3 OP. 90-100 gallons, and mix well together

From juniper berries 2½ pounds
Sweet fennel seeds 5 ounces
Caraway seeds 3½ ounces
Proof spirit 2 gallons
Corn Spirit 90 - 100 gallons

Whiskey Imitations

Scotch

Rectified whiskey 40 gallons
Scotch whiskey oil dissolved in 1 pint 88% alcohol

Bourbon

Irish

Genever

In the spring of 1922, a shipment of lamps from Germany arrived by steamer in Philadelphia. Customs appraisers found nothing out of the ordinary until one thought they seemed a bit, well, *heavy*. Upon opening one, he discovered a quart of "Holland" gin inside. Right then and there, the consignee lost the entire lot. "Unless Uncle Sam gets his hands on all shipments," noted a *Central Press* article, "German lampstands promise to become exceedingly popular in the land made famous by Mr. Volstead."[31]

The gin priming those lamps was not the familiar London dry style so popular today. It was an older, malted style also called genever, jenever, Hollands, genevieve, Schiedam (after the Dutch distilling center), and (incorrectly) Dutch gin. Since colonial days, Americans knew it as a Dutch specialty, though it is also made in Belgium and parts of Germany.

American distillers made semblances of genevers since at least 1809 when Pennsylvania distiller Samuel M'Harry published a recipe "How to make a resemblance of Holland Gin out of Rye Whiskey" in his *Practical Distiller*. Chief Gowanus New Netherland Gin from New York Distilling Company is a modern re-creation of M'Harry's recipe and worth seeking out. Confusingly, early bartending guides often refer to it simply as "gin." Using London dry gin, such as Beefeater or Tanqueray, makes some of those old gin drinks weird, unbalanced creations. What you want is malty, juniper-forward genever. Use it as you would whiskey.

KICK WITH EACH LAMP IS GERMAN TRADE BOOSTER

German "gin-lamp."

Philadelphia customs inspectors have just unearthed the latest device of rum smugglers. This is the use of German wooden lamp stands. The officers found that the lamp stands were expensive—but why not—each contained a quart of Holland gin.

Imitation Shiedam Gin

Dissolve 3½ drams oil juniper in sufficient 95% alcohol to make clear liquid. Add it to 40 gallons French spirits 10 above proof with 8 ounces orange peel flavoring. 1-quart syrup, add 30 drops oil sweet fennel.

Genever

Macerate 2 pounds juniper berries in 17 pounds of alcohol and 3 quarts of water for 2 days. Then distill off 19 pounds and compound distillate with 3 pounds sugar and filter

A slight error in transcription would make the two recipes on page 61 seem to be for English gin, but the original recipes are, in fact, for *English-made* genever, or Holland gin. They both come from the 1902 edition of *The Brewer, Distiller, and Wine Manufacturer*,[32] a British guide.

The bones of all proper gins and genevers are surely built from juniper, a tree that grows throughout Europe, north Africa, Asia, and parts of North America. Of the hundreds of varieties of juniper, the berry-like cones of *Juniperus communis* are most prized for the resinous, bracing aroma and flavor they bring. In North America, a taller related

Carvoli 2.5 g
Spiritus (95) 3 l
Sacchar. 1000.0
Coct cum Aquae 1000.0
Aquae 5.6 l

Genievre

Macerate 2 pounds juniper berries in 17 pounds alcohol and 3 quarts water for 2 days, then distil off 19 pounds, compound the distillate with 3 pounds of sugar and filter.

species called Western or Sierra juniper *(J. occidentalis)* bears a larger, bluer berry that is sometimes used in newer "Western style" gins, many of which contain non-traditional and hyper-local botanicals.

Just as they are now, juniper berries were easy enough to obtain from wholesale spice merchants. As always quality was key, and not just any berry would do. I asked David T. Smith, British coauthor of *The Craft of Gin* and irrepressible gin enthusiast, why the notebook specifies that juniper berries should be at least a year old for English genever. Smith holds that *Juniperus communis* berries actually need a full two seasons of growth, rather than one as the notebook specifies. Only then do the little blue-black balls have a great enough concentration of essential oils for use in gin.

Genever and Genever-Style Brands to Try

Anchor Distilling: Genevieve (US)

Bols: Genever (both 42% abv and barrel-aged versions) (Holland)

New York Distilling Company: Chief Gowanus New Netherland Gin

Notaris: XO Jenever (Holland)

De Vergulden Poort: Amsterdamsche Roggejenever, a 100% rye genever (Holland)

Wynand Focking: 5 jaar Geripte Genever (Holland)

ALAMAGOOZLUM

Alamawhoozlum? Alamagoozlum. It's a mouthful, and not just because the recipe—from Charles H. Baker Jr.'s 1939 *The Gentleman's Companion*—makes about a 10-ounce drink. A blend of herbal Chartreuse, malty genever, and a hefty dose of bitters, it's one you can share with a friend. Or two. Baker credits its invention to financier J. Pierpont Morgan, but in 1873 the Pelican Saloon in Los Angeles advertised drinks that included the Alamagoosier. Was it the same drink? Without a recipe, it's hard to say, though that *Bris Around the Corner* cocktail in the same ad gives me pause . . .

- 2 oz genever
- 2 oz plain water
- 1.5 oz Jamaican rum
- 1.5 oz Chartreuse (green is better here than yellow, but it's your call)
- 1.5 oz gomme syrup (page 147)
- 0.5 oz curaçao
- 0.5 oz Angostura bitters
- ½ egg white

Shake all the ingredients without ice for 10 seconds to emulsify the egg white. Add ice, shake again until shilled, then strain into a large coupe (or two smaller ones).

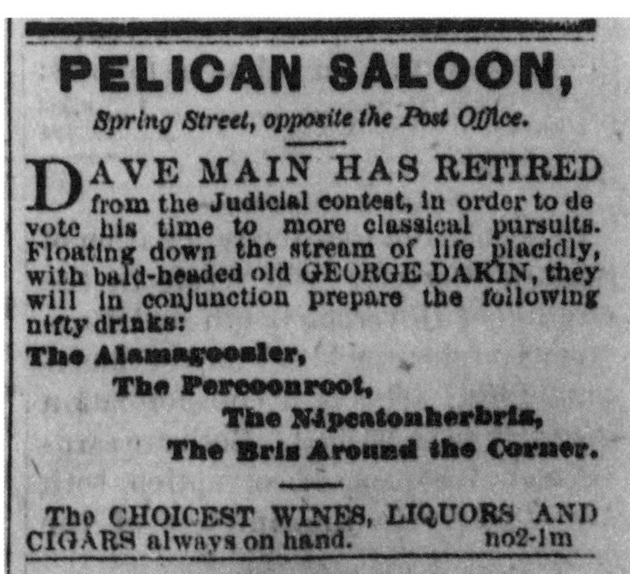

PELICAN SALOON,

Spring Street, opposite the Post Office.

DAVE MAIN HAS RETIRED from the Judicial contest, in order to devote his time to more classical pursuits. Floating down the stream of life placidly, with bald-headed old GEORGE DAKIN, they will in conjunction prepare the following nifty drinks:

The Alamagoosier,
The Percoonroot,
The Nipcatonherbris,
The Bris Around the Corner.

The CHOICEST WINES, LIQUORS AND CIGARS always on hand. no2-1m

THE COLLINS

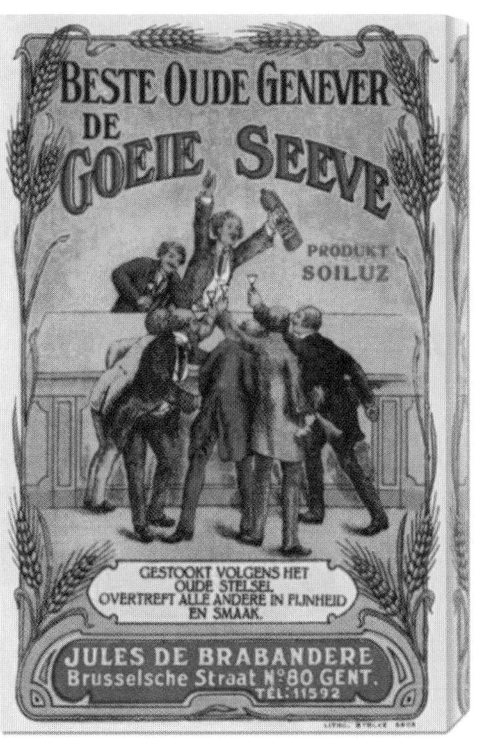

The Collins—Tom, John, or even Juan Collins, depending on who's doing the mixing—is an early 19th-century precursor to the French 75, using soda water rather than Champagne. Perfectly traditional with London dry or the lightly sweetened Old Tom gins, it shines with genever.

2 oz genever
1 oz fresh lemon juice
0.5 oz simple syrup (page 145)
Soda water, quantum satis

Shake the ingredients (except the soda water) with ice, strain into an ice-filled Collins glass, and top with soda water. Give it a brief stir, take a sip, and smile.

DEATH IN THE GULF STREAM

A stiff, bitter concoction from Charles H. Baker Jr.'s 1939 *The Gentleman's Companion*. Baker scored the recipe from his friend, famed author and boozehound Ernest Hemingway. Like the classic mai tai or a proper Cuba Libre, this one gets a boost of lime oil from the fruit's shell.

> Take a tall thin water tumbler and fill it with finely cracked ice. Lace this broken debris with 4 good purple splashes of Angostura, add the juice and crushed peel of 1 green lime, and fill the glass almost full with Holland gin . . . No sugar, no fancying. It's strong, it's bitter—but so is English ale strong and bitter, in many cases. We don't add sugar to ale, and we don't need sugar in a Death in the Gulf Stream—or at least not more than 1 tsp. Its tartness and its bitterness are its chief charm. It is reviving and refreshing; cools the blood and inspires renewed interest in food, companions and life.

Oh, go ahead and put a smidge of simple syrup (page 145) in it if the thing's too harsh for your tastes. Not enough to make it sweet, just to temper the high notes.

Rum

Of the 300-plus entries in Victor Lyon's notebook, not one includes directions for making actual rum, for starting with molasses or sugarcane, then fermenting, distilling, aging, and blending it. Every single one of his recipes involving rum either starts with that spirit as the base for making something else or is complete artifice. The thing is, Lyon wasn't some outlier compounding these sketchy fictions nobody had ever drunk or even heard of. During Prohibition, wealthy clientele often thought that while hoi polloi got cut, watered down, and faked spirits, *they* were getting the Real McCoy—but swells sometimes bought counterfeit wet goods the same as John Q. Public did; they just paid more for it.[33] Lyon's recipes fall firmly into an age-old tradition among rum merchants for deception. They reflect historical rums more accurately than many distillers would have us believe.

Most of the recipes from the notebook are for rum essences. Such essences were mixtures of alcohol and aromatic substances that, when added in small doses to plain spirits or blends of actual rum with spirits gave the general aroma and taste of aged rum. Such additions might have included vanilla, tea, caramel, sweet spirits of nitre, pyroligneous acid, ethyl butyrate, soot, sulfuric acid, various essential oils, gall tincture, and extracts of saffron. But, then, what constituted "actual" rum in the first place was an uncertain gamble.

According to New Orleans rum authority and collector Stephen Remsberg, Prohibition coincided with the beginning of the sale by distillers of their rum in a bottle with a proprietary label. "Before World War I," he wrote to me, "rum was shipped in the barrel. A tavern or grocer would buy a barrel and cases of empty glass bottles. The customer would buy or pay a deposit on the bottle, and the shop would fill it. If the merchant had a high-end trade, he would print a label with the customer's name. I have a few such bottles. In most cases, I doubt the customer ever knew the name of the distiller of the rum. He would tell the shop that he wanted 12 bottles of that Jamaican 'Wedderburn' rum he had bought in the past, identifying only the category of the rum on the London market. Under those circumstances who would know what 'genuine' was. You depended on the reputation of the local merchant."

And those merchants may not have been dealing with genuine rums even when they were unloaded in America, usually by way of London's rum market. At the dawn of Prohibition, American physician and pure food campaigner Harvey W. Wiley bemoaned the sad state of affairs. "As in the case of whiskey and brandy, rum has been subjected to all kinds of adulteration. So great has become the adulteration of rum shipped to England from Jamaica that for every barrel of rum sent 6 barrels were sold."[34]

Rum was not only widely adulterated, the spirit was itself an adulterant. By 1924, local rum could be had for as little as forty cents a gallon in Havana. One journalist writing from Cuba reported that a gallon of such rum mixed with a quart of Scotch yielded five quarts of Scotch. "It may taste a little raw," he wrote, "but the kick, in fact a good healthy wallop, is there, so why should anyone object?"[35]

Why indeed?

RUMESSENZ

This rum essence wasn't meant to be consumed *as* rum; it was intended to give rumlike aroma and flavor to plain spirits. Wholesalers, saloonkeepers, blenders, importers, exporters, bottlers, and others who handled bulk rum would use such essences for three main purposes: to fake rum completely from plain spirits, to reintroduce familiar rum smells and tastes to a batch that had been cut with plain alcohol, or to boost the appeal of rum that was subpar—perhaps because it had been already so massaged by previous handlers.

Through its history, rum has been a spectacularly adulterated and counterfeited spirit. Modern brands still regularly include ingredients to augment body and color that are forbidden in spirits such as straight whiskey. Chief among them is caramel for just the right color to suggest greater age than the spirit may actually have. In Lyon's recipe following, caramel is mixed with vanilla, cassia buds, salt, and birch tar. My advice? Just buy some nice rum. Great examples can be had for significantly less than French brandies.

Vanillae concisae (cut vanilla) 2.5
Olei Rusci (birch tar) 10.0
Radicis Tormentillae cincisae (cut tormentil root) 20.0
Korum cassiae contusurune (bruised cassia buds) 2.5
Fulginis splendentis pulveratae (powdered soot) 15.0
Salis culinaris (culinary salt) 25.0
Aetheris Formici (formic ether) . . .100.0
Spiritus Aetheris Nitrosi (nitric ether). 15.0
Spiritus (90%) (90% abv neutral spirit) 500.0
Tincturae Sacchari Tosti (caramel). . 50.0

Let macerate for 8 days—then filter. 15-20 grams are combined with 1 liter of neutral spirits at 53-55% (the original calls for "Weingeist," spirit of wine).

Rum essences formulas were wide-ranging, though they often include butyric and formic ethers for fruity, pineapple-like aromas; caramel, vanilla, and tea to imitate barrel-aging; and cassia to impart warmth. Recipes abound because types of rum did; Caribbean rums, for instance, may vary depending on whether the territories from which they hailed were colonized by French, Spanish, or British forces at different points in history with different distilling technologies. Some essence formulas evolved as understanding of ingredients—or quality of them—improved. Finally, many of them were just different paths to get to the same result. Or close enough.

Low grade Artificial Rum.

Plain spirits	40 gallons
Rum	5 gallons
Prune juice	1/2 gallon
Caramel	12 ounces
Rum essence	8 ounces

LOW GRADE ARTIFICIAL RUM

Plain spirits	40 gallons
Rum	5 gallons
Prune juice	½ gallon
Caramel	12 ounces
Rum essence	8 ounces

Saffron

Saffron, one of the world's most expensive spices, is the stigmata of a crocus flower that must be harvested by hand. Saffron has a rich, musky, floral scent and can impart varying shades of yellow to curries, cordials, and some vermouths. Its use as a colorant in spirits goes back at least 400 years. Old rum and whiskey recipes in particular rely on saffron for warmth, color, and a tinge of unearned age.

Aurantieae.
A
1
2
3
3a
4
4a
5
6
7
8
9
Citrus Limonum Risso.
8

Rum Cocktails

Lyon's recipes for rum shrubs are about as close as he gets to a cocktail in his entire notebook—and they are among my favorites. Until recently, shrubs were a nearly extinct line of beverages that once enjoyed immense popularity. In his excellent book *Shrubs*, Michael Dietsch focuses on vinegar-based examples of the fruit juice drinks (the name derives from the Arabic *sharab*, "to drink"). As bracing and refreshing as those are, a second mellow type of shrub without vinegar but made from fruit juice, sugar, and brandy or rum has been knocking around for centuries. Use it in punches or as you might curaçao.

RUM SHRUB

Lyon's two shrubs are among my favorite recipes in the notebook, each lifted from Joseph Fleischman's 1885 compounding manual. Both are good over ice (maybe with a bit more rum or iced tea for an impromptu punch) or as a cordial, and I've used them in margaritas to good effect. For each, Puerto Rican 151 is fine but Lost Spirits Cuban-style rum is grand. Here's a scaled-down and slightly tweaked version for home:

750 ml 151 proof rum
3.25 oz fresh orange juice
3.25 oz fresh lemon juice
Peel of 1/2 lemon, pith removed
Peel of 1/2 orange, pith removed
13 oz sugar
16 oz water

Combine the rum, juices, and citrus peels in a large swing-top jar. Seal and let macerate 24 hours in a cool place. Meanwhile, make a syrup by heating the sugar and water in a nonreactive pot. When cool, combine with the strained rum mixture, stir to blend, and bottle.

The West Indian shrub is identical, except that it uses fresh lime juice in place of both the lemon and orange juices.

Rum Essence

Alcohol 32 ℥
Sulfuric Acid 4 ℥
Manganese Dioxide 2 ℥
Pyroligneous Acid 4 ℥

is distilled and to 32 ℥ of distillate is add

Acetic ester 32 ℥
Butyric " 8 ℥
Saffron extract 16 ℥
Oil of birch 1/8 ℥

Saffron Extract

1 qt 95% alcohol
3 oz yellow saffron (flo
macerate for 3 days
and filter

Rum Shrub

To 1 gallon of rum add 1 pint each of orange and lemon juice and the peels of 2 oranges and one lemon. Digest for 24 hours in the cold strain and sweeten with syrup made by dissolving 4 pounds white sugar in 5 pints of water.

West India Shrub

Similar to above only replace orange and lemon juice by equal quantity of lime juice

Rum is 77% by volume.

From Fleischman's Art of Blending and compounding liquors and wines.

Fly Spray (Druggists Circular August 1930)

Eucalyptol
Acetic Ether
Water āā 100
lcohol suitably perfumed 400
incture of insect flowers 500
(Giorn di Farm) To be used with an atomizer

Rum Essence (see page 1)

Butyric Ether	15 parts
Acetic ether	2 parts
Tr. Vanilla	2 parts
Essence violets	2 parts
Alcohol	90 parts

TWELVE MILE LIMIT

As Prohibition was just getting its sea legs, the United States reckoned its laws held 3 miles into open water. Beyond that, just out of US jurisdiction, bobbed armadas. Dubbed "rum row," each was an amalgam of smuggler's ships, cutting plants, and offshore warehouses freighted with those intoxicating beverages forbidden onshore. When America later extended its territorial reach to 12 miles, rum row shifted further out and continued as before. In a nod to that shifting, permeable barrier, here's a stiff one to keep you afloat.

1 oz white rum
0.5 oz rye whiskey
0.5 oz brandy
0.5 oz grenadine
0.5 oz fresh lemon juice
Garnish: lemon twist

Shake with ice until chilled. Strain into a cocktail glass. Garnish with a lemon twist.

MICHAEL LAZAR'S MAI TAI

San Francisco bar manager and author Michael Lazar is a cautious advocate of essential oils in drinks. "Some have too narrow a flavor range compared to the fresh botanicals, but I look at them as different ways to get flavors in," he explains. "Galangal is so hard, it's impossible to work with, so galangal oil is great. And shiso is so incredibly delicate and very hard to keep fresh, especially in a bar setting, that the oil is a godsend." In his adaptation of Trader Vic's 1944 Mai Tai, Lazar combines fresh lime juice with lime-flavored simple syrup.

2 oz Appleton or El Dorado 12-year-old rum
1 oz fresh lime juice
0.5 oz Ferrand dry orange curaçao or Cointreau Noir
0.5 oz orgeat
0.25 oz lime simple syrup (recipe follows)
Lime wheel and sunflower petals, for garnish

Mix all ingredients and shake with ice. Strain over crushed ice, garnish with lime wheel and sunflower petals. For a more traditional approach, drop the spent lime shell in the drink and garnish with a sprig of mint

LIME SIMPLE SYRUP

1 liter 1:1 simple syrup (page 145)
5 to 10 drops lime oil

Mix the lime oil in cool or room temperature syrup. Stir to combine.

MARY PICKFORD

In Havana, rum-based cocktails were all the rage among Americans seeking respite from Prohibition. Among their favorites: the El Presidente (recipe follows), the Hotel Nacional Special, daiquiris, and this number named after "America's Sweetheart," actress Mary Pickford.

2 oz light rum
1 oz fresh pineapple juice
1 tsp grenadine
1 tsp maraschino liqueur
1 brandied cherry

Shake in a cocktail shaker with ice. Strain into a cocktail glass or a coupe. Garnish with a brandied cherry.

It wasn't just warm weather that drew Yankee snowbirds to Cuba during Prohibition. Havana was home to a robust year-round nightclub scene that catered to Americans thirsting for a proper cocktail. Or five.

EL PRESIDENTE

Named for Cuban president Gerardo Machado, the elegant El Presidente is a mix of rum, curaçao, grenadine, and one specific vermouth. Tropical drinks historian Jeff Berry notes in *Potions of the Caribbean* that Dolin Vermouth de Chambéry, a moderately dry French vermouth, works in an El Presidente, but that the other dry vermouths simply don't. He's right. In fact, it's a pretty bad drink with the French vermouths that dominate the market. If you can't find Dolin, do as Berry suggests and mix equal parts of dry French and sweet Italian vermouths.

- 1 oz aged rum (Añejo Havana Club if you have it)
- 1 oz Dolin Vermouth de Chambéry
- 0.25 oz orange curaçao
- Orange peel
- 1 booze cherry

Stir the rum, vermouth, and curaçao in a mixing glass with ice. Strain into a chilled coupe. Twist the orange peel over the drink, drop it in, and garnish with a cherry.

Arrack (Spiritus Oryzae)

Like rum, proper Batavia arrack from Indonesia, also known as arak or rack, is distilled from sugarcane. Unlike rum, it has a healthy dose of red rice added to the mash. The aromatic spirit—much like a funky, locker-room rum—was core to punch recipes until the 19th century, when its popularity waned. Although it remained something of a back-shelf staple in parts of northern Europe, arrack was all but impossible to find in the United States until importer Eric Seed began bringing in Batavia Arrack van Oosten. Middle Eastern arac and Turkish raki, two anise-flavored spirits, have similar names, as does Sri Lankan arrack made from fermented and distilled coconut flower nectar, but the arrack here is the Indonesian/Dutch variety.

ARRAKESSENZ

A decade ago, if you really wanted to try your hand at replicating old punch or cocktail recipes that called for arrack, I would have advised looking to a formula like this one to mimic the sugarcane- and rice-based spirit sometimes called *spiritus oryzae* in medical literature. Here, Lyon would have us mix 20 to 25 ml of a blend of vanilla, Pekoe tea, catechu, and formic ether (so-called rum ether) to a liter of spirit.

Vanillae concisae (cut vanilla) 2.0
Herba Thea Peaco
(Orange Pekoe tea) 50.0
Cateshu Pulverati
(powdered catechu). 10.0
Olei Florum Aurantii guttae (drops of
neroli, e.g., oil of orange flowers) . . .2
Aceti Pyrolignosi rectificat
(rectified pyroligneous acid) . . . 50.0
Aetheris Formici (formic ether) . . .100.0
Spiriti Aetheres Nitrosi crudi
(nitric ether). 10.0
Spiritus (90%)
(90% abv neutral spirit) 350.0

Macerate for 8 days, then strain and filter. 20–25 grams added to 1 liter of 35% alcohol produces produces artificial arrack.

note

The original German has an uncorrected error and calls this artificial rum.

SWEDISH PUNCH

Swedish or "caloric" pun(s)ch is a classic use for Batavia Arrack, good for drinking on its own as a Christmas punch, mixing in cocktails, or spiking baked goods. I haven't been without a bottle of two of this cardamom-scented citrus punch since bartender and blogger Erik Ellestad laid down a DIY framework almost a decade ago on his blog, SavoyStomp.com. Ellestad calls for Appleton V/X rum, a blend of 15 different rums. I prefer the funkier five-year-old El Dorado Demarara. Your call.

2 lemons, sliced thinly
2 cups well-aged rum
1 cup Batavia Arrack
2 cups hot strong spiced tea (4 tsp black tea, 6 crushed green cardamom pods, brewed in 2 cups water for 6 minutes, then strained)
2 cups raw or natural sugar

Put the lemon slices, along with any accumulated juice, into a ½-gallon nonreactive container with a sealable lid (e.g., a big ol' Mason or swing-top preserving jar). Add the rum and arrack. Macerate for 6 hours. Don't leave it all day or overnight; you don't want to extract too much of bitterness from the lemons.

Meanwhile, pour the hot spiced tea over the sugar. Stir to dissolve and let it cool to room temperature.

After 6 hours, pour the rum off the lemon slices and combine it with the syrup. Filter and bottle in a clean, sealable container. Let it mellow for a day.

WILLIAM KITCHINER'S MOCK ARRACK

William Kitchiner's 1817 tome *The Cook's Oracle* contains one of the earliest references to potato chips. It is a paragon of 19th century English make-do attitude. Of his many cordial and spirits recipes, this one offers another semblance of proper arrack by deploying benzoic acid in rum.

Dissolve two scruples of flowers of benjamin [benzoic acid] in a quart of good rum, and it will immediately impart to it the inviting fragrance of "Vauxhall nectar."[36]

Caramel

Also called burnt sugar, burnt sugar coloring, or sometimes black sugar in older manuals, caramel is one of the oldest coloring agents still used in modern beverages. Almost every bit of blended Scotch, for instance, has a touch a caramel to achieve a darker hue than the secondhand bourbon barrels—which are required for Scotch—can give. Lyon's notes concern both making caramel and detecting it in spirits that may not have been aged as long as their vendors presented.

Of the two types of caramel that dominate old recipes, the first, and more prevalent, has almost no taste at all in the minuscule quantities used. This style is sometimes called "French" caramel and readily imparts a reddish-brown color (and the suggestion of barrel-aging) to rums, brandies, and whiskeys. A rectifier might use it to correct coloring just as a chef uses salt or pepper to correct a dish before serving it. Such coloring is made by heating sugar or sometimes glucose, occasionally with some alkali. The longer caramel cooks, the less sweet and viscous it becomes. This is darker and thinner than the sweet, gentle caramel we know from candied apples or *dulce de leche* ice cream.

CARAMEL FOR COLORING

To be honest, I had mixed feelings about giving a recipe for making caramel to color spirits. If the goal is to fake age, then I just wanted to wash my hands of it. However, caramel coloring can give a nice dark color—in judicious amounts—to bitters, cordials, and other homemade wet goods. Come to think of it, when it's known as browning, a few drops of the exact same caramel gives a bit of color to soups, stews, and gumbos that otherwise might have turned out a bit pale.

- 8 oz plain white sugar
- 6 oz water, divided

Open the windows, turn on a fan, and be ready for some smoke. Or make this one outdoors. In a deep, heavy, nonreactive pot, heat the sugar and 2 ounces of the water over medium-high heat until the sugar melts. It will turn amber, then darken like an old penny. Keep cooking, but watch carefully. When it has turned a deep, dark brown—almost, but not quite black—remove from the heat and add the remaining 4 ounces of water. It will hiss, steam, spit, and seize up. Don't get burned. Stir the mass until it liquefies, over more heat if necessary. Store at room temperature.

The second type of caramel, in the following recipe, is not cooked as long as black sugar; it retains the taste and aroma of cooked sugar. Added in somewhat greater quantities, it lends pleasant, rounded caramel notes to rums—and rum cocktails—in particular.

CARAMEL LEMONADE

In 2014, I gave a talk about mainland and Hawaiian moonshine at Tiki Oasis, San Diego's annual gathering of tiki enthusiasts. There, we blended caramel syrup with white whiskey from Death's Door in a wickedly good boozy lemonade. You may want to open your kitchen windows when making this caramel and, if you have a particularly twitchy smoke detector, unplug it; things can get smoky.

1.5 oz Death's Door White Whiskey
4 oz Front Porch Lemonade (recipe follows)
2 teaspoons Sweet Caramel Syrup (recipe follows)

Mix the whiskey, lemonade, and caramel syrup over ice. Garnish with mint if you're feeling extra fancy.

FRONT PORCH LEMONADE

5 parts fresh lemon juice
5 parts water
3 parts 1:1 simple syrup made with Demerara or white sugar (see page 145)

Stir until blended in a jar, pitcher, or gallon jug.

SWEET CARAMEL SYRUP

12 oz white sugar
15 oz water

Slowly heat the dry sugar in a deep, heavy-bottomed pot (I use an unlined copper one, but use what you've got). When it reaches a rich amber color, immediately (and carefully) pour in all the water. Be careful: It will spatter and steam. The whole mass will seize up in a hard candied blob. No worries. Lower the heat to low and continue to heat the mixture, stirring now and then, until the sugar dissolves. Some water will have evaporated as steam, so when the whole thing is liquid and cool, transfer it to a measuring cup and add just enough water to make the total volume 25 percent more than the original volume of sugar. In this example, 12 ounces (100%) plus 3 ounces (25%) = 15 ounces. Just top off with cool water until the total volume is 15 ounces. Easy-peasy.

COPPER DISTILLED BOURBON

A devious recipe. Clearly, this isn't distilled bourbon at all, but a facsimile given an authentic-sounding name.

Copper sulfate dissolved in H_2O	1 dram
Proof spirit	40 gallons
Peach flavoring	1 gallon
Brandy flavoring	1 gallon
Wine vinegar	1 pint
Glycerin	1 pound
Oil cognac dissolved and alcohol	12 drops

Color with caramel.

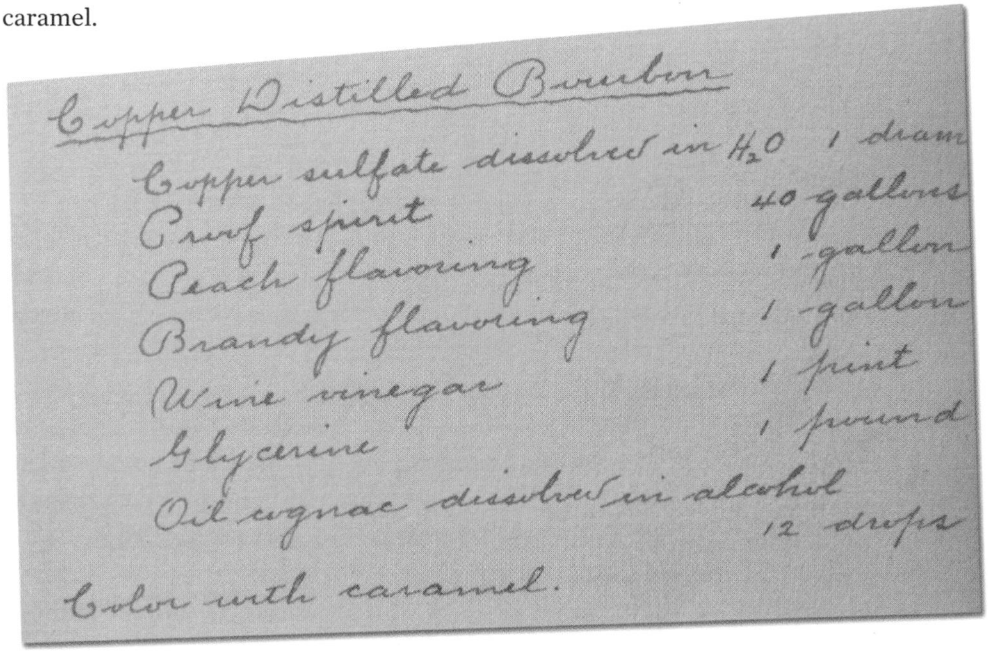
Copper Distilled Bourbon
Copper sulfate dissolved in H_2O 1 dram
Proof spirit 40 gallons
Peach flavoring 1 gallon
Brandy flavoring 1 gallon
Wine vinegar 1 pint
Glycerine 1 pound
Oil cognac dissolved in alcohol 12 drops
Color with caramel.

Whiskey

Well before Andrew Volstead was born, Americans were flavoring, sweetening, spicing, coloring, and otherwise adjusting their whiskeys. To this very day, families macerate peaches, apples, cinnamon, blueberries, and other fruits and botanicals in whiskey. In moonshining families, jars of such concoctions are boons of the Yule season. Some of the most famous bars in the country feature exactly such concoctions. Well. Maybe not that blueberry one.

Lyon's whiskey entries are a mishmash of compounded whiskey recipes, formulas for essences or oils that would have been added to rectified spirits, and notes on making actual whiskeys, including rough grain bills for bourbon and notes on malting. Although some of his notes call for commercial products—Fritzsche Bros. were renowned flavor

It was soon realized that, by mixing freshly made spirit, perfectly colorless, and which, therefore, had received no value from storage, with a small quantity of whisky and coloring it by means of caramel to resemble old whisky and adding certain flavoring agents made by chemists, or such substances as prune juice, so-called blending sherry, etc., a liquor could be made resembling in color and flavor old whisky. The compounder could make up hundreds of barrels of this liquor in a day and place it upon the market in such a guise that the unsuspecting consumer would be certain he was buying an old and valuable product . . . So great was the extent of this adulteration that it has been estimated by some authorities that at the time of the passage of the food law in June, 1906, more than 90 percent of all the so-called whiskies sold upon the American markets were of the kind described above.

—Harvey Washington Wiley,
Beverages and Their Adulteration (1919)

importers whose firm was eventually subsumed by Swiss flavor conglomerate Givaudan—many call for compounding disparate aromas and flavors as needed. Creosote would have lent a charred, smoky taste to factitious whiskeys. Oils of clove, wintergreen, and Cognac are common, while peach flavoring, honey, and glycerin smoothed the taste of raw liquor. It's not surprising that many of the whiskey recipes are imitations of rye, an immensely popular whiskey before Prohibition that is coming back into vogue now.

We whiskey drinkers can get testy when someone adds syrup, flavors, and color to our supposedly pure drams. Nonetheless, cinnamon-flavored whiskeys, themselves an old cordial against cholera and other diseases, have cut a huge swath into the drinking habits of Americans in the last few years. In truth, whiskey has been one of the most fantastically adulterated spirits in the history of the world. Nineteenth-century compounding manuals testify to the sorts of mixtures once passed as whiskey, but long before essential oils and extracts of creosote were deployed, what people drank as whiskey bore only a fleeting resemblance to what we know today.

USQUEBACH, five
AQUA VITÆ,
Hibernis popularis.

℞ Aquæ Vitæ generofioris, libras viginti quatuor.
Illis per quatriduum infunde.
Rad. Glycyrrhizæ libram unam.
Uvarum paffarum exacinat. libram dimidiam.
Caryophyllorum unciam dimidiam.
Macis,
Zingiberis, ana drachmas duas.
Servetur colatura in ufum.

Take, for instance, the *usquebach* from the *Pharmacopoeia Londinensis* published in 1618. The stuff went under a number of names, including *usquebaugh* and *uisge beatha*, but each was a Gaelic rendition of the Latin *aqua vitae*, the water of life. Scotch and bourbon drinkers may know where I'm headed with this, but modern drinkers would recognize the word as *whiskey*. Or *whisky*. Whichever. But the name is about the only thing that they would recognize; whiskeys of the time were nothing like what we drink today. They were outlandishly flavored with big flavors, such as mace, ginger, licorice, and—especially—saffron. See page 69 for more on that last one.

I Need to Check Your ID

Most of the outright fake whiskey from the 19th century through today, despite the particular style or even brand their makers try to reproduce, boils down to faking one thing: age. From early experiments with X-rays to soaking wood chips and sawdust in whiskey to modern experiments with smaller barrels or exposing new spirits to ozone, distillers, blenders, wholesalers, and bootleggers have tried either to speed aging or give the impression of a spirit older than it really is, even though probably more than half of a whiskey's taste comes from the barrel. New, raw whiskey is a solvent that does three important things as it ages in oak barrels:

1. It extracts compounds from the barrel's wood itself (which varies depending on whether and how much the interior may be toasted or charred, whether it may have held wines or other spirits, and what species of oak is used).

38 FRITZSCHE, SCHIMMEL & CO.

No. 41.

RYE WHISKEY

(For 40 gallons.)

Rye Whiskey Essence	3	ounces.
or of the		
Rye Whiskey Oil	1½	ounces.
Glycerin, chem. pure	2	pounds.
Cologne Spirit, proof	40	gallons.

Color with Sugar Coloring.

No. 42.

SCOTCH WHISKEY

(For 40 gallons.)

Scotch Whiskey Essence	3	ounces.
Glycerin, chem. pure	1	pound.
Cologne Spirit, proof	40	gallons.

No. 43.

IRISH WHISKEY

(For 40 gallons.)

Irish Whiskey Essence	3	ounces.
Glycerin, chem. pure	2	pounds.
Cologne Spirit, proof	40	gallons.

2. During long oxidation, it breaks down some compounds and transforms them into all-new pleasant-smelling and -tasting chemicals that did not exist in the new spirit.

3. Through evaporation through porous wood, whiskey loses volume, but becomes more concentrated.

But such aging takes years. Even then, some batches turn out better than others. One of the ways bootleggers sidestepped proper aging was to infuse raw whiskey, sugar moonshine, or neutral spirits with oak sticks or chips (often made from genuine broken-down whiskey or beer barrels). After a few hours (or weeks if they were true back-alley artisans): voilà—whiskey! Not really, of course. Such "chipped" whiskey lacked the suave complexity of properly aged spirits. I've sampled whiskeys made this way. They just never taste better than alcohol flavored with wood extracts. Thin, hot, weak examples that won't satisfy discerning drinkers. Of course, such extracts, along with other compounds, can be deployed in otherwise decent whiskey in hopes of improving it. Those are more successful cheats I warrant most whiskey drinkers have unknowingly—and perhaps happily—consumed.

Whiskey Cocktails

ROCK & RYE

Admittedly, winter sniffles and sneezes aren't the pressing concern here in San Diego that they can be in other places. Still, we like our remedies against chilly nights and this is a good one.

Before, during, and after Prohibition, enough temperance advocates made allowances for booze-heavy tonics and bitters that their prevalence in ostensibly dry houses became a running joke. While a slug of plain whiskey would almost surely have been met with tightly pursed lips, who could argue that rock candy sugar and fruit wouldn't be wholesome additions? A touch of horehound—an herb that, as everyone knows, is such balm to a sore throat—was exactly what the doctor might've ordered to keep winter's bane in check.

A few years back, we planted blood orange and lemon trees in the garden. When I—*cough, cough*—feel a cold coming on, I'll raid the trees for a few fruits to soak in rye whiskey with hard horehound candy for the perfect remedy.

- 750 ml rye whiskey
- 6 to 8 oz horehound candy (see note)
- 3 oz dried sour cherries
- 2 (4-inch) sticks of cinnamon
- Zest of 1 orange (blood orange if you've got it)
- Zest of 1 lemon
- 3 whole cloves

Mix the ingredients in a 1- to 2-liter lidded glass jar. Macerate at room temperature, giving the jar a swirl now and then, for 2 to 5 days until the candy is fully dissolved and the cordial is fragrant with citrus and spice. Strain into clean 1-liter bottle.

A few confectioners, such as Hammond's in Colorado, still make horehound candy. If you can't find any, swap regular or yellow rock candy and add 1 teaspoon of dried horehound. If you can't find horehound, you could add a star anise fruit or two, but don't sweat it.

WARD 8

Although it predates Prohibition, the Ward 8, a rye and orange juice *potus*, remained popular under Volstead. Tipplers then would have used old stocks of Pennsylvania or Maryland rye, smuggled Canadian whisky, or even synthetic stuff. Ratios are all over the board for this one, but here's the version I like:

2 oz straight rye whiskey
0.75 oz fresh lemon juice
0.75 oz fresh orange juice
0.25 oz grenadine, or to taste
Sparkling water

Shake the first four ingredients with ice and strain into a chilled glass. Add a splash of sparkling water to give the whole thing a lift.

Poisoned Liquor

Some of Lyon's recipes are good, others are better left to professionals, others still just don't result in spirits as good as what we can buy from even modestly stocked modern stores. A few, however, stand out as recipes you must not re-create. One of them is rye ether. Ethers are distinct class of compounds, but as used by rectifiers and blenders, the term also referred to combinations of essential oils, ethers, alcohols, acids, and other aromatic compounds that gave the characteristic smell of different fruits or spirits—raspberry, for instance, pear, bourbon, strawberry, apple, etc. Such ethers are harmless in and of themselves, but Lyon's recipe calls for a small amount of methyl alcohol, the notorious "wood alcohol" that blinded and killed so many in the late 19th and early 20th centuries.

I am sorry to learn that [Germans] have just invented a method of making brandy out of sawdust. Now, what chance will prohibition have when a man can take a rip saw and go out and get drunk with a fence rail? What is the good of prohibition if a man is able to make brandy smashes out of the shingles of his roof, or if he can get delirium tremens by drinking the legs off his kitchen table?

—Mark Twain,
quoted in *Los Angeles Times*, March 8, 1908

RYE ETHER

Anise oil	1 part, ʒi	
Acetic ether	5 parts, ʒv	
Amyl alcohol	5 parts, "distil" ʒv	
Nitrous ether	5 parts, ʒv	
Methyl alcohol	2 parts, ʒii	
Alcohol	100 parts, ℥xiiss	

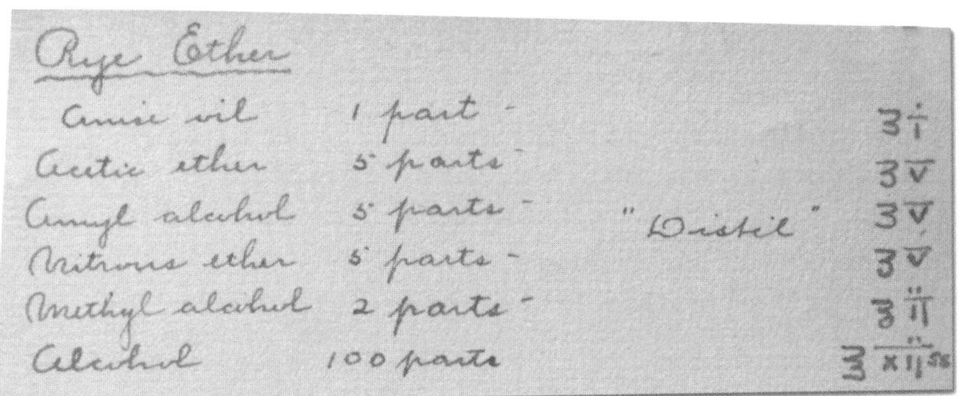

Rye Ether

Anise oil	1 part -		ʒi
Acetic ether	5 parts -		ʒv
Amyl alcohol	5 parts -	"Distil"	ʒv
Nitrous ether	5 parts -		ʒv
Methyl alcohol	2 parts -		ʒii
Alcohol	100 parts		℥xiiss

Later, Lyon gives a recipe for brandy essence that likewise calls for methanol under the name "rectified wood spirit." This essence isn't something anyone would drink as is, but which would be added in minuscule amounts (1 part to 1,600 parts of an alcohol-water mixture). Methanol at that concentration and in the amount a drinker would likely consume probably would be harmless—but the stuff is toxic even when inhaled or absorbed through skin, so skip it.

You wouldn't want to drink it—in fact, it is *imperative* that you not—but alcohol that looks and tastes just as clean and pure as vodka can be distilled from lumber and sawdust. Low concentrations of methanol (CH_3OH), also called wood alcohol, is common in many foods (including alcoholic beverages). It even courses through our own bloodstream. Such small amounts are harmless, but a toxic dose for humans may be as little as 8 grams[37]—about a teaspoon. In the words of New York City's chief medical examiner in 1928, "wood alcohol is not 'poison' liquor. It is simply poison. If it gets into liquor, the liquor is poisoned."[38]

In the 19th and early 20th centuries, pharmacists, physicians, and those in the trade believed that wood naptha, as crude distillates of wood were called, was so vile, so disgusting, that no one would willingly consume it. The smallest part, so the thinking went, would taint drinking alcohol. For the most part, they were right. Until about the 1890s, only isolated instances of methanol poisoning show up in medical literature.

Brandy Essence

15 parts Acetic Ether
12 parts Spirit Nitrous Ether
1 part rectified wood spirit (16)

5 parts Oil of grapes
4 parts Acetic Ether
1 part Tincture Allspice
3 parts Tincture of Galls
100 parts Alcohol

Take 1 part of either of these essences to 1000 parts alcohol with 600 parts water.

Or.
2500 - 3000 parts 80-90% alcohol
1700 - 2000 parts Water
10 parts Spirit Nitrous Ether
5 parts Tincture Allspice
1 part Acetic Ether
2 parts Tannic Acid

Detection of Methyl Alcohol

Dissolve 0.5-gram of sodium salicylate in 1-gram of alcohol to be tested and add 5-drops concentrated sulfuric acid during 1 minute. A distinct odor of methyl salicylate is noticed if methyl alcohol is present.

Then new production methods came along that yielded the light, colorless methanol we know today. It was widely used in hundreds of products from paints to cosmetics and was one of the chief additives that the US government permitted in several regulated formulas to create "denatured" alcohol, supposedly unfit to drink. After high-profile mass poisonings,[39] awareness spread among physicians that methanol could blind and kill those who drank it. Even then, the general public wasn't aware of the threat until well into Prohibition, when ignorant or indifferent bootleggers began using it in, or even as, bootleg liquor.

The results were devastating. After 30 people were poisoned from drinking contaminated whiskey in New York in 1918, toxicologist Alexander Gettler issued a clarion call about the dangers of wood alcohol poisoning in the *American Journal of Pharmacy*. Those who drink or inhale the poison or absorb it through their skin may experience nausea, headaches, weakness, vomiting, and temporary visual distortions. A less fortunate drinker may suffer permanent blindness as her body slowly metabolizes it over several days into more toxic formaldehyde and formic acid, leading to coma and organ failure. The inevitable fate of those who consume too much: death. Six of those poisoned did, in fact, die. Gettler's message was that such poisoning would skyrocket. Doctors and health officials needed to warn everyone.

A decade later, Gettler's boss, New York City medical examiner Charles Norris, published an excoriating essay on policies that led to the widespread use of wood alcohol among bootleggers. "Nearly ten thousand in [New York City] will die this year from strong drink," he wrote. "Our national casualty list for the year for this one cause will outstrip the toll of the War. These are the first fruits of Prohibition—not in terms of savings banks or factory efficiency or the votes of pussy-footing legislators, but in terms of life and death . . . This is the net dividend of our noble experiment—in extermination."[40]

Korn

Distilled from rye, barley, or sometimes wheat, *Korn* is a bit of a stranger in the US, but the grain spirit has a long history in Germany. In German, *Korn* refers to grain more broadly rather than American corn (*Zea mays*). The nose and taste of these minimally aged schnapps are clearly cereal. Think less vodka and more grain moonshine or white dog. A shot of chilled *Korn*, served either alongside a glass of beer or mixed into it, is known in Germany as a *Herrengedeck*, a sort of Teutonic boilermaker.

Hot and Spicy

After water and neutral spirits, capsicum and grains of paradise rank among the most common spirit adulterants since the 19th century—especially in gin, whiskey, and schnapps. Old manuals are rife with compounded recipes calling for them. Capsicum generally referred to cayenne pepper, but it may also indicate other hot chiles. Capsicum is almost universally derided as a particularly low adulterant in old texts.

Methanol by Any Other Name

Methanol has been known by a slew of names over the last century and a half, including wood alcohol, methyl alcohol, wood spirits, pyroligneous spirit, pyroxylic spirit, methylic alcohol, Columbian spirit, colonial spirit, eagle spirit, carbinol, wood naptha, methyl hydroxide, and methyl hydrate.

Any beverage recipe calling for any of these should never be followed as written. Let me repeat: Do not, under any circumstances, add methanol to any food or drink. Either read such a recipe as an historical curiosity or, assuming it has no other problems, swap out the methanol with high-proof ethanol, such as grain alcohol or overproof vodka.

Unscrupulous blenders who watered down whiskey, so the story goes, used chile peppers to simulate a higher proof, to "sharpen" the spirit.

While the practice does seem to have been widespread, the problem with that simple interpretation is that chiles don't simulate high proof. The taste may distract drinkers from the aqueous nature of overly hydrated whiskey, but some drinkers enjoy the painful/pleasurable kick that cayenne adds to a drink. Certainly pharmacists, physicians, and mothers alike before and during Prohibition used cayenne as a medicine—at the very least, the burn it imparted felt like it was doing *something*.

In fact, Lyon's two German recipes for *Kornschärfe* are for doing exactly that—giving a bit of bite to the grain spirit *Korn* with capsicum and grains of paradise. The recipe is lifted from *Spezialitäten und Geheimmittel*,[41] a 1906 German text.

KORNSCHÄRFE

To fortify artificial grain schnapps.

A – Prepare a capsicum extract 1:10 with 92-93% alcohol.

B – An extract comprising
4 T. [*Theilen* or parts] capsicum
1 T. [parts] grains of paradise
40 T. [parts] alcohol 92-93%

Kornschärfe
Zum verstärken Künstlichem Korn schnapps.
A - Ein Paprika-auszug 1-10 mit 92-93% Weingeist bereitet
B. - Ein Auszug aus
4 T. Paprika-shoten
1 T. Paradies Körner
40 T. Weingeist 92-93%.

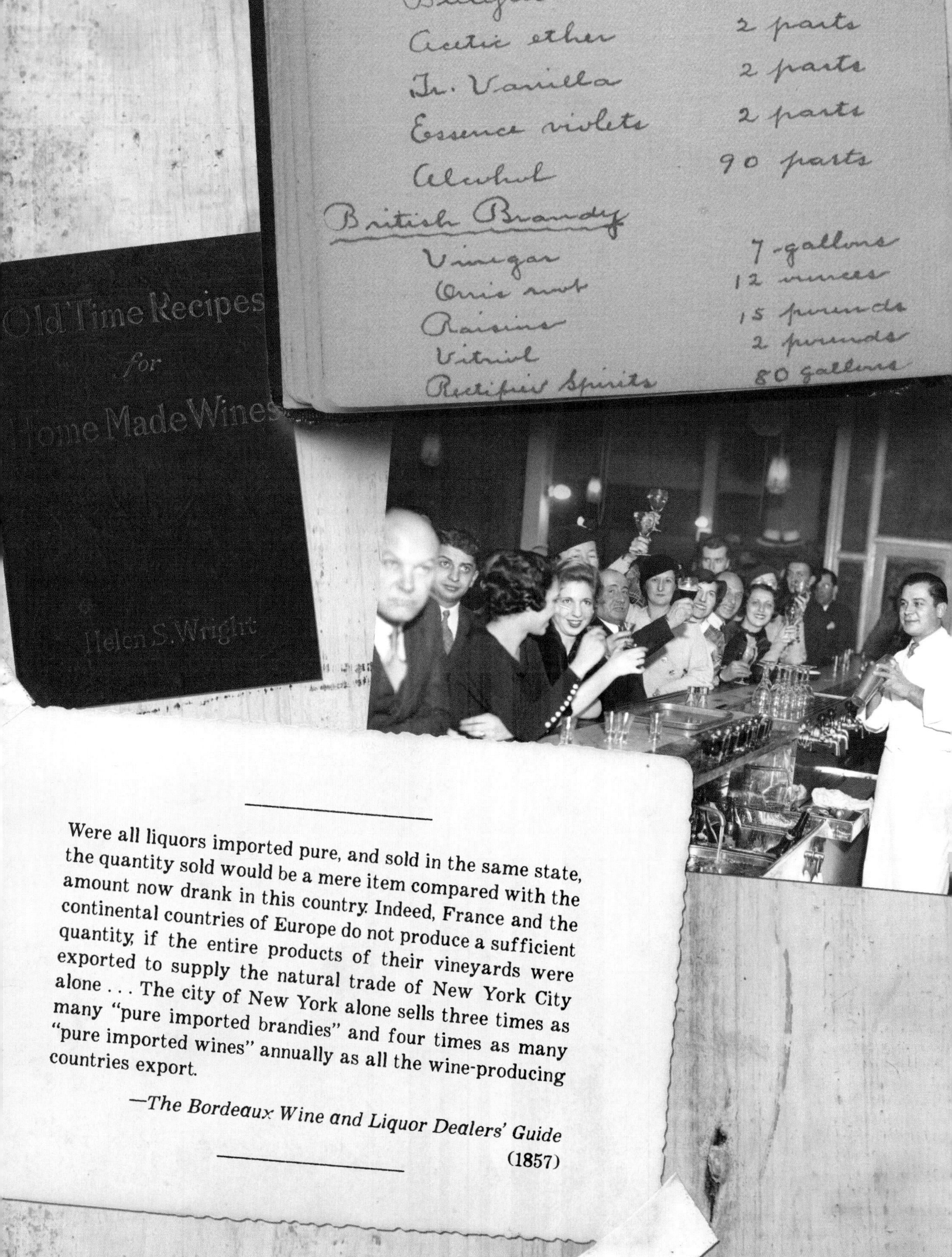

Were all liquors imported pure, and sold in the same state, the quantity sold would be a mere item compared with the amount now drank in this country. Indeed, France and the continental countries of Europe do not produce a sufficient quantity, if the entire products of their vineyards were exported to supply the natural trade of New York City alone . . . The city of New York alone sells three times as many "pure imported brandies" and four times as many "pure imported wines" annually as all the wine-producing countries export.

—*The Bordeaux Wine and Liquor Dealers' Guide* (1857)

Chapter four

Brandy, Wine, and Cider

Not all mixtures or blends of spirits are frauds

Brandy

In the early years of the Republic, American distillers adapted their craft to New World ingredients, creating recipes that struck notes of genuine pride in the New World's overwhelming bounty. They often strove to provide spirits every bit as good and wholesome as those from Europe—at a fraction of the cost. Eighteenth- and 19th-century spirits formulas repeatedly call for making this or that spirit "as good as imported" or "in the style of XYZ spirit." Samuel M'Harry's 1809 manual *Practical Distiller,* for instance, gives directions for making "a Brandy resembling French Brandy" from clarified whiskey or apple spirits blended with 25%–33% genuine French brandy. In a New World mashup of pride and thrift, he notes that, if kept a few years, it will be more sound and salutary than French brandy alone. Thrift, pragmatism, and nationalism all rolled into one.

Practical Distiller

Samuel M'Harry's manual was so clearly written—and printed just as Americans were migrating west and south into the Appalachian mountains—that its directions for distilling on pot stills informed much of American folk distilling (i.e., *moonshining*) right into Prohibition years. In fact, I've interviewed moonshiners who still follow M'Harry-style recipes more than 200 years after they were published.

French distillers probably would have taken issue with M'Harry's estimation of such domestic wet goods, but they would have recognized his methods immediately—as would have their colleagues in Germany, Britain, the Netherlands, and other countries with commercial distilling sectors. Blending a portion of genuine brandy, whiskey, or rum into

Brandy

I

Powdered catechu	100 grams
Sassafras wood	10 "
Balsam of tolu	10 "
Vanilla	5 "
Essence bitter almonds	1 "
Well flavored alcohol (85%)	1 litre

II

Malt Spirit (17 U.P.)	100 gallons
Nitrous ether	2 quarts
Ground cassia buds	4 ounces
Bitter almond meal	5 ounces
Sliced orris root	6 ounces
Cloves in powder	1 ounce
Capsicum	1½ ounces
Good vinegar	3 gallons
Brandy coloring	3 pints
Powdered catechu	2 pounds
Full flavored Jamaica rum	2 gallons

Mix in an empty Cognac cask and macerate for a fortnight with occasional stirring. Produces 106 gallons at 21 or 22 U.P.

neutral spirits (sometimes called stretching or cutting the spirit) was a well-established technique well before Prohibition. By then, though, it became a standard maneuver with less and less genuine spirit involved—and oftentimes none at all. In 1864, Charles Tovey inveighed against just such practice about casks of spirits coming from Holland, Germany, and Mediterranean ports

> bearing most impudently the brand of Cognac; in fact, it is known to the writer that many houses send over to Hamburg freshly emptied casks, having the original brand of some of the best shippers of Cognac brandy. These casks are filled with Hamburg Spirit, pale or brown, at a cost of about 3 [shillings] per gallon for proof, and those who are not acquainted with the manoeuver, are too often deceived by the external appearances. (Charles Tovey, *British & Foreign Spirits: Their History, Manufacture, Properties, Etc.* [London: Whittaker & Company, 1864])

Barrels filled with spurious German potato or sugar beet spirits would go on to bonded warehouses abroad from where customers who sought the surety of bonded liquor were fleeced as surely as the punter quaffing a dram of counterfeit whiskey at the corner pub or saloon. Alternately, German firms would send barrels of such spirits to France, whence they were shipped out from the land of Cognac with new identities.[42] A bit like money laundering, but with booze.

But not all mixtures or blends of spirits are frauds. French distillers in particular have added a variety of substances to their brandies—stellar, world-class, award-winning brandies, mind you—for centuries.

Boise

Boise (pronounced bwaz-AY) is a wood extract, commonly made of oak, but may be of other woods, and fortified with spirits. It is blended with spirits (typically brandies, but at times with whiskeys and others) in small amounts to get them ready for market. They add color as well as tannins and other compounds to help "round" and "shape" the final product. For cheaper brandies, the extract can be quite new, but some in use today are 100 years old—or more.

Distiller Hubert Germain-Robin's family has been in the brandy business for centuries in France. One of the first things he did when he arrived in California was to make boise. "When people are making boise," he recently explained, "it's just a special place where you don't visit. It's not known. It's not like a Cognac house where you can visit the tasting rooms." In its earliest incarnations, boise was simply chips from barrels. "That was it. It started like that. Then, after people started to make boise, to sell boise in the Cognac region, there were different ways to do it. Sometimes it is just an infusion and they boil it gently, and evaporate and concentrate it and use that." Some distillers buy boise, but Hubert makes his own. He prefers American or French oak, but says that some

Duplais - Best Cognac Imitation

Alcohol (85%)	54 litres
Rum (good quality)	2 litres
Syrup of raisins	3 litres
Infusion green walnut hulls	2 litres
Infusion shells of bitter almonds	2 litres
Catechu in powder	15 grams
Balsam Tolu	6 grams
Pure water	37 liters

Mix and color with caramel.

Brandy

Cologne Spirits (red to P.)	40 gallon[s]
Oil of Cognac	1/6 ounce
Burnt sugar coloring	1½ pint
Tannin	1/4 ounce
Brandy essence	1 part
Alcohol	1000 part
Water	600 part

Cognac Oil

mixture of Amylic Alcohol
Oenanthic Ether

Beading Oil

Sweet oil of almonds 48 ounces
C.P. Sulfuric Acid 12 8 ounces
neutralize with ammonia adding double volume of proof spirit and distilling the mixture.

Brandy Ager

Old rum	2.00 liters
Old Kirsch {Brandy distilled from cherry wine}	1.75 "
Infusion walnut hulls	.75 "
Syrup of raisins	2.00 "

Add to 100 liters. For aging or improving new brandy for immediate use.

Cognac Oil

Melted cocoanut oil	16 ounces
Sulfuric Acid	8 ounces
Alcohol	16 ounces

Mixed and distilled.

Cheapest Brandy Imitation

Spirits	45 gallons
Caramel	6 ounces
Cognac Oil	1/8 ounce

Cognac - Charente Type.

A. - Typage

Black Ceylon Tea -	5 ounces
Vanilla beans -	5 ounces
Stoned dry plums -	8 pounds
Oak wood -	10 pounds

Percolate after allowing to stand 14-days with 8-gallons proof wine distillate. Result 6½ gallons extract called - Typage.

B Syrupage for Cognac

16½ pounds sugar are boiled with 2½ gallons water with addition of 2½ pounds caramel.

Result 3½ - gallons.

C Syrup Charentais for Cognac Basis

6½ - gallons Typage and

3½ gallons Syrupage are mixed to the final result of 10 gallons of which ¼ gallon is sufficient for 10 gallons Cognac

Whiskey Mash

18-26 gallons of water 140°F per bushel of the finely ground cereal in suitable vessel. Small amount of malt sometimes added

In prim
of ¼ gall
and colo
distillate
lowest li
Ordinary
is 17 U.P.
understo
or if hig
must be

Pure ev
consists

Syrup
Pure genuine
Distilled

(see page

Oenanth
Formic
Acetic a
Grape j
Glycerine
Alcohol

have even used bitter galls to make boise. "You get very different character with the different woods. A good boise is thirty, forty years or more. I want one with at least fifteen years so I can use different boises with different characteristics the same way I use different types of brandy in a blend."

Lyon uses oak in a few recipes to approximate barrel-aging and some astringency, such as in the cognac recipe (below) which called for oak sawdust (yeah, don't follow that one; sawdust extracts are among the most unpleasant natural oak flavorings—all harsh edges and thin astringency with none of the richness of toasted oak barrels or staves). He also makes a run at an ersatz boise with his recipe for Cognac Charente Type:

COGNAC CHARENTE TYPE

A. — TYPAGE

Black Ceylon Tea . . . . 5 ounces
Vanilla beans . . . . 5 ounces
Stoned dry plums . . . . 8 pounds
Oak wood . . . . 10 pounds

Percolate after allowing to stand 14 days with 8 gallons proof wine distillate. 6½ gallons extract called Typage.

B. — SYRUPAGE FOR COGNAC

16½ pounds sugar are boiled with 2½ gallons water with the addition of 2½ pounds caramel.

Result 3½ gallons.

C. — SYRUP CHARTENTAIS FOR COGNAC BASE

6½ gallons Typage and 3½ gallons Syrupage are mixed to the final result of 10 gallons of which ¼ gallon is sufficient for 10 gallons Cognac.

In principle cognac is a mixture of ¼ gallon Syrup Charentais, sugar and color with genuine wine distillate of any strength. The lowest limit is about 19 U.P.

Ordinary manufacturing strength is 17 O.P. The wine distillate is to be understood to be of proof strength or if higher alcohol strength it must be diluted to 17 under proof.

PURE COGNAC OF 17 UNDERPROOF CONSISTS OF

Syrup Charentais . . . . ¼ gallon
Pure genuine proof
wine distillate . . . . 7 gallons
Distilled water . . . . 3 gallons

About 10 gallons

The yield on this recipe is "about" 10 gallons, when it would seem, from simple math, to make exactly 10.25 gallons. Math isn't so simple when mixing alcohol and water because when the two are blended, the alcohol contracts. To make exactly 10 gallons of finished product, compounders would have to add more than 7 gallons of proof spirit to 3 gallons of water.

Aged Syrups

Lyon's recipe for Cognac syrups (page 99) may well be what German and American distillers used to imitate French brandies through Prohibition. Shoot, it might even be what some French producers were making. But that's not how serious brandy makers do it. Notwithstanding purists who eschew as chicanery any syrup, boise, caramel coloring, and other additives in their spirits, those who make fine brandies in the French style with such additives age not only the brandy, but the various components as well. "When I use a tiny bit of syrup or caramel in my blend," says Hubert Germain-Robin, "I don't mix in something that is not the minimum age of my blend. It is more integrated already because it is aged."

Dan Farber, who makes magisterial grape and apple brandies at Osocalis in the hills of Soquel, California, agrees. "Syrups can be very, very old. I have syrups that are fifteen, maybe sixteen years old: way too young." Farber explains that vintage syrups (and boise) age at different rates and in different ways from brandy, becoming far more complex and nuanced over years in barrels. "Yes, people can do things that we might not like. They can take zero-aged *eau de vie*, blending it with wood extract and sugar syrup and caramel color to make something that's not great—but that doesn't mean you should throw the baby out with the bathwater. Therefore *all* things that have *anything* but the most pure essence of spirit are somehow flawed? That's a crazy way of thinking and it's sad in a way."

Common British brandy is prepared by adding to plain spirit French wine vinegar, alcoholic extract of prunes, burnt sugar for colouring, and a little foreign brandy. Sometimes the liquid procured by distilling spirit with the marc or refuse of the grape press, mixed with argal, or crude wine stone, is added to plain spirit, and the colour and flavour brought up by the addition of fruit tincture and caramel (burnt sugar).

—William Loftus,
Loftus's New Mixing and Reducing Book (1869)

Vinegar in Brandies

I enjoy vinegar-based fruit shrubs, vinegar pie, drinking vinegars, and vinaigrettes. Filipino chicken adobo, a dish swimming in vinegar, garlic, and soy sauce is one of my favorite dinners. But vinegar in brandy? Absolutely not. It's a characteristic I consider not just a flaw in brandies, but an insurmountable one. Nevertheless, old formulas for compounded brandies often include small amounts of acetic acid or vinegar. Why?

After talking to several distillers who were equally flummoxed, I have an idea. When fermentations turn sour with acetic acid, the flaw carries over into the distillation. The spirit cannot be salvaged. Before refrigeration, mashes that got too hot or were not distilled in time could have turned acetic more commonly. Perhaps, just as Belgians grew to dote on sour beers, locals (especially in Britain where many such recipes originated) developed a taste for that vinegar twang in some brandies, conflating it with age.

That's not to say vinegar doesn't have its place in mixed drinks. Try apple cider, champagne, raspberry, or other vinegars in your brandy as an alternate to lemon or lime juice. Call it *a gastrique* if you like. Just . . . not in your nicest brandies, eh?

Brandy Cocktails

Lyon's brandies are, by and large, not the kind we're likely to see on today's commercial market. Sure, even some world-class brandies are made with small amounts of caramels, vintage syrups, or boise, but the days of completely fake, imitation, or factitious brandy made from wine, grain, beet, or potato spirits are largely past. His ginger brandies are another matter. See page 170 for Lyon's Ginger Brandy No. II, a bracing cordial we put to good use. In the meanwhile, here's a trio of brandy cocktails popular in the Volstead days. Do try them with genuine brandies.

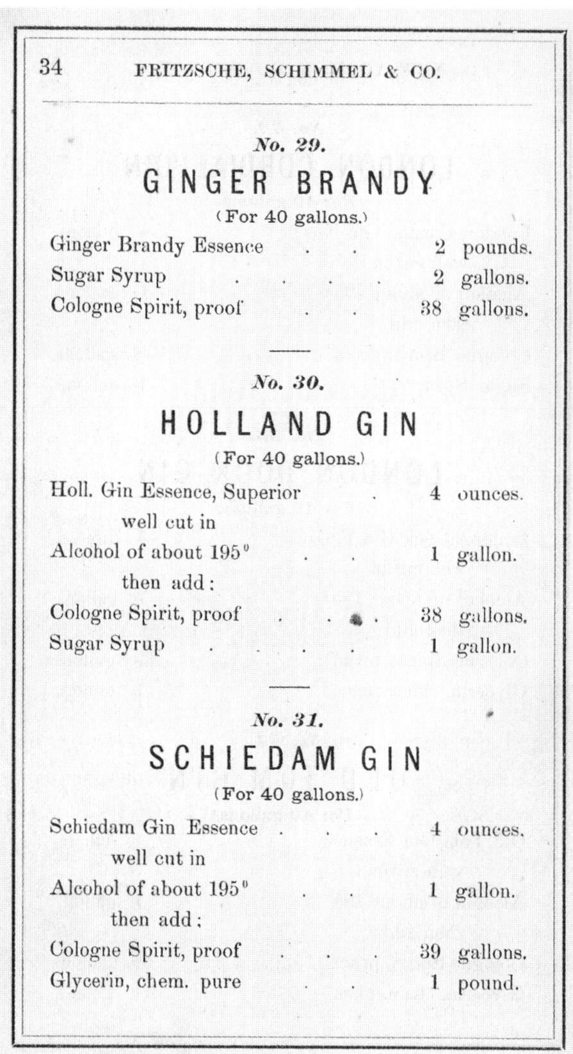

34 FRITZSCHE, SCHIMMEL & CO.

No. 29.

GINGER BRANDY

(For 40 gallons.)

Ginger Brandy Essence	2	pounds.
Sugar Syrup	2	gallons.
Cologne Spirit, proof	38	gallons.

No. 30.

HOLLAND GIN

(For 40 gallons.)

Holl. Gin Essence, Superior	4	ounces.
well cut in		
Alcohol of about 195°	1	gallon.
then add:		
Cologne Spirit, proof	38	gallons.
Sugar Syrup	1	gallon.

No. 31.

SCHIEDAM GIN

(For 40 gallons.)

Schiedam Gin Essence	4	ounces.
well cut in		
Alcohol of about 195°	1	gallon.
then add:		
Cologne Spirit, proof	39	gallons.
Glycerin, chem. pure	1	pound.

Old Peach

Clean alcohol, seventy gallons; water, fifty-five gallons; one and a half ounces of English saffron, or the same of gamboge; five gallons of honey, or sixty pounds of white or clarified sugar; this is to be dissolved in the above mentioned water before adding; add fifteen drops of creasote [sic]; balsam of Peru, half ounce; essence of lemon, a wine glass full; essence of orange peel, half ounce. The saffron or gamboge should be suspended in the spirit, which will obviate the necessity of straining the liquid.

Burnt sugar, &c., is no longer used for peach brandy, but those preferring it can color as for other brandy.

The above receipt furnishes a really fine sample of "old peach." It will have a fine body, pleasant taste, and approved flavor. This is sold for a distilled spirit, and is branded on the head to the effect that it is the product of some high sounding, though imaginary, distillery.

—Pierre Lacour,
The Manufacture of Liquors, Wines, and Cordials without the Aid of Distillation (1853).

SIDECAR

The Sidecar is a versatile cocktail for your arsenal, and is one of my favorites. Even the thought of one feels like pulling on a comfortable old sweater. Originally made with equal parts of brandy, Cointreau, and lemon juice, this one gets tinkered with a lot by modern bartenders. It's stiff, bracing, tart, and (if you give the glass a sugar rim) a bit sweet. Here's a stiffer modern version with more brandy and softened with dollop of syrup:

- 1.5 oz Cognac or other brandy
- 0.75 oz Cointreau
- 0.75 oz fresh lemon juice
- 1 teaspoon 2:1 rich syrup (page 145) or 3.2 compounder's syrup (page 145)

Shake in a cocktail shaker with ice. Strain into a cocktail glass or a coupe. Garnish with orange zest. If using apple brandy, swap out the syrup with a bit of maple syrup or boiled cider: just enough to soften it a bit.

BRANDY FIX

From *Barflies and Cocktails*, a 1927 vade mecum of mixed drinks published in Paris by Harry McElhone (of Harry's Bar) and illustrated by Wynn Holcomb, here's a vestige of 19th-century bracers that gooses brandy with cherry brandy—which could be read as either a sweet, dark cherry-flavored brandy such as Heering or as a clear, dry kirschwasser. Go with the latter.

Pour into a small tumbler 1 teaspoonful of sugar, 1 teaspoonful of Water to dissolve the sugar, Juice of a half Lemon, ½ Liqueur [glass] of Cherry Brandy, 1 Liqueur [glass] of Brandy.

Fill the glass with fine ice and stir slowly, then add a slice of Lemon, and serve with a straw.

In modern measures, try it like this:

1.5 oz VSOP Cognac
0.75 oz kirschwasser
Juice ½ lemon (0.5 to 0.75 oz)
1 teaspoon simple syrup (page 145)
Lemon twist

Shake with cracked ice and pour it, ice and all, into a tumbler. Garnish with fresh fruit—if garnishing is your bag—and a lemon twist.

HARVARD COCKTAIL

Given the brandy, bitters, and just enough fizz to lighten and lift the whole drink (the Harvard Cocktail is sometimes called a Harvard Fizz), we'd expect this northeast stalwart to be served in a highball glass, but no: the stemmed cocktail or martini glass is the classic way to serve it.

1.5 oz Cognac
1 oz Italian vermouth
2 to 3 dashes of bitters (Angostura or Fee Brothers, barrel-aged)
Club soda

Stir the Cognac, vermouth, and bitters together in a shaker with ice. When cold, strain into a chilled cocktail glass or coupe. Gently pour in 1 to 2 ounces of club soda and give it a brief stir.

Cider

In the lead up to national Prohibition, many winemakers, brewers, and cider makers assumed that they would be permitted to carry on once the nation went dry. Makers who considered their beers and wines "temperance" beverages reckoned that Prohibition would target only distilled spirits, such as whiskey, gin, and "demon" rum. They were in for a shock. With a few exceptions, the National Prohibition Act outlawed every intoxicating beverage over 0.5 percent alcohol. Apple cider was one of those exceptions.

In 1920, after much confusion in cider-making areas about what was permitted, John Kramer, the federal prohibition commissioner, clarified that anyone manufacturing "nonintoxicating cider and fruit juices exclusively for use in his home"[43] needed no permit. Sugar, molasses, raisins or other dried fruit were prohibited since those were ways to boost alcohol content and (presumably) prepare "a mash fit for distillation."[44]

Prohibition wrecked America's cider-drinking traditions. Farmers could sell sweet cider by the glass, but if customers took some away and it later hardened, the farmer could be held accountable for having produced an intoxicating beverage. Home vinegar making was permitted, but commercial producers were required to secure a bond and permit. Many threw in the towel on cider, tore out their orchards, and either sold the land or planted other crops.

Cider Cocktails

For many Britons and Americans who may not have been able to get or afford imports, apple cider formed the basis of traditional imitation wines and spirits from abroad. Lyon's cider "Champagne" is one such venerable imitation. In an unusual twist, the recipe calls for fining the mix—that is, clearing it of particulates—with milk. Home brewers commonly fine with gelatin or isinglass, but modern bartenders have rediscovered fining with milk only recently. Some call it milk washing. When milk is added to spirits, it curdles and traps little floaty bits that would otherwise accumulate in the bottom of barrels or bottles. It also smooths some of the spiky flavors, making a rounder resulting beverage. When the cider is clear, it is carefully racked off the top of the curdled milk.

John Conacher's 1919 cartoon, *The Sacred Cider Grove*, gives a broad wink at the difficulty of keeping Americans away from intoxicating beverages as Prohibition approached. "Are those good eating apples?" asks the gentleman rider. "No, Mister," responds the farmer, "not this year they ain't. This year them apples is good drinkin' apples."

...t

...nces
...nce
...ttle
...uart.

...nse

...nces
...achm
...achm
...nce
...nces

...mac Essence

1/4 ounce
1/4 ounce
3 1/2 ounces
4 ounces
8 ounces
2 1/2 pounds
2 1/2 pounds
4 pounds
10 pounds

5 ounces
4 1/2 gallons
6 gallons

Sherry Wine

Prepared cider	20 gallons
Spirits	1 gallon
Raisins	1/2 pound
Good sherry	3 gallons
Bitter almonds in alcohol	1/2 ounce

Let it stand 10 days and draw off carefully, fine it down and again rack it off into another cask.

Cider Without Apples

Put in a barrel 5 gallons hot water 30 pounds brown sugar, 3/4 pound acid tartaric, 25 gallons cold water, 3 pints of hop or brewer's yeast worked into paste (3/4 pounds flour and one pint of water will be required to make this paste) put all together in a barrel, which it will fill and let it work 24 hours, the yeast running out at the bung all the time, by putting in a little occasionally to keep it full. Then bottle, putting in 2 or 3 broken raisins to each bottle and it will nearly equal champagne

Cider Champagne

Good cider	10 gallons
Spirits	1/2 gallon
Sugar	3 pounds

Mix and let rest for 2 weeks. Fine with 1 pint skimmed milk. Often sold for champagne

CIDER CHAMPAGNE

Put in a barrel 5 gallons hot water[,] 30 pounds brown sugar, 3⁄4 pound acid tartaric, 25 gallons cold water, 3 pints of hops or brewer's yeast worked into paste (3⁄4 pounds flour and one pint of water will be required to make this paste) put all together in a barrel, which it will fill and let it work 24 hours, the yeast running out at the bung all the time, but putting in a little occasionally to keep it full. Then bottle, putting in 2 or 3 broken raisins to each bottle and it will nearly equal champagne.

CIDER WITHOUT APPLES

Lyon's Cider Without Apples, while a traditional recipe, doesn't stand up to the fine ciders we can get today from the United States, France, Spain, and the United Kingdom. Its saving grace is raisins, which help give a little fizz when they ferment in the bottle. Do try the Cider Champagne, though. If you omit the sugar and milk fining, you're on the way to have a batch of good old Cider Oil.

Good cider. . . . . 10 gallons
Spirits. . . . . 1⁄2 gallon
Sugar . . . . 3 pounds

Mix and let rest for 2 weeks. Fine with 1 pint skimmed milk. Often sold for champagne.

Cider Oil

Cider oil. Cider royal. Cyder-oil. Cider ile. What even is that stuff? Depends on who's talking. Often it was a blend of hard or sweet cider and apple brandy (or sometimes whiskey) popular in colonial America similar to Lyon's Cider Champagne. But it was also sometimes what we call applejack today. In his 1810 *Sketches of a Tour to the Western Country*, Fortescue Cuming mentioned stopping along his trip for "a bowl of excellent cider-oil . . . stronger than Madeira . . . obtained from the cider by suffering it to freeze in the cask during the winter, and then drawing off and barreling up the spirituous part which remains liquid, while the aqueous is quickly congealed by the frost." Records show George Washington served it to voters in 1758 in his bid for the Virginia House of Burgesses. He won. You could do worse than serve up a bowl to friends.

Rosaceae. (Pomeae.)
2
3
1
9
6
A
7
5
8.
B
4
W.Müller n.d.Nat.
Pirus Malus L.

THE STONE FENCE

In *The History of Applejack*, Harry B. Weiss notes a stiff drink from northern New Jersey's "apple belt" called the Stonewall Jackson: 4 ounces of applejack in 8 ounces of hard cider. "After swallowing this, the drinker wouldn't know if he were in Sussex, England, or Sussex, New Jersey." It's a stiffer version of the Stone Fence (or Stone Wall), a colonial-era drink still popular in some quarters:

2 oz apple brandy
(or, in a pinch, rum or whiskey)
Hard cider

Pour the apple brandy into a pint glass over a few ice cubes. Fill with hard cider. Orange and/or aromatic bitters are optional newfangled additions to this ancient quaff. Served hot, it benefits from a slice of lemon and a few cloves or a cinnamon stick.

CIDER SHERRY FLIP

Flips, a class of drinks that mix eggs with sugar and spirits or wine, are coming back into vogue after decades of neglect. Bartenders of the past, including Pennsylvanian George Murray, weren't always punctilious about including the eggs. In the 1890s Murray served a cider sherry flip that Pittsburgh's businessmen snapped up to stave off the summer heat.[45] During Prohibition, that "sherry" might well have been an imitation sherry such as Lyon described. Murray's original made about a 2-ounce drink—but our summers seem to be hotter. Let's nudge the volume just a bit higher.

1.5 oz pale sherry
1.5 oz cider champagne
1 tsp simple syrup (page 145)

Stir in a shaker with ice. Strain into a chilled coupe.

Applejack, Jersey Lightning, and Spirits of Cider

Unlike urban moonshining that so often relied on sugars, distilling apple spirits has always tended to be a rural pursuit. While Harlem doctor Victor Lyon secretly recorded recipes that might have landed him in jail if he had tried to publish them, illicit distillers in nearby New Jersey cranked out untold gallons of applejack, the region's traditional spirit, to slake New York's thirst. Supplies also ran to Philadelphia, Baltimore, and points south, though Virginia and North Carolina apple distillers kept the flame alive in the upper South.

Prohibition very nearly put an end to the tradition, but Americans had been downing apple distillates and blends for centuries under a variety of names: applejack, apple whiskey, Jersey Lightning, cider brandy, spirits of cyder, cider royal, and others. What came to the cities during the 1920s and early 1930s was often new and raw, a roughness that helped kill our taste for it. After repeal, Charles H. Baker Jr. advised readers,

> Don't get Jersey Lightning that some friend has put down in the wood since last fall, get it at least four or five years old. It is a very deceiving fluid, and when not watched will induce a happy state from the waist down, closely approaching voluntary paralysis. (*The Gentleman's Companion* Derrydale Press: New York 1939)

For much of American history, **applejack**, **apple whiskey**, and **apple brandy** indicated the same thing. But not always and not everywhere. In casual use, many say "applejack" to designate aged, American-style, charred-oak apple brandy. It may also refer to a rough winter spirit later dubbed *Yankee antifreeze*, obtained from freezing hard (i.e., fermented) apple cider and repeated breaking through the icy surface to extract unfrozen higher-proof liquid underneath until what's left simply fails to freeze. This type of applejack has disappeared from the commercial scene, but a few modern distillers experiment with the form.

The final type of applejack is, like many of Lyon's whiskeys, brandies, and rums, more than half vodka. So-called **blended applejack**, popularized by New Jersey distillers Laird & Company starting in 1968, actually predates Prohibition. In 1954, Harry B. Weiss noted in *The History of Applejack* that blending apple brandy with grain spirits allowed pre-Prohibition distillers to compete against cheaper corn and rye whiskey.

Apple Brandy Cocktails

Unless they are intended to replicate some specific beverage such as sherry or port, always consider swapping out the "spirits" called for in cider compounding recipes with apple brandy to emphasize the apple taste and aroma. A little barrel char adds agreeable character as well. Alternately, if barreling your own apple spirits isn't in the cards, you would do well to shake one of the big apple drinks of Prohibition: the Jack Rose.

THE JACK ROSE

The Jack Rose predates David Embury's 1948 *The Fine Art of Mixing Drinks*, but Embury pegged it as one of the best-liked apple brandy drinks of its day. It's still a good one.

- 2 oz American barrel-aged apple brandy
- 0.5 oz fresh lemon or lime juice
- 0.25 oz real pomegranate grenadine

Shake vigorously with plenty of cracked or crushed ice and strain into chilled cocktail glasses.

Embury notes that "a nice touch" is frosting the glass by dipping its rim in grenadine, then in powdered (i.e., fine, not confectioners') sugar before straining the drink into the glass.

In 1926, US "dry czar" General Lincoln C. Andrews admitted that his forces captured only 10% of the "family stills" in America. Here, agents in San Francisco dismantle one of millions of such illicit stills.

> "Liquor for non-beverage purposes and wine for sacramental purposes may be manufactured, purchased, sold, bartered, transported, imported, exported, delivered, furnished and possessed..."
>
> —National Prohibition Act, Title II, Section 3

Wine

Just around midnight one frigid February night in 1925, five cars rolled up to a Chicago, Milwaukee & St. Paul Railroad warehouse in Chicago. Out poured 15 men, armed raiders who pressed the facility's lone watchman into service to help them load more than 40 barrels of port into their cars. The value of their haul? $12,000.[46] In today's economy, that's about $162,000 worth of fortified wine. The appeal for bandits is undeniable—that is, after all, a lot of money—but here's the thing: wine was actually legal during Prohibition. At least some of it was. The wine in the warehouse wasn't some bootleg rotgut, but a perfectly legal agricultural product owned by the Italian Vineyard Company.

The wine loophole in the Volstead Act was a doozy, the scams it spawned breathtaking. The act explicitly permitted wine for sacramental purposes but didn't delineate what was sacramental and what wasn't. The intention was to make national prohibition more palatable to Catholics, who drank modest amounts of wine during Mass, and to Jews who drank in somewhat greater quantities at home. With each group thinking that Prohibition would not prohibit that sacred juice, the thinking was that they would give less resistance.

Rabbis willing to endure onerous paperwork could secure access to 10 gallons of wine for every Jewish family in America. But what was "wine?" Port or claret? Hock or Champagne? What about vermouth? Inveterate Prohibition agent Izzy Einstein once seized $35,000 worth of sacramental Dubonnet, a sweet fortified aperitif from France, in a Harlem garage.[47]

Framers of the Nation Prohibition Act failed to take into account the informal structure of rabbinical ordination. Determining whether a Catholic priest was, indeed, a priest was relatively straightforward: ask his superiors. "Compared to Christian religious institutions," writes historian Marni Davis, "the American rabbinate was loosely organized and minimally supervised." If a man said he was a rabbi, in other words, who's to say he wasn't? Counterfeit rabbis claimed new, robust congregations, notes Davis, "filled with members named Houlihan and Maguire." They culled members from lists of the dead or made them out of whole cloth. In Alameda, California, the city's mere 50 Jewish families constructed a fictitious congregation of over 500 names.

The Wine Doctor

In a widely reprinted article from the *London Daily News,* Armiger Barclay wrote of his encounter with a local *licoriste* who pointed to rows of bottles and promised he could recreate any wine or cordial from abroad Barclay might like.

> "See those? Wine in embryo. Tons of it! Give me good water"—he indicates an innocent looking tap in the corner—"and I'll turn you out a bottle of anything you like to name—while you wait!" . . . "Mind you," he goes on, "I don't object to the real wine in moderation. My own best qualities have a base of sound Sherry or Burgundy. Take claret, for instance. Why send to Bordeaux when, with a gill of Australian Burgundy or Spanish Rioja, water—watch while I do it—a few drops of French vinegar and 25 per cent of potato spirit that's colorless and odorless and only costs a few pence per gallon, I can give you chemically the same thing with more alcoholic strength?"
>
> Presto! It is done. He pours some of the result into a wine glass and hands it to me. It has the look, smell and taste of the wine for which I pay one and six pence a bottle.
>
> "Total cost is a fraction over three pence, bottle and label included," he exults . . . From the bottles on the shelf he takes benzoic acid, benzoic ether, acetic acid and ether, oenanthic ether and glycerine—a drop or two of each—and fills up the glass with the ever indispensable alcohol. I raise the colorless mixture to my lips and behold! It is Maraschino! ("Tricks of the Wine Doctor," *Salt Lake Herald,* August 18, 1907, 6)

During Prohibition, men and women alike smuggled liquor into public spaces hidden in thousands of different containers from hot water bottles and canning jars to flasks disguised as books, ample bellies, high heels, cigars...and walking sticks.

TO COLOR CLARET WINE

Take as many as desired of damasciennes [i.e., damsons] or black sloes and stew them with some dark colored wine and as much sugar as will make it into a syrup. A pint of this will color a hogshead of claret. It is also suitable for new port wines and may be kept ready for use.

TO COLOR PORT WINE

Raspings of red sanders
  wood . . . . 6℥ [ounces]
Spirits of wine . . . . .1 quart

Infuse 14 days and filter for use. Produces a beautiful red color for port.

Don't Get Caught Up on Names

Some drinks are patently bad no matter what we call them; their salvation does not lie in nomenclature. Others may be perfectly fine, but bad examples of what they purport to be. Don't get caught up on names. There's a trap into which we can fall when we project our current understanding onto terms and concepts of the past.

Take Lyon's "port wine." Real port is phenomenal stuff. Compared to them, Lyon's attempt isn't just subpar; it's off-spec. If a bartender served me that when I asked for ruby port, I'd send it back. As a drink, though, stripped of its counterfeit name, I like it. That huge bump of hard cider made me think immediately of cool-weather punches. Then it hit me that it's a sort of distaff cousin to Spanish sangria or Scandinavian glögg. With that in mind, I studded an orange with cloves to make an old-school pomander, roasted it, and poured Lyon's heated concoction over it for a hot, jammy punch during one of our cold and wet spells in San Diego.

At the same time, don't go off the rails. You can make a liter of lavender, black pepper, and nutmeg cordial that's got 450 grams of sugar in it if that's what gets your motor revving, but if you insist on calling it port (or triple sec or eggnog), that's not artistic license; you've just straight-up got it wrong.

Port Wine

Worked cider	21-gallons
Good port wine	6 gallons
Good brandy	1½ gallons
Pure spirits	3-gallons

Mix. To give color elderberry and sloes and hawthorn berry gives a fine color.

Port Wine

Prepared cider	20 gallons
Good port wine	3 gallons
Wild grapes in clusters	5 quarts
Bruised rhatany root	1/4 pound
Loaf sugar	1½ pounds
Spirits	1 gallon

Let stand 10 days. Then rack off and fine. If color is too light add tincture rhatany root.

Madeira Wine

Prepared cider	40 gallons
Tartaric acid	½ pound
Spirits	4 gallons
Loaf sugar	3 pounds

Let stand 10 days and draw off carefully.

TO PREVENT A BAD TASTE AND SOURNESS IN WINE.—Put in a bag the roots of wild horse radish, cut in bits. Let down into the wine and leave it two days ; take this out and put in another until the wine is restored—or use wheat.

TO PREVENT A BAD TASTE AND SOURNESS IN WINE

Horseradish makes a surprise appearance in the formulary as a clipping pasted into the book's pages. Not usually associated with spirits, here it's used "to prevent a bad taste and sourness in wine." My advice? Skip it. Instead, infuse about a cup and a half of *fresh* horseradish (please: not jarred) in a 700 to 750 ml bottle of vodka for about 4 hours, strain it, and use the bracing fluid in Bloody Marys. It also works in tequila and gin, but it would be a shame if such a strong flavor overtook your finest spirits. Use the everyday stuff. And if your everyday stuff *is* the finest, well, bully for you!

Dealcoholized Wine and Cider

The problem with fruit juices—or the whole point of getting your hands on some, depending on how you look at it—is that yeasts tend to attack them, devouring their sugars and churning out alcohol as a waste product. If you let apple or grape juice ferment, you've got hard cider or wine on your hands. There's more to it, than that, of course, and much depends on the blending of appropriate varieties. Your wine or cider won't necessarily be the best you've ever had, but it will have a kick, not something to sneeze at when your government deems intoxicating beverages of all stripes contraband.

Those in the business of selling "fresh" ciders during the Volstead years, though, were often at pains to make sure that their products contained less than 0.5% ethanol, the maximum permitted under the laws of the time. In 1920, the *National Bottlers' Gazette* offered straightforward advice to its readers who wanted to steer clear of governmental entanglements: boil the juice as wine makers did to make "dealcoholized" wine. As any distiller can tell you, ethanol has a lower boiling point than water. Either bringing vats of cider to a boil or turning live steam into suspect juice would heat it enough so that all but trace amounts of alcohol present would be carried away with the vapor.[48]

Who knows how many vintners and cider makers bothered to collect that alcohol-rich vapor? But that would be pretty rough brandy. And wholly illegal.

PORT WINE ESSENCE

Not all nonalcoholic wines began as proper wines, though. Lyon's Victorian-era port wine essence could have been used either to simulate real port or to make an alcohol-free version for children's parties or to flavor syrups for ices.

- Tartaric acid . . . . 3 drams
- Tincture of orange . . . . 3 drams
- Concent[rated]. Decoction logwood . . . 4 drams
- Glycerin . . . . 4 drams
- Oenanthic ether. . . . . 20 minims
- Acetic ether. . . . . 20 minims
- Sp[iri]ts [of] nitrous either . . 30 minims
- Syrup qs ad [enough to equal a total of] . . 3 ounces

This quantity to be added to 1½ pints (Imp) of water to make nonalcoholic port wine (English formula)[.] Sherry wine essence is made in the same manner omitting the logwood and using sufficiency of caramel.

Wine Cocktails

DIY SUMMER CUP

In *Boardwalk Empire*, HBO's series set in Prohibition-era Atlantic City, Steve Buscemi's character Nucky Thompson uses a classic gin and vermouth aperitif from England in a power play with a corrupt senator. Pimm's No. 1 (there have been several iterations over the years) is the base for Pimm's Cup, a summertime refresher loaded with fruit. Of course, you could buy Pimm's No. 1, but making a DIY summer cup hardly even qualifies as work. Over oysters and cocktails one afternoon at San Francisco's Ferry Building, Martin Cate, owner of the rum bar Smuggler's Cove and beloved in tiki circles for his championing of tropical drinks, shared me with his base recipe for a summer cup in the style of Pimm's No. 1. His version is as straightforward as they come:

- 2 parts sweet vermouth
- 2 parts gin
- 1 part curaçao

Mix and store in a cool, dark place. I add about 2 ounces of this to a glass with ice, top off with sparkling lemonade or ginger beer (Cate likes bitter lemon), and garnish with fresh cucumber spears, mint, hulled strawberries if we have them on hand, and a tuft of lemon balm or borage. For the curaçao, consider Lyon's Rum Shrub (page 71) or swap it out with Lyon's Ginger Brandy (page 171) for a drink with more bite.

Mash for Whiskey (14)
Crushed barley malt 10 bushels
Corn meal 20 bushels
Ground Wheat 20 bushels
Water 900 gallons

Mash for wheat whiskey
Crushed malt 25 bushels
Coarsely ground wheat 125 bushels
Water 2700 gallons

Mash for rye Whiskey
Malted rye 45 bushels

So-called "local options" allowed towns and counties to vote to go (officially) booze-free before the Volstead Act fell on the nation. Some places have yet to repeal those laws.

SONNENTANZ

While prohibition had taken hold in parts of America, but Prohibition proper was still a few years off, members and guests of Philadelphia's Union Club drank Zeeland Cocktails: a bit like a rum Manhattan with a splash of kümmel. Okay, but no great shakes. Treat it like a summer cup, though, and you're onto Something Else. Ladies and gentlemen: the Sonnentanz.

- 1.5 oz Jamaican rum
- 0.75 oz red vermouth
- 0.5 oz strong cold tea
- 0.5 oz orange curaçao
- 1 bar spoon kümmel

Stir with ice until well chilled and strain into a chilled glass.

KÜMMELLIKÖR

Mix 40 loths of fine white sugar with 1½ drams of pure caraway oil. Dissolve the mixture in 1½ quarts of water, and mix in 6 pounds of alcohol. After a while, filter this liqueur through blotting paper.

note

The *Loth* is an old German measurement equal to 0.5 ounce. A retail pound is equal to 16 ounces, 32 *Loth*, or 128 *Quentchen*.

Tweaking Brandies One Note at a Time

Brandy manufacturers have had a battery of compounds for adjusting aromas and flavors at their disposal for hundreds of years. Some are used even still; a dose of aged wood extract, caramel coloring, and vintage syrups are among the traditional tools a distiller

The "brandy" here is from physician Andrew Ure's 1837 Dictionary of Arts, Manufactures, and Mines. Compounders typically based so-called British brandies on neutral or malt spirits rather than grapes.

may legally use to "shape" such brandies as Armagnac, Cognac, and Calvados—to give them the body, aroma, mouthfeel, and taste customers find pleasing.

Other ingredients are either lesser known or have fallen by the wayside. The faked brandies of Prohibition owe their formulas to French, Dutch, and German blenders of the 18th and 19th centuries. Cognac oil, ethyl butyrate, tannins, vinegars, raspberry syrup, and various fruit "ethers," when added in judicious amounts, can impart the taste of old brandies to something quite new. In imitation of boise (see page 99) achievable only with great age, blenders have resorted to infusions of hickory nuts, almonds, and walnuts, to neroli, bitter almond oil, vanilla, and prune and raisin syrups. Meanwhile, the raw, fiery taste of new alcohol can be tempered with sweeteners, such as syrups, honey, or glycerin. For astringency: galls, oak extracts, infusions of nut hulls, teas, catechu, and kino. Ambergris, a highly aromatic secretion of sperm whales that has been softened by years of oxidation on open ocean waters, was once used to achieve a "particularly fine" flavor, but it is both hideously expensive and prohibited now in many countries.

When discussing the clinical effects of thujone and absinthe, it should be kept in mind that the majority of the data available was derived from clinical observations made in the late 1800's and are therefore lacking reliability and clinical significance.

—Stephan A. Padosch,
"Absinthism: a Fictitious 19th Century Syndrome with Present Impact," 2006

A DISSERTATION ON ABSINTHE BY MOOR

Sale of Absinthe In Morocco Prohibited by French Resident General—Moors Pleased

Paris, June 15.—One of the first things that General Lyautey, the French resident general in Morocco, did in taking office was to prohibit the sale of absinthe. This measure, aimed at both the French troops of occupation and the natives, considerably affected business interests and steps were taken to try and stir up a movement of opposition.

An old Moor to whom a trader tried to explain the tyrannous nature of the general's order, took a wholly unexpected attitude: "Absinthe,' he said, "is an invention of the Evil One. On its roots he pours the blood of a peacock; then, when the leaves begin to grow, he sprinkles them with the blood of a monkey; then he dips the stalks in the blood of a bear; lastly he mingles with the juice of the plant the blood of a pig.

"So that when the faithful drinks absinthe, at the first glass his appetite awakes, and he arises, proud as a peacock; at the second glass, he becomes excited and gesticulates like a monkey, at the third he becomes quarrelsome and spiteful, like a bear; at the fourth he becomes besotted and falls to the earth, and rolls like a hog in the mire.

"May Allah protect us; Sidi Lyautey is right."

Wild Cherry Liquor

of either good Monongahela Whiskey. Jamaca Spirits or Brandy. Use 2 qts Cherries to 1 Gall Liquor The Demijohn can be replenished several times with liquor. Jamaca Spirits which is very fine is only half price of Brandy. Telegraph.

Currant Wine

Chapter five

Absinthe, Cordials, and Bitters

The ban was not so much lifted as it disappeared

Brandies fabricated with nothing but grain alcohol, wood extract, sweeteners, and colors are the antithesis of artisanal distilling. Likewise, manufactured "whiskeys" that are blends of vodka, aromas, colors, and flavors are straight frauds. There's not much (legitimate) reason to make them when such good examples can be had at any decent-size grocery or liquor store.

Cordials and bitters, on the other hand, are something else. Some cordials, such as anisette and crème de menthe, are made routinely, even by respectable firms, with essential oils or essences derived from them. In this chapter, we'll round up the sweetened alcoholic beverages from Lyon's notebook and some related concoctions. In particular, we'll look at caraway, anise, mint, and ginger. We'll throw in cinnamon, coumarin, orange, and some bitters. Some use essential oils; some, spices and herbs.

But first: absinthe.

ABSINTHE IMITATED, INCLUDING THE KICK

Nancy Man Finds Cheaper Formula, but Cafe Owner Is Fined.

Special Cable to THE NEW YORK HERALD.
Copyright, 1922, by THE NEW YORK HERALD.

New York Herald Bureau, Paris, May 13.

France, like America, is having trouble with booze substitutes, but, unlike the land of thirst, the French police are complaining that the chief fault is that the substitute imitations of strong drinks are really better than the prewar brands.

For more than a year the thirst of American visitors has been quenched by a chemical product with a base of aniseed, masquerading as absinthe. The law has provided a complicated standard to define the point where it ceases to be anise and commences to border on absinthe: namely, when it remains opaque when four times its own volume of water is added. At Nancy this week, however, the inspectors discovered a new brand which is enjoying the reputation of providing a first class joyfest.

After a few libations the investigation proved that the manufacturer had found a formula cheaper and stronger than those of his competitors and was getting rich quick. The law provided no penalty for the maker, but the owner of the cafe where the drink was purveyed had his stock confiscated, was heavily fined and his license canceled.

This is where the case is at present—quite triangular. The Police Commissary still has his eye on the musician. The musician virtuously has nothing to do with bars. The bars never heard a note of the musician's music. And if any tourist says that prohibition of absinthe does not work in France—real bona-fide absinthe, with from 40 per cent. to 60 per cent. alcohol and distilled aromatic, narcotic, nerve-stimulating plants—let him try to get some in the Nice or Paris bars.

Absinthe

When it comes to spirits in the United States, it's hard to find one more maligned and romanticized than domestic moonshine. But one runs a close second: the famous green fairy of the belle époque, absinthe. Like many beverages in the old notebook, absinthe has—at least tenuously—a medicinal aspect. Lyon includes more than a dozen entries on the spirit. The high-proof spirit has been reviled for the better part of a century, accused of causing a particularly virulent (and clinically dubious) form of alcoholism 19th-century physicians dubbed *absinthism*, but its early success is due in part to the French army's issuing absinthe as an antimalarial. French soldiers developed a taste for the spirit and spread an affinity for the stuff to cities across the country.

Although absinthe was popular on both sides of the Atlantic in the years before American Prohibition, numbers from France demonstrate the surge in its popularity from the late 19th century until just before World War I. In 1875, total French consumption of *la fée verte (the green fairy)* was 15,500 hectoliters—about 410,000 gallons of pure alcohol. In 1908, the volume increased tenfold to over 4 million gallons. By 1913, the volume had grown to 6,327,000 gallons, a whopping 60 liters per inhabitant—more than half a cup of absinthe per person each and every day of the year.[49]

SCHWEIZER ABSINTHÖL [SWISS ABSINTHE OIL]

Like most of Lyon's recipes, his "Swiss" absinthe oil is pinched from someone else. In 1925, the identical recipe is included in a long list of wormwood preparations deep in the bowels of *Hagers Handbuch der Pharmazeutischen Praxis*, a German druggists' manual. The recipe is an example of a compound oil. Rather than blending so much of various essential oils with alcohol, a compound oil made of multiple oils would simply be added to a base alcohol and perhaps syrup. Recipes like this one are sometimes called essences or concentrates.

Anisöl (anise oil) . . . . .350 g
Fenchelöl (fennel oil) . . . . 130 g
Röm. Kamillenöl
(Roman chamomile oil) . . . . 6 g
Sternanisöl (star anise oil). . . . . . . 133 g
Wermuthöl (wormwood oil) . . . . .300 g
Wermuthessenz
(wormwood essence). . . . . . . [40 g]
Veilchenessenz (violet essence) . .àà 40 g

With diluted spirits of wine, makes Swiss Absinthe.

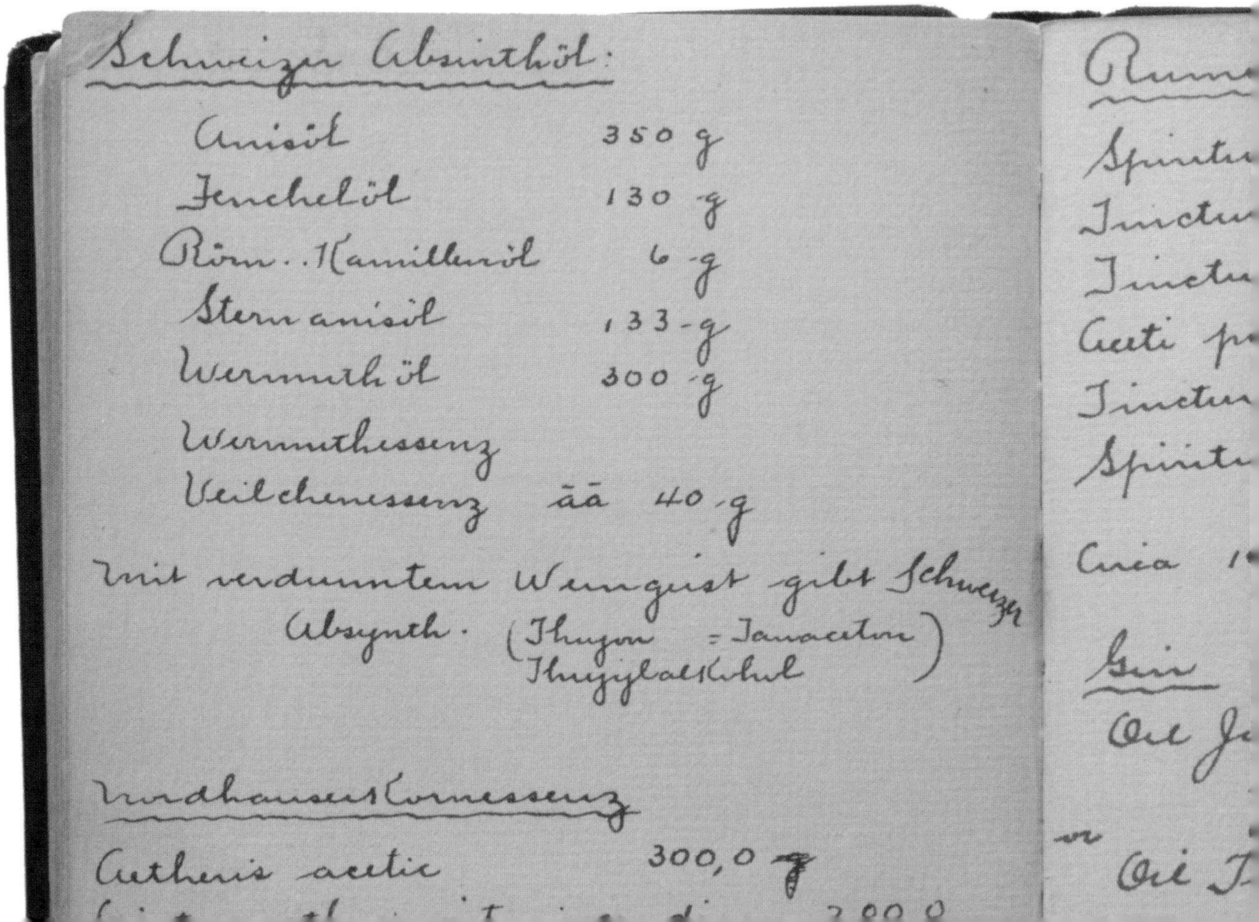

O, for a Ruse of Fire!

Toward the end of the 20th century, fire arrived on the absinthe scene—such as it was—a sort of marketers' sleight of hand. I'm not an absinthe purist and have no compunction about using the high-proof spirit in such cocktails as a Sazerac or a Death in the Afternoon. I stand, however, with absinthe historian Marie-Claude Delahaye who declared flaming absinthe "a heresy from the Eastern countries."[50] See, fire was never part of traditional absinthe preparation in bars or cafés in Europe or America. The pyrotechnics were a 1990s ruse designed to distract novice drinkers from the low quality of so-called Bohemian absinth(e)—cold compounded wormwood-flavored spirits from the Czech Republic, usually lacking absinthe's other traditional botanicals, such as fennel and anise. Flames also highlight the stuff's high alcohol content.

The maneuver is simple; place a sugar cube on a perforated spoon over a thick glass containing the spirit, moisten the cube with a bit more, and set the booze-soaked sugar alight. The sugar melts and falls into the glass where it sets the spirit on fire. A dose of cold water extinguishes the flame and it's stirred until the whole thing may (or not) achieve a mild louche. The routine ruins spoons, makes glassware hard to clean, and introduces off flavors. It is a maneuver calculated to delight rubes and newbs.

Since we are neither, we do *not* set our absinthe on fire.

Absinthe Cheat Sheet

Just as whiskey, rum, and gin have definite styles, classic absinthe varieties can be broken down a few ways. In broadest strokes, there are green (*verte*) which typically are colored by a maceration of herbs after distilling and white (*blanche*) types which are not. But that's a crude measure. Differences also derive from botanicals used to prepare each. First, let's look at what they have in common.

The Flavor

Classic absinthe is a lightly bitter, high-proof spirit flavored with anise, fennel, and wormwood. Variation among the botanicals yields several styles (see "Different Styles," page 127) and plenty of recipes exist that may omit one or more of the aforementioned trio—though purists might not deem them true absinthes. The best absinthes are distilled spirits, but there was once a robust market for cold compounded versions made with oils. The majority of absinthe aficionados regard such compounded absinthes as beneath notice. The green color so common to absinthe comes from steeping botanicals in the distilled spirit (which is as clear as water otherwise), a final adjustment of flavor and look before bottling.

High Proof

The highest grade absinthes are strong spirits, usually 65% to 72% abv. Exemplars of green/*verte* absinthes are usually called *absinthe supérieure*, while the highest grade of white/*blanche* are *absinthe suisse* ("Swiss" absinthe). A step down from that was *absinthe fine* with slightly lower proof. Below that was *demi-fine*, which ranged from 40% to 53% abv. *Absinthe ordinaire* was an everyday/for-the-masses version subject to much adulteration and often made with inferior spirits. The categories were not hard and fast, but as rough analogs similar to today's premium, midrange, well, and bottom-shelf spirits, they give you a broad feel for what each means without getting bogged down by the particulars.

Unsweetened

Many drinkers, especially in my home, sweeten their absinthe in the glass by melting sugar cubes suspended over the surface with cold water, but the spirit itself has no sugar. A lower-proof cordial version called *crème d'absinthe* did have syrup added.

Different Styles

Anise, fennel, and "grand" wormwood (*Artemisia absinthium*) are sometimes thought of as the "Holy Trinity" of absinthe botanicals. Three more complement them in most absinthes: petite wormwood, hyssop, and melissa (lemon balm). According to *A Treatise on the Manufacture and Distillation of Alcoholic Liquors*—the premier 19th-century distillation manual by Pierre Duplais—variations in the amounts and other botanicals account for differences in style named after the French cities in which they were once popular.

Absinthes

	Wormwood	Anise	Fennel	Petite wormwood	Hyssop	Melissa	Veronica	Angelica	Coriander	Mint	Elecampane
Besançon	×	×	×	×	×	×	×		×		
Fougerolles	×	×	×	×	×	×	×	×			
Lyon	×	×	×	×	×	×	×	×	×		
Montpellier	×	×	×	×	×	×				×	×
Nîmes	×	×	×	×	×	×	×				
Pontarlier	×	×	×	×	×	×					
Suisse	×	×	×								

Compound Liqueur Oil
French Absinthe

Oil Coriander 9 drams
Oil Cloves 9 drams
Oil Cassia Cinnamon 9 drams
Oil Fennel 1 ounce
Oil Star Anise 2 ounces 5 drams
Oil Wormwood 11 ounces
1 lb

Absinthe Exotica

We rarely see whiskey aficionados mixing different whiskeys in one glass. Gin lovers are loath to stir a martini with multiple gins. But the tiki crowd has no compunction about blending two, three, or even more rums in one glass (or mug or bowl) in an effort to get just the right flavor for a drink. They also deploy, from time to time, drops and dashes of absinthe to get the right flavor in such tropical libations as the Cobra's Fang, the Cuba Kula, and the Zombie, all from the 1930s. Anywhere from 3 to 6 drops of absinthe can lend an indefinable something to a drink, an *I-can't-quite-put-my-finger-on-it* exoticness that even people who profess not to like absinthe can dig. More than 6 drops, though, and the cat's out of the bag.

COMPOUND LIQUEUR OIL FRENCH ABSINTHE

Compounders and rectifiers embraced essential oils centuries ago for making spirits and cordials with varying degrees of success, but wormwood oil often proved problematic. As far back as 1805, Richard Shannon called it "one of the more ungrateful oils" that smelled of wormwood, but had "little or nothing of its bitterness."[51] Modern users have called wormwood oil flabby, vegetal, and rank—unsuitable for making essential oil-based absinthes.

When I asked Gwydion Stone, distiller of Marteau absinthe and fellow tiki connoisseur, whether he knew formulas for respectable oil-based absinthes, he said that it's possible in theory to make a decent absinthe by cold-compounding oils, and there were apparently some made in the pre-ban era. "The problem these days," he explained, "is that there's no absinthium oil being produced for the beverage trade; it's all made for medicinal applications. Consequently there's more focus on capturing the therapeutic elements and none on good flavor and aroma." One ounce of this compound oil flavors a gallon of spirit.

Oil Coriander. . . . . .9 drams
Oil Cloves . . . . .9 drams
Oil Cassia Cinnamon . . . . .9 drams
Oil Fennel . . . . 1 ounce
Oil Star Anise. . . . . . . 2 ounces 5 drams
Oil Wormwood. . . . . .11 ounces
Total: . . . . 1 lb

The Louche

Oil and water, so goes the old saying, don't mix. And that makes a very nice effect for people who like anise-flavored alcoholic beverages, such as pastis, raki, sambuca, and ouzo. Like them, absinthe turns translucent when brought down to drinking strength. Just as adding high-proof spirit can clear cloudiness in some spirits made with essential oils, cold water creates an emulsion of an essential oil that had been dissolved in the high-proof spirit. The main component of that essential oil is trans-anethole,[52] an ester with a strong anise aroma. It's highly soluble in ethanol, hardly at all in water. At a target 5:1 ratio of water to absinthe, the alcohol content is about 12 to 14 percent, the same as in a glass of wine. But the result with so much cold water is cloudy, slightly milky, almost opalescent, shot through with swirls of whites, greens, and even faint blues. Watching a swirling louche form is particularly mesmerizing as the afternoon sun splays through a window and into the glass.

Water 26 quarts

Absinthe

Leaves and tops of wormwood plant 4 pounds, Angelica root, calamus root, anise seed and dittany leaves 1 ounce each. Brandy or spirit (12 U.P.) 4 gallons.

Macerate 10 days add 1 gallon water. Distill 4 gallons at gentle heat and dissolve in the distilled spirit 2 pounds white crushed sugar Flavor with few drops of anise.

ABSINTHE

With its sugar and anise oil added to a nonstandard botanical bill (where's the fennel?), this recipe might turn off aficionados, but it's in line with many of the sorts of absinthe variants in older books—and among today's home distillers.

> Leaves and tops of wormwood plant 4 pounds, Angelica root, calamus root, anise seed and dittany leaves 1 ounce each. Brandy or spirit (12 U.P.) 4 gallons.
>
> Macerate 10 days add 1 gallon water. Distill 4 gallons at gentle heat and dissolve in the distilled spirit 2 pounds white crushed sugar[.] Flavor with few drops of anise.

Calamus is a sweet-smelling plant that grows along waters' edges across most of Europe, into Asia, and parts of North America. Its root (a rhizome really) imparts a bitter flavor with overtones of cinnamon and ginger in countless 19th century bitters, cordials, and spirits formulas. Calamus is not approved as a food additive in the US because some varieties may be carcinogenic and cause vomiting.

Absinthe: An Early Victim of Prohibition

So many absinthes are available to modern shoppers. Even a modest liquor store might offer a half-dozen choices. In a shop where the proprietor takes a personal interest, that number easily could double or treble. Some bartenders and journalists will tell you that that's because "the ban" on absinthe was lifted only recently. They might even pinpoint the year to 2007 and National Absinthe Day, a publicity ploy that originated with savvy absinthe company Lucid. It's a tidy little story, but that's not how it went down. In fact, no ban was lifted, no laws were changed, no regulations updated. Yet now we have absinthe and 15 years ago we didn't. What changed?

Absinthe was indeed banned in the United States at one time. Following the leads of Holland, Belgium, Switzerland, and Brazil, the US Department of Agriculture outlawed the spirit with Inspection Decision 147 in 1912, making it an early victim of the burgeoning temperance movement. Italy did the same in 1913. France itself, the heart of absinthe drinking culture in Europe, followed in 1915 on fears that the vast consumption weakened its military readiness. Knowing the ban was coming, many dedicated drinkers hoarded supplies, making the 1913 bottling one of the more common vintage expressions on today's vintage spirits market. Germany finally made absinthe verboten in 1923.

The thing is, sometime—probably in the 1960s, according to *absintheur* Gwydion Stone (see "Serving Absinthe," page 132), though nobody seems quite sure exactly when—absinthe's ban in America seems to have fallen through the cracks in a bit of bureaucratic reorganization. Absinthe has been perfectly legal for more than 40 years, but until the 2000s, nobody thought to challenge conventional wisdom that dictated that it wasn't.

The ban wasn't lifted so much as it disappeared—probably before Neil Armstrong first stepped on the moon.

Absinthe Will Make You Hallucinate!

Sigh. No. No, it will not. The notion that absinthe caused fin de siècle drinkers to have psychedelic experiences is entirely a fiction of the Watergate era when Americans were experimenting with drugs as never before (well, discounting alcohol, opium, tobacco, etc.). The idea that thujone, a minor component of absinthe derived from wormwood, is an hallucinogen took hold then and has proven particularly hard to shake. Thujone is not an hallucinogen. High doses can, however, be toxic, so never ingest undiluted wormwood oil.

Absinthe Cocktails

SERVING ABSINTHE

Last Spring, I visited Gwydion Stone and his wife, Trinity, in Seattle. Stone distills Marteau absinthe and is cofounder of the Wormwood Society, an absinthe appreciation group. Our long afternoon at their home elided into evening, eased along in part with a bottle of 1913 Pernod Fils absinthe. We didn't break the seal and we didn't kill the bottle, but the food, conversation, and generosity combined to make one of my favorite memories of 2014.

We drank that pre-WWI absinthe in the classic manner with nothing more than ice water and a little sugar—and some specialized gear. Absinthe glasses usually have a mark or reservoir for a specific measure of the spirit, usually one ounce. If you don't have one, a wine glass is perfectly fine. The sugar is optional. Some like it, some don't. You will note, however: no fire.

4 to 5 oz water
1 oz absinthe
1 sugar cube (2 if they're small)

Fill a carafe with ice and water. Pour the absinthe into an absinthe glass, and place a perforated absinthe spoon on top, spanning its rim from side to side. Place the sugar cube on the spoon. Drip a bit of ice water over the sugar cube until it is soaked through. Then slowly drip more water over it, dissolving the sugar until the absinthe louches—turns completely opaque, a pale opalescent green. Stir briefly. Sip. Revel in the sensation of being the cat's pajamas.

The "save the children" trope is nothing new. Shutting down saloons was positioned early on as pro-family, anti-crime propaganda.

{see page 16 for essence formula}

Absinthe Formulas

French: For 10-gallons

% alcohol under proof		19
Essence (Page 27)	2½	10 ounces
Alcohol 38° over proof	1	4-gallons
Sugar syrup 60%	¼	1-gallon
Water	1	5¼-gallons

Color green

German

Alcohol under proof	19
Essence	10 ounces
Alcohol 38° over proof	4-gallons
Water	6¼-gallons

Color green

Swiss

Alcohol under proof	12
Essence	10 ounces
Alcohol 38° over proof	4¾-gallons
Water	5½-gallons

Color light green

Crème Absinthe

Essence Wormwood	3¼-drams
" English Mint	3¼ drams
" Anise	1 ounce
" Sweet Fennel	4½ drams
Distilled Essence Lemon	1 ounce

ABSINTHE SUISSESSE

This New Orleans brunch classic is not as well known outside the city as the Sazerac or Ramos Gin Fizz, but it's as good an introduction to absinthe cocktails as you're likely to get. Well . . . after the Sazerac, perhaps. Although modern recipes are apt to omit it, crème de menthe harkens back to 1930s versions of the drink.[53] If mint's not your bag, ditch it, then double both the orgeat and the half-and-half.

1.5 oz absinthe
0.5 oz white crème de menthe (or any of the mint cordials in this book)
0.25 oz orgeat
1 fresh egg white
1 oz half-and-half

Dry-shake all the ingredients (i.e., in a shaker without ice) until blended, 10 to 15 seconds. Add ice and shake again until well chilled. Strain into a chilled cocktail glass. Alternatively, combine the ingredients in a blender with ½ cup of crushed ice and blend for 5 seconds. Pour unstrained into a rocks or highball glass.

MONKEY GLAND

While Prohibition raged in the United States, the French surgeon Serge Abrahamovitch Voronoff gained first fame then notoriety for his procedure that grafted tissues from monkey testicles to men's testicles. Oh, laugh it up, but Voronoff made a huge name—and tidy fortune—for himself doing it as a way to increase vitality. The gin-and-absinthe cocktail named after his procedure may not provide quite the same boost, but do make sure the OJ is fresh. If you have it, blood orange or Cara Cara is the way to go.

New Cocktail in Paris Is the Monkey Gland

(Special Cable Dispatch)

Paris, April 28.—Preparing for a busy tourist season, Frank, the noted concocter behind the bar of the Ritz, has devised a new series of powerful cocktails, favorite of which is known as the "monkey gland."

Like Frank's "soixante quinze" gloom raiser, the "monkey gland" requires absinthe to be perfect, but its amateurs have found anise a substitute with a sufficient kick.

For the benefit of friends over in America, who have not exhausted their cellars, here is the recipe: Half and half gin and orange juice, a dash of absinthe, and a dash of raspberry or other sweet juice. Mix well with ice, and serve only with a doctor handy. Inside half an hour the other day Frank purveyed 40 of these, to the exclusion of manhattans and martinis.

1.5 oz gin
1.5 oz fresh orange juice
1 tsp grenadine
1 tsp absinthe

Shake the ingredients with ice; strain into chilled coupe or cocktail glass.

ABSINTHE ONIONS

If the closest the old notebook comes to cocktail recipes is a brace of rum shrubs (see page 71), it's no surprise that Lyon is reticent about garnishes. I'm pretty sparing with them myself. Every few months, though, I put up a small jar of briny cocktail onions in absinthe. In ones and threes, I drop them rather than an olive into a martini for a bitter twist on a Gibson cocktail.

I use 120-proof Absinthe Verte from St. George Spirits in this, but use what you've got.

Drain the brine from one 8–fluid ounce/237 ml jar of pickled cocktail onions. This should be about 4 ounces/120ml. Pitch the brine (or take it as a pickleback if you're into that sort of thing). Top off the onions with the same volume of absinthe, reseal the jar, and pop it in the fridge. These onions keep for months, but should be good to use in 3 to 5 days.

Bitters

Pennsylvania physician Jacob Hostetter developed a recipe for bitters to combat constipation, colic, and fever in the early 19th century. When he retired in 1853, his son David began to manufacture and sell the nostrum. Young David for years poured most of his profit into advertising. By the time the Civil War broke out, the name Hostetter was so well known that the Union Army routinely ordered it by the train carload as medicine for its troops, leading to a handsome fortune for the Hostetter family. Dr. Hostetter's concoction—which came in at a whopping 47% alcohol—enjoyed decades of strong sales, even if the proof was reduced in later years. Prohibition, however, dealt a blow to the company from which it never recovered. By the 1950s, it was history.

In intervening decades numerous recipes arose which emulated the famous stomach bitters. Bitters like these are not the same as cocktail bitters such as Angostura, Fee Brothers, Abbott's, or Peychaud's. Rather, they are more akin to medicated wines meant to settle rumbly bellies and subdue a variety of complaints. Its bitterness (derived from orange peel, gentian, and cinchona) is about on par with tonic water—but with a decided orange punch. I use it sometimes as a nightcap or, if I've had too many nightcaps, first thing as a morning pick-me-up.

Even before Prohibition, there was grumbling and grousing from bartenders and temperance advocates alike about druggists who sold, in addition to medical spirits, all sorts of boozy bitters, tonics, and nostrums to a thirsty public.

Stomach Bitters equal to Hostetter's for one quarter cost.

European Gentian root	3/4 ounce
Orange Peel	1 1/4 ounces
Cinnamon	1/8 ounce
Anise seed	1/4 ounce
Coriander seed	1/4 ounce
Unground Peruvian bark	1/4 ounce
Gum Kino	1/8 ounce

Bruise all these and put in half pint best alcohol. Let it stand for a week and pour off. Boil the dregs in one pint of water. Strain and press out all the strength. Dissolve 1/2 pound loaf sugar in the hot liquid adding 1 1/2 quarts cold water and mix with the tincture first poured off.

Ginger Wine

Best ginger root (bruised)	1/2 ounce
Capsicum	2 1/2 grains
Tartaric acid	1/2 dram

Put into one pint 95% alcohol, let it remain one week and filter. Then add 1/2 gallon water which has been boiled with 1/2 pound crushed sugar. Mix when cold. To give color boil 1/4 ounce cochineal 3/8 ounce cream tartar, 1/4 ounce saleratus 1/4 ounce alum in 1/2 PINT water.

119795

D. HEMMETTE, 68½ Liberty St., N. Y.

PARK BENJAMIN,

GTON'S

MY AND NAVY

OLVER!

he Government.

ny other Pistol of the kind.
olvers. Sold by the Trade

TON & SONS,
Ilion, N. Y.

34 DR. C. W. ROBACK'S MEDICAL ALMANAC.

DR. ROBACK'S STOMACH BITTERS.

A new and delightful Stomachic and Cordial, for giving tone to the Stomach, and for the prevention of bilious complaints incident to the Western country.

As a morning drink, to assist digestion, it has no equal. There is in it nothing nauseous, which is a characteristic of nearly all the so-called Bitters. On the contrary, it is exceedingly pleasant to the taste, imparting a glow and stimulus to the whole system. It is slightly Aromatic, which quality is highly beneficial in removing all symptoms of Flatulency.

An "ounce of prevention is worth a pound of cure," is an old saying, but none the worse for age. Then, if you would save many a doctor's bill, keep these Bitters constantly in your houses.

If you have symptoms of Dyspepsia, take them freely. Half a wine-glassful is an ordinary dose, but a much greater quantity can be taken with safety. In short, the amount should be regulated to agree with your nervous system—hardly any two being alike in that respect.

In cases of great prostration, or in that feeling described as a sense of "goneness," it needs only a trial to effect a perfect restoration, and a bracing up of the nervous system. Its exhilarating properties are not excessive, like the vile compounds with which the country is flooded, under the names of Schiedam Schnapps, Cordial Gins, etc., containing few medicinal virtues of any value, and which are intended merely as an evasion of restrictive Maine Laws; but, instead of so large a proportion of alcohol, these Bitters derive their stimulus from the powerful tonic nature of the roots and herbs of which they are composed.

The formula of these Bitters has remained in the hands of one of our most eminent medical practitioners of the West, with whom it originated, and in whose private practice it has been constantly made available in that class of disease where there is a General Depression of the Nervous System, a Loss of Muscular Energy, Weakness, Lassitude, Want of Appetite, Faintness, Chilly Sensations, and Aching of the Bones, which precede attacks of Fever and Ague, etc.; and the present proprietor, believing it would be a blessing to the human race, has concluded to make its virtues publicly known.

It will soon be for sale by all of Dr. Roback's numerous Agents, the country over. In the meantime, orders will be filled direct from Cincinnati, in any quantity, and at the lowest rates. It is put up in Quart Bottles, and securely packed in one doz. cases. Half doz. sample cases will, however, be packed and sent to any address, if desired.

Retail Price, $1 per Bottle, or Six for $5.

DR. C. W. ROBACK'S ALMANAC.

MAGAZINE

AND

of Fashion,

MBER, 1864,

IN ATTRACTION!

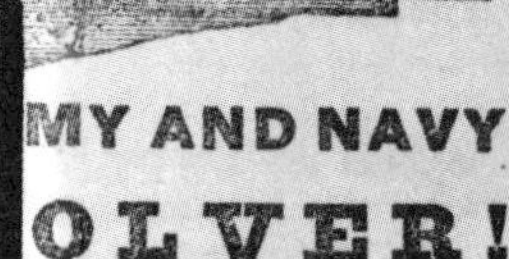

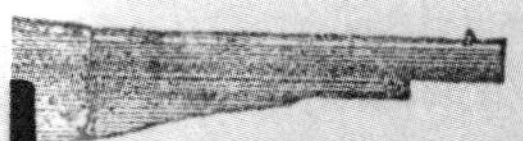

HOSTETTER'S

CELEBRATED

STOMACH BITTERS.

A TIMELY WARNING TO THE SICK.—It is especially important at this time, when the markets of the United States are flooded with the direst poisons, under the name of imported liquors, and when domestic compounds purporting to be medicinal, but not a whit less pernicious, are heralded to the world as "sovereign remedies," that the public should fully understand the facts. Be it known then, that while all the diffusive stimulants called *liquors* are impure, and all the *Tonics* containing alcohol are manufactured with a fiery article containing *amyl* or *fusel oil*, a *mortal poison*; HOSTETTER'S CELEBRATED STOMACH BITTERS contain none of these things, but are a combination of pure Essence of Rye with the pure juices of the most valuable stomachic, anti-bilious and aperient herbs and plants, and that as a safe and rapid remedy for Dyspepsia and all its kindred complaints, this preparation stands before the world without a rival or competitor. Its sales to-day are equal to the combined sales of all the other Tonics advertised in the United States, and the certificates which authenticate its usefulness are signed by individuals of the highest standing in every professional calling and walk of life. Beware of imitations and impostures.

Sold by all Druggists and Family Grocers.

Hostetter's Stomach Bitters,

PREPARED AND SOLD BY
HOSTETTER & SMITH, PITTSBURG, PA.
NEW YORK OFFICE, 59 CEDAR STREET.

$10 AGENTS $10

Cooley's Cabinet

FOR

Merch

And
best

GOURA

Italian Medic

It is well known—cures
Eruptions, Prickly Heat,
Chaps, Chafes and all cuticul
GOURAUD'S POUDRE SUBTI
foreheads or any part of the
GOURAUD'S LILY WHITE fo
GOURAUD'S LIQUID VEGETA
GOURAUD'S HAIR DYE and
sories, found at the old estab
DR.

Also of BATES, 129 Washingt
South Eighth Street, Philade
CALLENDER, Philadelphia; H
and Druggists generally.

"Self Preservation
book, containing Secrets rela
Life, which no man, young o
Price 50 cents. Address
5374, P. O., New York.

Stereoscopic Views a
1,000 different kinds. Sen
000 VICTOR DELA

$60 A MONTH!—I wa
expenses paid, to
cils, *Oriental Burners*, and
culars free. JOHN F. LORI
452-64

MATRIMONI

BRIDAL SETS, BRIDAL
MAIDS' SETS, OST
AND PARIS

At TUCKER'S.

$100 per Month.
Agents in the Army and eve
lucrative business known.
Address or apply to
457-67 T. & H. GAUGH

HOSTETTER(ISH) BITTERS

Gum kino provided astringency and a bit of color to 19th-century cordials and bitters. Astringency is not bitterness exactly, but more like a "dryness" in drinks that's often associated with tannins. Some red wines, for instance, can seem dry. A century after Lyon lived, kino is an elusive ingredient, so I've swapped it out for one that's as close as the nearest grocery: black tea. Not just any tea, mind you; *overbrewed* tea. Three to five minutes of steeping, depending on the kind of tea, will give you a decent cuppa. Let that same tea steep for half an hour, though, and you've got a mouth-twisting dryness that will earn you the stinkeye from finicky tea drinkers (including me). That's exactly what you want here.

TINCTURE

Bitter orange peel, dried . . . . .36 g
Gentian. . . . . .21 g
Cinnamon. 3. 5g
Anise seed. .7 g
Coriander seed . . . . .7 g
Cinchona, crushed . . . . .7 g
Spirit 96% abv . . . . .237 ml

TEA

Loose-leaf black tea . . . . 3 Tbl
Boiling water. . . . . .1.5 quarts

Day One: bruise all spices in a mortar and put into a clean, dry, wide-mouth jar. Rinse the mortar with half the spirit. Pour this onto the bruised spices in the jar. Repeat with the remaining alcohol. Let it all infuse for 1 week to create a tincture.

Day Eight: brew the tea an hour or two before proceeding with the rest of the recipe. Pour the boiling water over the tea leaves in a pot, and cover off the heat. Allow to steep for 30 minutes, then strain and set aside to cool. Discard the leaves.

Next, strain the spice tincture into a clean jar. Set aside. Put the dregs—the spice remnants you strained from the now-dark tincture—into a medium pot. Add 16 fluid ounces/474 ml of water. Bring the mixture to a boil, cover, lower the heat to medium-low, and simmer for 20 minutes.

Meanwhile, put ½ pound/227 g of sugar into a 2-liter jar. When the 20 minutes are up, strain the hot liquid from the dregs into the sugar, pressing the wet mass with the back of a spoon to extract every last bit of liquid (within reason; you want to be thorough, not manic). Alternately, run the mixture through a Büchner funnel (see page 38) Discard the dregs. Stir to dissolve. Add the tincture you set aside earlier. Add the cool tea. Stir to make sure the sugar is completely dissolved.

Prune flavor for Liquors

Mash 25 pounds, infuse 15 days with 6 gallons proof spirit stirring it every day, press and filter.

Orange Peel flavoring

Steep 1 pound orange peel in 1 gallon 95% alcohol for 15 days. Filter

Peach flavoring for whiskey

Steep for one month 10 gallons dried peaches, 10 gallons oak sawdust and five pounds black tea in 40 gallons proof spirit, strain & filter.

Flavoring compound for brandy

Mash 25 pounds raisins, 12 pounds prunes 6 pounds figs and 1 pineapple sliced. Infuse for 15 days in 20 gallons proof spirit stirring every day and then filter.

Syrup for cordials

1 pint of water for every 2 pounds of sugar. This makes fine syrup about 32° Baume. Beat up whites of 2 eggs (for 10 pounds sugar or in proportion) until very frothy and mix with rest.

Cordials

In North America, the terms *cordial* and *liqueur* tend to be used interchangeably. Each refers to sweet, flavored spirits. The sugar content may be as low as 2.5 percent or run higher than 60 percent in older recipes. That much sugar makes a cordial little more than a highly aromatic syrup, shudderingly saccharine to modern tastes. Today, we favor much less sweet cordials, about 200 to 300 grams of sugar per liter. In the UK, *cordial* may refer to sweetened, nonalcoholic beverages. British recipes calling for elderflower, lime, or other cordials may then instruct readers to slip some booze into the glass, or may not. They should be read closely.

Orange peel flavoring allowed rectifiers to add additional layers of orange aroma and flavor to curaçaos cold-compounded solely of citrus oils, syrup, and alcohol. Peach flavoring often contained oak sawdust to emulate barrel aging. A better use of your resources? Snag a bottle of peach-flavored whiskey from Colorado distillers Leopold Bros., who actually age their spirits in barrels.

Making the Grade

Before Prohibition pulled the rug out from under absinthe as the de facto spirit of bonhomie in the first years of the 20th century, distillers and compounders frequently divided cordials, such as anisette or curaçao, into different grades the same way they categorized commercial absinthe. The distilling industry didn't enforce exacting standards about what set one grade of the spirit apart from another; such things fell to individual distillers or compounders, custom, and what the market would bear, but higher grades, however they were determined, commanded higher prices. We don't use grades the same way today, but if you've used *bottom-shelf* rum, a *good starter* whiskey, or an *ultra-premium* gin, you get the gist of booze hierarchy. That last category is a bit of marketing hype, but, then, so was *absinthe supérieure*. The point is that knowing about old-fashioned grades is a useful framework for understanding vintage spirits and, consequently, why old cocktail recipes sometimes don't work with modern spirits. Old and modern ingredients might share a name, but alcohol content and ingredients might have shifted considerably over the decades or centuries since recipes were written.

Five variables stand out, though, in old formulas that affect the grade of a spirit or cordial. The first is the **production method**. Was the stuff distilled or cold compounded? With rare exceptions—for instance, in the case of mint cordials, which were almost universally made from mint essential oil and spirit—producers and customers alike regarded distilled spirits as superior to nondistilled made from essences, extracts, and oils. Distilled spirits consequently commanded higher prices. The second feature is **alcohol content**. The third, for cordials rather than spirits, is the amount of **sugar syrup** used to sweeten it. Higher grades used greater proportions of alcohol and sugar. For some cordials, 600 grams of sugar per liter was normal: pretty sweet for modern tastes when you consider that today's orange liqueurs often run around 250 grams of sugar per liter. Often, especially when compounding spirits, the number and amount of **aromatics**, such as essential oils or botanicals, factor in the "fineness" of a particular batch. Old cocktail recipes that call for a dash or two of curaçao or kümmel make more sense when you realize that such mixers might have far more intense flavors and aromas than modern examples that simply get lost in mixed drinks.

The last—and perhaps most important—element was the **alcohol** itself. Not just the amount of alcohol per liter, but its inherent characteristics. Did a formula call for Cognac or other brandy? Genuine rum? Or did it specify "silent" neutral spirits? The greater the proportion of neutral spirits in formulas, the lower the final grade tended to be.

Less carefully distilled alcohol that contained heads and tails thick with unwanted compounds would often be used in lesser grades of spirits. There really weren't enforceable standards in the distilling industry that set one grade of the spirit apart from another, but some general rules held.

Specific measurements to distinguish grades of cordials from one another vary among classic textbooks, but French usage dominates in professional manuals. In general, the highest grades were *surfine* (super fine) with the most and best-quality alcohol and highest concentration of sugar. After that was fine, then *demi-fine* ("half" fine), and finally *ordinaire*.

Pierre Duplais's *A Treatise on the Manufacture and Distillation of Alcoholic Liquors* is a monumental work of distilling knowledge that went through seven editions from 1855 through 1900. It remains *the* go-to manual for 19th-century absinthe recipes. Its success bred innumerable imitators and "Duplais" (as the book is often called) was widely plagiarized. According to Duplais and others, the following ratios of ingredients hold for every 10 liters of cordial (about 2.64 US gallons).

LIQUEURS ORDINAIRES

Alcohol 85% abv.	2.5 liters
Sugar	1.25 kilograms
Water	6.6 liters

LIQUEURS FINES

Alcohol 85% abv.	3.2 liters
Sugar	4.375 kilograms
Water	3.9 liters

LIQUEURS DEMI-FINE

Alcohol 85% abv.	2.8 liters
Sugar	2.5 kilograms
Water	5.5 liters

LIQUEURS SURFINES

Alcohol 85% abv.	3–4 liters
Sugar	5.6 kilograms
Water	2.6 liters

Doppel, Doppelt, or **double** cordials tend to be stronger and less sweet (analogous to *liqueurs surfines*) with stronger flavors and aromas.

Syrups

Syrups are concentrated solutions of sugars in watery fluids. More often than not, that means plain water and white table sugar. When water and sugar are the only ingredients, the result is called "syrup" or "simple syrup." The "simple" here refers to its two ingredients, not a specific proportion of sugar to water, which may vary widely depending on the profession, the practitioner, and the method of measuring ingredients.

That "watery fluid" could be nearly anything: tea, coffee, milk, wine, or infusions of spices and/or herbs such as cinnamon, star anise, or fennel are just the beginning. The first mint julep I was ever served used a syrup made with sugar, water, and fresh mint. It's the way I made them for years after (but please don't tell my father, a Kentucky colonel, of those unorthodox youthful indulgences).

The sugar? Well, that could be maple, Demerara, or palm sugar, to start. But don't stop there. Agave nectar gets a lot of play in bars these days and honey practically demands blending with water to make it mixable enough for drinks.

sliced. Infuse for 15 days in 20 gallons proof spirit stirring every day and then filter.

Syrup for cordials

1 pint of water for every 2 pounds of sugar. This makes fine syrup about 32° Baume. Beat up whites of 2 eggs (for 10 pounds sugar or in proportion) until very frothy and mix with rest.

On Measuring Syrups

Bar syrups can get awfully fancy, what with exotic spices, tropical fruits, unusual sugars, essential oils, and whatnot, but the simplest of them is nothing more than a solution of equal parts of plain white sugar and water (see “A Trio of Syrups for Drinks and Cordials,” page 145, for how to mix this and other proportions). Volume is a crude measure for sugar, though; the true amount of sugar (hence the final syrup’s sweetening power) depends on how tightly packed or settled it may be. Think of how many baking recipes call for tightly packed brown sugar rather than just scooped; it makes a difference. In recent years, bartenders have taken to weighing their ingredients to assure greater uniformity.

Some bartenders take a page from old cordial makers and measure the degrees **Brix** (°Bx) of their syrups. Brix measures the mass concentration of solids as a percentage of the final solution’s total mass. Fifty grams of sugar in 100 grams of solution is the standard 1:1 simple syrup. Sixty-seven grams of sugar (rounded up) in 100 grams of syrup is 2:1 rich syrup. The compounder’s standard 60% syrup is 60 grams of sugar in every 100 grams of final solution or 60°Bx.

SYRUP FOR CORDIALS

One pint of water for every 2 pounds of sugar. This makes fine syrup about 32° Baumé. Beat of whites of two eggs (for 10 pounds of sugar or in proportion) until very frothy and mix with rest.

Eggs

Eggs (usually chicken, but also quail, duck, and other species) are either used whole or separated into whites and yolks for different preparations. Egg whites are frequently used in shaken cocktails both to give a smoother mouthfeel and to soften the edges of rougher spirits. They are also mixed with wines to "fine" or remove suspended particles before sending to market. Yolks, on the other hand are turned with great advantage into Eierlikör or advocaat, German and Dutch drinks roughly analogous to English and American eggnog. As everyone knows, the chalazae (those white, squiggly cords that attach fresh yolks to shells) are the most repellent things in the world. Pluck them out with the edge of a broken shell, mix and strain the yolks, or blend the hell out of your egg drinks; nobody wants one of those vile things slithering across their lips.

Degrees Baumé, B°, Bé°, or simply Baumé (with or without the accent on *e*) is an older system used to measure density of liquids compared to distilled water (which is 0 °Baumé). Thirty-two degrees Baumé is a 59% sugar solution, which is pretty dang close to the old compounders' standard of 60% sugar syrup (recipe follows).

A TRIO OF SYRUPS FOR DRINKS AND CORDIALS

To make **simple syrup** (1:1 or 50% sugar), combine 600 grams each of sugar and water (or, really, any equal mass of the two). No need to heat it. Shake, stir, or blend in a blender until the sugar dissolves. Prepared simple syrup will keep several weeks under refrigeration. Optional: add an ounce or so of vodka or neutral spirits per liter to help prevent mold growth. Or maybe next time, just don't make so much.

Compounder's syrup (3:2 or 60% sugar) must be heated to dissolve the sugars. To make it, combine 600 grams of sugar and 400 grams (milliliters) water. Proceed as with rich syrup, below. When using compounding syrup in cordials, first mix cold sugar syrup with any water called for, then add the alcohol. After that, blend essential oils dissolved in high-proof alcohol and other aromatic compounds, wines, or juices. Adjust the color with caramel, cochineal, saffron extract, or other colorants.

Rich syrup (2:1 or 66.7% sugar) also needs to be heated. To make it, combine 600 grams of sugar with 300 grams (milliliters) of water in a pan (or, again: whatever amounts you want as long as you keep that 2:1 ratio). Heat the mixture slowly, stirring as needed, until the sugar is dissolved. Add spirits as above if you like, but rich syrup is not likely to develop molds if kept at a cool room temperature in a dark place.

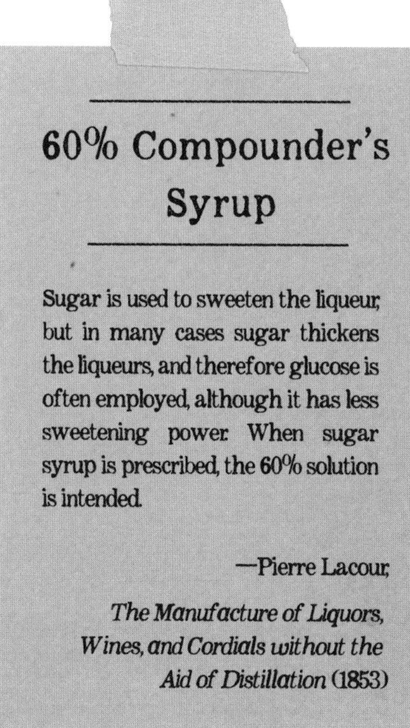

60% Compounder's Syrup

Sugar is used to sweeten the liqueur, but in many cases sugar thickens the liqueurs, and therefore glucose is often employed, although it has less sweetening power. When sugar syrup is prescribed, the 60% solution is intended.

—Pierre Lacour,

The Manufacture of Liquors, Wines, and Cordials without the Aid of Distillation (1853)

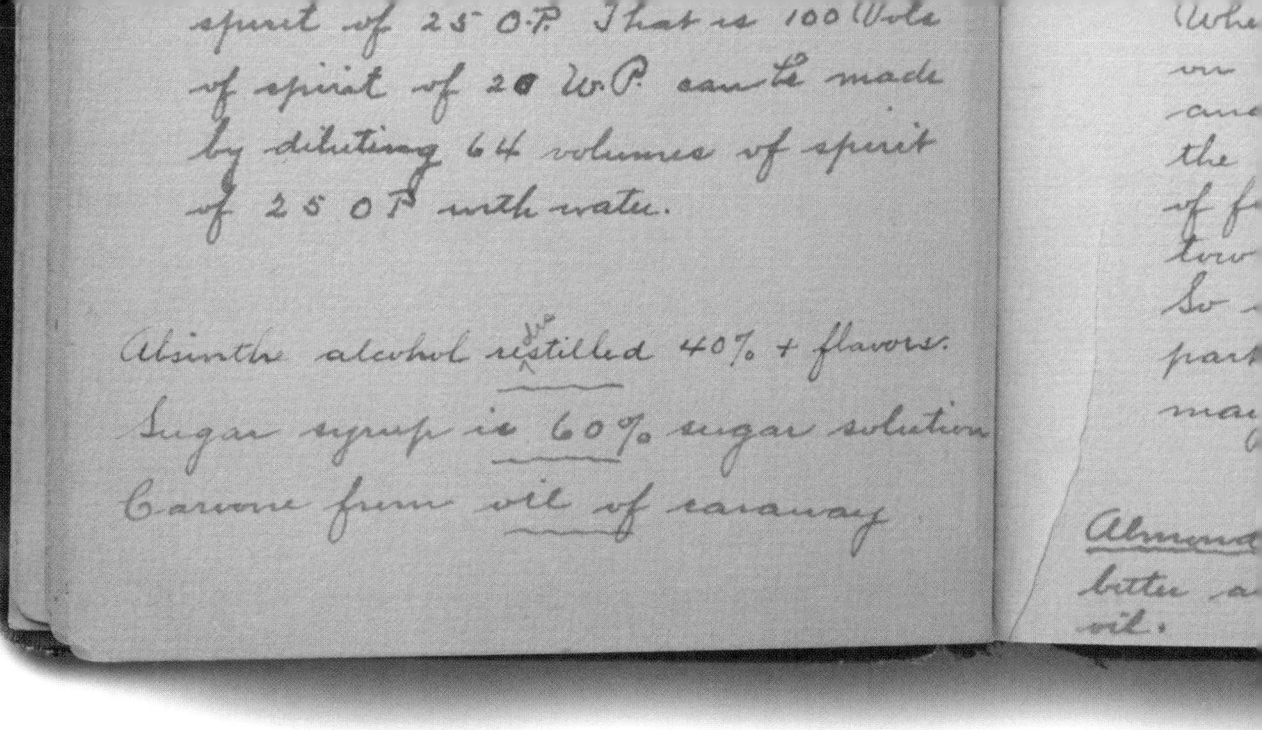

Brandy makers, especially those who follow French methods that call for adding small amounts of sweeteners to balance the final spirit, often age their syrups for decades. Just as whiskeys, rums, and other spirits change over the years, syrups aged in toasted oak transform, becoming more complex and richer. Thirty-, 50-, or even 100-year old syrups are not practical for most homes, but with small oak barrels on the market, and a little patience, more modest aged syrups are achievable.

Flavoring Syrups with Essential Oils

Some bartenders will add scant drops of essential oils to granulated sugar, let the mixture rest a bit, then stir in hot water until the sugar dissolves. And it's easy to see why they would. After all, the *oleo saccharum* ritual that starts off so many bowls of punch is just such a mashup of oils and sugar. The name literally means "oil-sugar" (well, in dog Latin, even if classicists take exception to the term). But ever since David Wondrich's *Punch*, a grand exploration of proper flowing bowls, came out in 2010 and reintroduced drinkers to the practice, making an *oleo saccharum* has become de rigueur among cocktail types. Mashing sugar and oils together just *feels* right.

But don't do that. Yeah, sure, you'll get a syrup, but you're not making the best use of sometimes pricey ingredients. Keep in mind that essential oils are also called *volatile oils*; the reason they smell so strongly when you open a bottle of, say, orange or cumin oils, is that molecules break free from the main body of oil and disperse in the air. Adding heat—whether it's hot water or other liquids such as tea or milk—increases the rate of reaction and sends even more aromatic compounds into the air. Smells nice, but you want that in your drink, not wafting into the ether of your kitchen or prep area.

Rather, add oils to *cold* or room-temperature syrup made in advance. Doing so helps to keep essential oils stable. It also results in clear syrups, unclouded with oils.

GUM SYRUP

While it hasn't returned as a staple in every bar, sugar syrup known as *gomme*, or gum, has made a comeback in craft cocktail bars. Gum is thickened with dried and ground resin of various acacia species.[54] The rehydrated resin gives syrups a round, supple mouthfeel. If, as some observers would have it, some 90 percent of pre-prohibition American whiskeys were adulterated by the time they reached consumers' lips, such "gum" syrup would have helped some of the rougher burrs. Harsh spirits or no, the velvet feel cocktails and cordials made with gum syrup are well worth reviving.

2 oz/55 g gum arabic
6 oz/180 ml water, divided
12 oz/340 g superfine sugar

In a small container, combine the gum arabic and 2 ounces/60 ml of the water. Stir to blend, and cover. Let sit for 48 hours, or until the gum arabic is completely dissolved.

In a small saucepan, combine the sugar and remaining 4 ounces/120 ml of water. Heat gently until the sugar begins to dissolve, and then fold in the gum arabic mixture. Remove from the heat immediately, let cool, and bottle. Store in the refrigerator indefinitely.

Kümmel

Poor, ignominious kümmel. Moonshine may be sneered at, absinthe misunderstood, but kümmel has languished, practically forgotten, for the better part of a century. The war, of course, is to blame. When World War I erupted in 1914, Americans—their patience already tested by what they felt were the divided loyalties of German Americans—demonized all things Teutonic. Even speaking German on a telephone could get a call disconnected. Speaking it in the street? Why, that could get you beaten. As a readily identifiable German tipple with that insufferable . . . nay, even treasonous *umlaut*, the caraway-flavored cordial took a big hit; by the 1960s mostly old-timers drank it. When they died off, so did sales.

At its most stripped-down, kümmel (a.k.a. kummel and kimmel) is unsweetened brandy flavored with caraway seeds. Bartenders who once concocted their own caraway brandy might have used such a barebones version in dashes and squirts to flavor drinks, much as they used bitters or dashes of clove tincture. When bottled for sale, however, it was often sweetened. Ice caraway is a particularly lovely expression in bottles so rimed with sugar crystals that the whole thing seems frosted. Caraway was often kümmel's dominant flavor, rather than the only one. Fennel and cumin frequently appear in old recipes, but so do coriander, star anise, cinnamon, rose, bitter almond, lemon, orange, and other flavors. Of modern brands, my favorite is Combier's Doppelt Kümmel Extra, but making your own gives additional latitude for personalizing this old cordial.

Lyon's notebook contains over a dozen recipes for making this once-important beverage. But the Germans weren't the only ones drinking caraway-spiked spirits and cordials. English and American bartenders in the 19th century used strongly flavored caraway cordials. An 1855 report on wood alcohol-spiked ethanol ("methylated spirit") in England noted that while a large pub may retail 1,200 gallons of gin in a month, it may only sell 10 to 12 gallons of cordials:

> The substances chiefly used in flavouring cordials are caraway, cloves, and aniseed. The methylated spirit could not be used for any of these liquors. Indeed, from their being generally made use of to give an extempore flavour to gin at the option of the customer, more than usual attention must be paid to their own purity of flavour. (Graham, Hofmann, and Redwood, "Report on the Supply of Spirit of Wine Free of Duty for Use in the Arts and Manufactures," *Pharmaceutical Journal and Transactions*, 14, no. 9 [1855]: 556, 562)

From the 1905 *The Hoffman House Bartender's Guide*, here is a simple kümmel for dashing into drinks:

CARAWAY BRANDY

Steep one ounce of caraway seed, bruised, in one pint of brandy. In one week strain. Add six ounces loaf sugar.[55]

Caraway also gets extensive play in northern European drinks. It is the cornerstone of aquavit, a distilled Scandinavian spirit whose history goes back centuries and whose name (also rendered akevitt and akvavit) is derived from Latin *aqua vitae* ("water of life").

Doppel (also ***Doppelt*** or **double**) kümmels are stronger, drier, and may have more botanicals or oils. Historic recipes tend to run 45%–50% abv and about half the sugar (10%–12%) one could expect from an everyday kümmel.[56]

Doppel Kümmel

5 gallons 94% alcohol add 4 ounces oil caraway, ½ dram oil of anise, 5 drops oil coriander 5 drops oil bitter almonds 10 drops oil calamus. Add 20 gallons French proof spirit and 15 gallons water in which 10 pounds white sugar have been dissolved. This will make 40 gallons Kümmel of 36¾% strength. If for cordial more sugar may be added

Doppel Kümmel

Dissolve separately in little 95% alcohol ½ dram oil of anise and 5 drops each of oil calamus bitter almonds and coriander. Dissolve also one to 1½ ounce of oil caraway in sufficient 95% alcohol to make clear solution Incorporate these with 40 gallons French proof spirit and add 10 pounds sugar dissolved in 5 gallons water

Caraway Cordial

Dissolve 1 dram oil caraway in 3 gallons 95% alcohol. Add a syrup made by dissolving 42 pounds sugar in 4¾ gallons water. Filter

SIMPLE CARAWAY VODKA

It's not the same as the genuine article, but a simple, stripped-down kümmel (or is it an akvavit?) can be made with nothing more than caraway seeds and vodka. Soften it if you like with up to a tablespoon of syrup. Small additions of fennel, star anise, or lemon zest are not hateful.

- 1.5 to 2 tbl caraway seeds, lightly crushed
- 750 ml vodka, 40%–50% abv

Combine the caraway and vodka in a 1-liter jar and macerate anywhere from 4 hours to a week. Strain into a clean bottle. Serve cold from the freezer.

TWO HISTORIC KÜMMEL RECIPES[57]

Fill three quarts of cognac or kirschwasser, six ounces of broken caraway, and 2⁄5 of an ounce of star anise into a glass bottle, close it with a bladder, and place it in a pot partly filled with cold water; now heat this, and let boil for half an hour; take the pot from the fire, and let the bottle get cool in the water, then sweeten the liquor with two pounds of refined sugar; filter, bottle and cork well.

With the aid of oils the method of manufacturing is as follows: dissolve 30 drops of caraway extract, 2 drops of fennel oil, 1 drop of cinnamon oil in one ounce of spirits; mix this to four quarts of cognac and three pounds of refined sugar; filter and bottle.

KÜMMEL

From *The Druggists' Circular* (1913) comes a recipe that more closely cleaves to Alasch, a Russian kümmel variant:

Oil of anise	2 drops	Tincture of vanilla	2.0 grammes
Oil of bitter almond	2 drops	Sweet spirit of niter	20.0 grammes
Oil of parsley	6 drops	Alcohol (90%)	3650.0 grammes
Oil of rose	8 drops	Sugar	3000.0 grammes
Oil of caraway	2.0 grammes	Water	3500.0 grammes

Dissolve the oils in the alcohol, and add the tincture, spirit of niter, and the water in which the sugar has been dissolved.

PICAYUNE KÜMMEL

From the 1910 edition of *Picayune's Creole Cook Book*, a straightforward caraway cordial that uses essential oil. Like all good cordials, this one benefits from a rest to let the flavors marry and stabilize. Consider small additions of different essential oils—just a few drops—oils of fennel, star anise, lemon, orange, or other oils. Fresh dill or dill seeds make a hybrid oil-and-spice compound that drifts into the realm of Scandinavian aquavit.

- 1 quart of the best rectified alcohol
- 30 drops of kümmel oil [1–1.5 ml caraway essential oil]
- 1 quart of boiling water
- 2 pounds of the finest white loaf sugar

Pour the boiling water over the sugar and stir till dissolved. Bring to a boil, and let it continue boiling from 15 to 20 minutes. Strain, and when lukewarm, add the oil and the alcohol. Bottle and keep for at least two months before using. The oil is obtained from druggists.[58]

Ice Caraway

Boil 50 pounds hard crystallized sugar with 2 gallons of water to a syrup, filter through flannel and while still hot add 6 gallons strong alcohol, and 10 ounces Russian caraway essence. Filter hot and as quickly as possible and fill into white glass bottles to 3/4 of their content The bottles are stoppered and placed in a vat filled with crushed ice mixed with some table salt. While cooling the sugar crystallizes slowly, and the more slowly the more beautiful are the crystals The bottles are finally filled with any desired caraway liqueur of high alcohol content (see page 19)

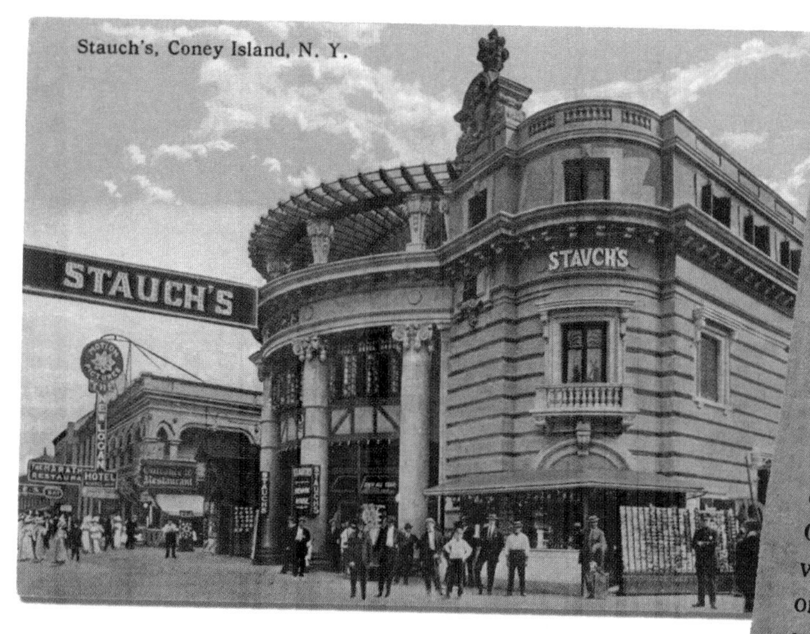

In 1906, Stauch's Restaurant on Coney Island boasted one of the biggest dance halls in the world. Three thousand couples, it was said, could dance there at once. In the cavernous dining hall, the bill of fare offered dishes that would have been familiar to well-heeled diners of the day: oysters 16 different ways, local bluefish, lobsters, Delmonico steaks, mutton chops, and turtle soup.

Four styles of schnitzel, eels in jelly, Bismarck herring, and Pomeranian goose breast, however, revealed a German hand in the kitchen. The bar menu shows the same touch. To cap a meal after Champagne and wine, owner Louis Stauch offered cordials, including Chartreuse, Benedictine, and violet-hued Crème Yvette. But one drink stood out: ice kümmel, a version of which Victor Lyon wrote out as "Ice Caraway."

ICE CARAWAY, OR ICE KÜMMEL

Unlike everyday kümmel, which was simply flavored with caraway oil or essence, distillers prepared the ice version by first filling clear bottles with a hot, supersaturated sugar solution. Over the course of days, delicate crystals grew, covering the bottles' interiors. Distillers then poured out the syrup and filled each bottle with kümmel. The result was a beautiful "frosted" bottle of cordial.

Boil 50 pounds of hard crystallized sugar with 2 gallons of water to a syrup, filter through flannel and while still hot, add 6 gallons strong alcohol, and 10 ounces Russian caraway essence. Filter hot and as quickly as possible and fill into white glass bottles to three-quarters of their content. The bottles are stoppered and placed in a vat filled with crushed ice mixed with some table salt. While cooling the sugar crystallizes slowly and the more slowly, the more beautiful are the crystals. The bottles are finally filled with any desired caraway liquor of high alcohol content.

ICE LIQUOR

The old German favorite ice kümmel is easy to make at home. The hardest thing about it is waiting patiently for days as sugar crystals form. Once crystals frost the inside of the bottles, fill them with commercial kümmel, white rum, gin, or an aquavit, such as Krogstad's from House Spirits in Portland, Oregon. Don't like caraway? Not a problem. Use another flavoring—cinnamon or peppermint oils, for instance, maybe with a bit of citrus oil or menthol—to flavor high-proof vodka or white dog. For ease of calculations, I've increased the metric amounts slightly.

6.25 lbs/3 kilos sugar
1 quart/1 liter filtered water
2 to 3 drops essential oil (e.g., caraway, peppermint, or cinnamon) (optional)
700 to 650 ml clear spirit

Combine the sugar and water in a large pot. Bring to a boil over medium-high heat and stir frequently until all the sugar dissolves. Stir in the essential oil, if using. While still hot, pour the syrup through a funnel into two clean 750 ml bottles, then stopper each bottle. At this point, either place them aside in a cool space where they can remain undisturbed for several days or put them in an insulated cooler surrounded by crushed ice mixed with a handful of kosher or rock salt. When the bottles are fully "frosted" with sugar crystals, carefully decant the remaining syrup and fill each bottle with any spirit you like.

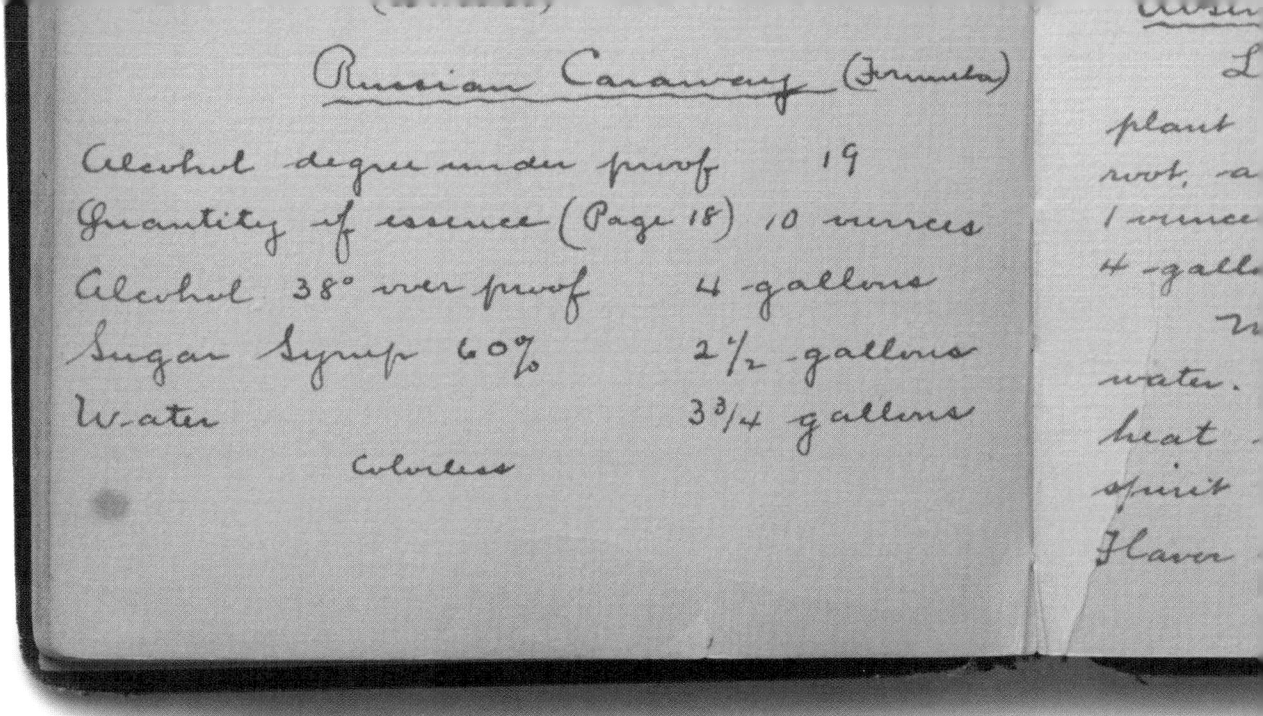

Russian Caraway (Formula)

Alcohol degree under proof	19
Quantity of essence (Page 18)	10 ounces
Alcohol 38° over proof	4-gallons
Sugar Syrup 60%	2 1/2-gallons
Water	3 3/4 gallons

Colorless

RUSSIAN CARAWAY

The journal contains two recipes for Russian Caraway, one for the essence, and the other for the liquor created with the essence (denoted as "the formula"). The essence calls for 13 ounces of carvol, also known as carvone, a compound with two forms, both of which dissolve readily in alcohol. One tastes of caraway and dill; the other, of spearmint. First isolated in 1849, each form is still used in food and candy making. Because pure d-carvone, the primary constituent of caraway oil, may be difficult to find, essential oil of caraway is an acceptable substitute.

Kümmel Cocktails

THE KÜMMEL FIZZ

When tending bar at Expatriate in Portland, Oregon, Jacob Grier devised the Kümmel Fizz as a "Diplomatic Pouch" drink (the bar's version of bartender's choice). Yet another reason that Portland really is a fine city in which to bend elbows.

- 1.5 oz kümmel
- 1 oz fresh lime juice
- 0.5 oz blackberry liqueur

Shake, serve on rocks, then top with soda. Garnish with a lime wedge.

SAM WARD'S RECIPE

The Sam Ward Cocktail is a sweet little number either invented by or named after the son of the New York City Temperance Society's first president. Sam Junior didn't seem to take much after Pops and was a bit of a gourmand. Despite its many variants, the drink always has lemon and yellow Chartreuse. It may be as simple as a bit of yellow Chartreuse and chipped ice in a hollowed-out lemon half, but bartender Tim Daly's recipe from 1903 combines those elements with Cognac—and kümmel:

Peel a bright clean lemon in one long string; arrange same around inside of a fancy stem glass; fill centre with shaved ice, fill one third full of kümmel, fill one third full of yellow chartreuse; add Cognac to fill glass, and serve with small straws.

This delicious decoction was devised by the famous New York connoisseur, after whom it was named; and by gentlemen who are on affectionate terms with their palates and stomachs is as fondly considered as their wives and sweethearts.[59]

THE APPLE NAP

The Sam Ward is similar to a drink from William Schmidt's 1891 manual *The Flowing Bowl*. "The Only" William's recipes are a mixed bag; some work and some don't. With Cognac, his Nap cocktail is nothing special. But it got me to thinking of an old dish: apples baked with caraway and sugar. Using Laird's 100-proof apple brandy makes all the difference. A strong, spicy drink the color of chamomile tea—and head and shoulders above your dance club appletinis. Do give it a try.

0.5 oz kümmel
0.5 oz green Chartreuse
0.5 oz Laird's 100-proof apple brandy

Stir with ice until well chilled. Strain onto fresh ice and serve. A dash of rose water or rose liqueur (such as Crispin's Rose Liqueur from California distiller Crispin Caine) is an optional, but nice, touch.

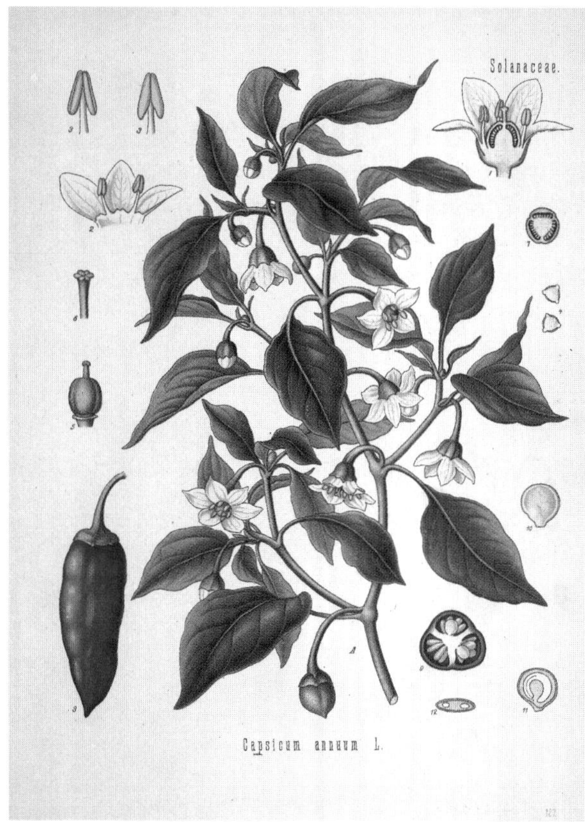

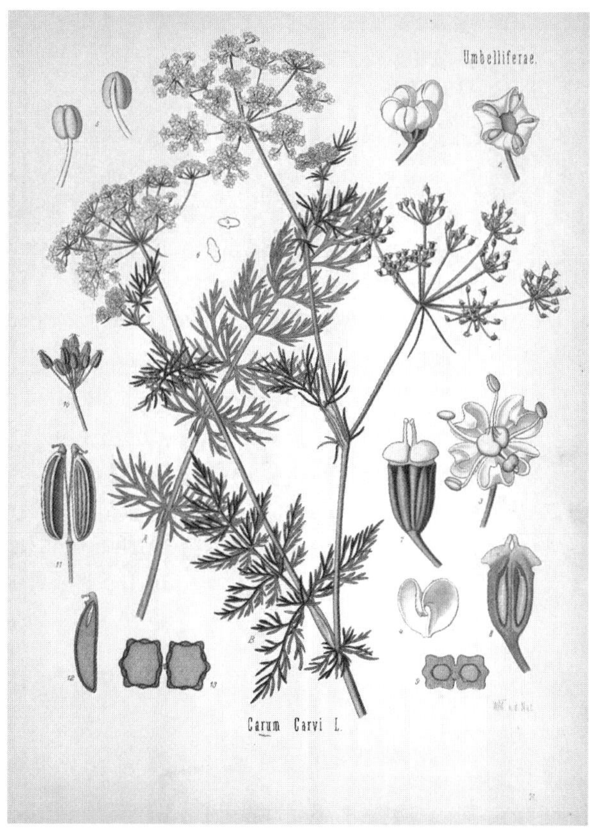

MISSION BELL

Portland bartender Tommy Klus uses more than dashes of kümmel; his modern Mission Bell is distaff cousin to margaritas, with caraway cordial in place of orange liqueur. Although it's not in his original, I like this one with a float of brick-red Ancho Reyes, an ancho chile–flavored cordial from Mexico. See page 89 for notes on chiles in old recipes.

1.5 oz Pueblo Viejo Reposado
0.75 oz Combier Doppelt Kümmel Extra
1 oz fresh lime juice
0.25 oz agave syrup

Shake all the ingredients with ice in a cocktail shaker. Strain into a chilled coupe and serve with no garnish.

EPICUREAN

Paul Clarke, editor of *Imbibe* magazine and author of *The Cocktail Chronicles*, took a stab at a Cognac and kümmel drink from David Embury's classic *The Fine Art of Mixing Drinks*. "Embury doesn't call for it," he notes, "but a slender wisp of lemon zest emancipated from the fruit and sent, with a quick twist, into the depths of the drink, certainly isn't a bad idea."[60] No. Not bad at all.

2 ounces Cognac
1 ounce dry vermouth
0.5 ounce kümmel
Dash of Angostura bitters

Stir with ice until well chilled and strain into chilled glass.

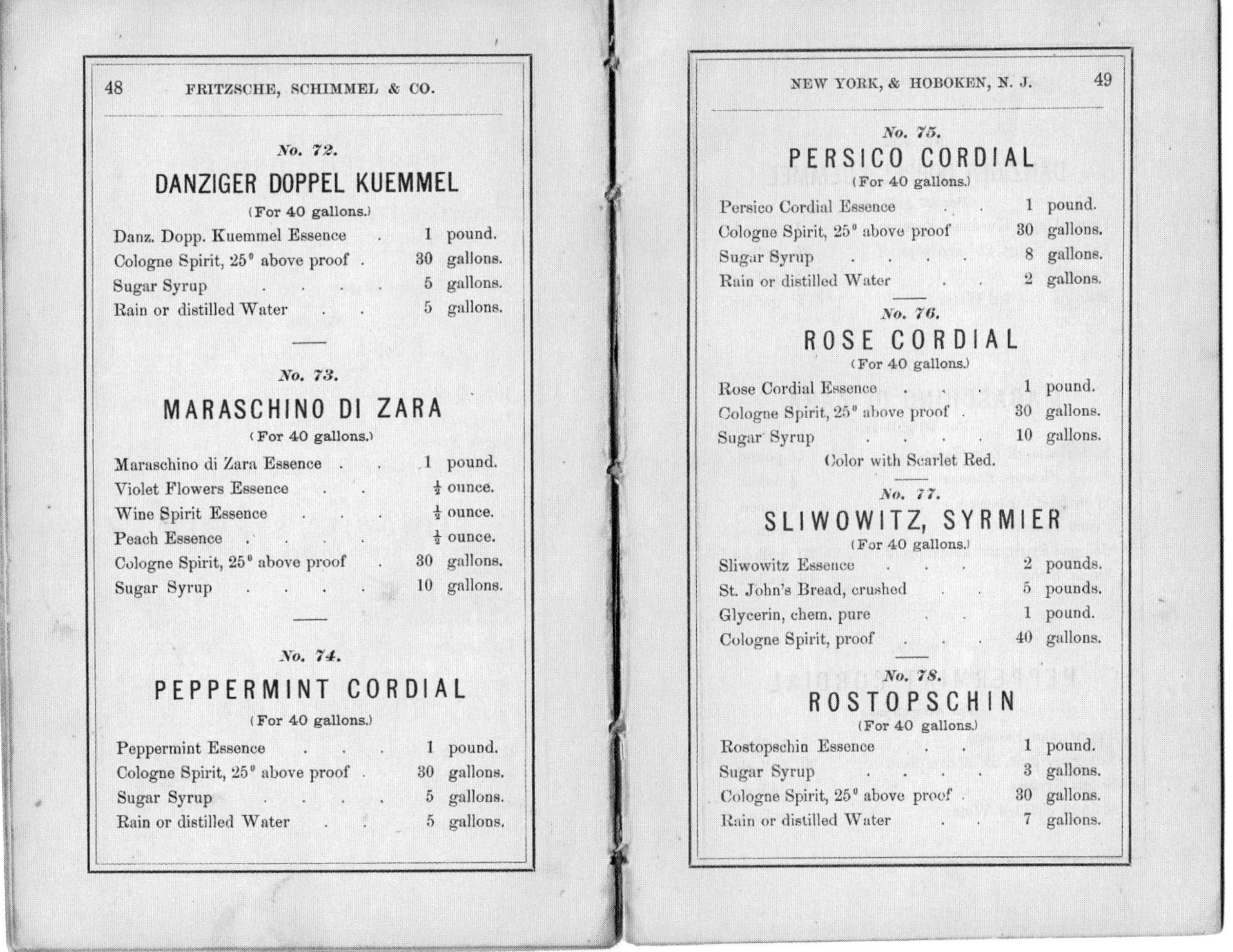

48 FRITZSCHE, SCHIMMEL & CO.

No. 72.

DANZIGER DOPPEL KUEMMEL

(For 40 gallons.)

Danz. Dopp. Kuemmel Essence	1	pound.
Cologne Spirit, 25° above proof	30	gallons.
Sugar Syrup	5	gallons.
Rain or distilled Water	5	gallons.

No. 73.

MARASCHINO DI ZARA

(For 40 gallons.)

Maraschino di Zara Essence	1	pound.
Violet Flowers Essence	½	ounce.
Wine Spirit Essence	½	ounce.
Peach Essence	½	ounce.
Cologne Spirit, 25° above proof	30	gallons.
Sugar Syrup	10	gallons.

No. 74.

PEPPERMINT CORDIAL

(For 40 gallons.)

Peppermint Essence	1	pound.
Cologne Spirit, 25° above proof	30	gallons.
Sugar Syrup	5	gallons.
Rain or distilled Water	5	gallons.

NEW YORK, & HOBOKEN, N. J. 49

No. 75.

PERSICO CORDIAL

(For 40 gallons.)

Persico Cordial Essence	1	pound.
Cologne Spirit, 25° above proof	30	gallons.
Sugar Syrup	8	gallons.
Rain or distilled Water	2	gallons.

No. 76.

ROSE CORDIAL

(For 40 gallons.)

Rose Cordial Essence	1	pound.
Cologne Spirit, 25° above proof	30	gallons.
Sugar Syrup	10	gallons.

Color with Scarlet Red.

No. 77.

SLIWOWITZ, SYRMIER

(For 40 gallons.)

Sliwowitz Essence	2	pounds.
St. John's Bread, crushed	5	pounds.
Glycerin, chem. pure	1	pound.
Cologne Spirit, proof	40	gallons.

No. 78.

ROSTOPSCHIN

(For 40 gallons.)

Rostopschin Essence	1	pound.
Sugar Syrup	3	gallons.
Cologne Spirit, 25° above proof	30	gallons.
Rain or distilled Water	7	gallons.

Does It Ever Occur to You

How handy is a bottle of just the proper remedy at the proper time ? When any of your family is taken with Cholera, come direct to our drug store and have something excellent in the way of

holera Cure or Cinnamon Cordial,

For Cholera, Dysentery, Cramps, Pain in the Stomach etc. Also Neutralizing Cordial for derangement of stomach and bowels in children while teething. These preparations are unequaled. Price 25c Per Bottle.

Gladding, Jr., Druggist,

FREEMAN'S BLOCK, CHURCH STREET. Telephone.

BRIGHT and PECHIN,

Have for Sale, on very reafonable Terms, at their Store in Water-ftreet, about Midway between Race and Vine-ftreet,

A LARGE Quantity of very good Carolina Soal Leather, Cotton, Mufcovado Sugar, Beaver, Indigo, Bees-wax, dreft Deer-fkins, Annifeed and Cinnamon Cordials, Country made Mill-ftones, and a large Quantity of choice Live-oak Ship Timber, &c. &c.

TEN DOLLARS Reward.

Cinnamon Cordials

Even when they're not the dominant flavors, cinnamon and the related spice cassia are immensely popular in old cordial recipes. Lyon includes cinnamon in about a dozen recipes, including imitation rye, absinthe, rum essence, gin, brandy, and one simple cinnamon cordial.

Their essential oils provide a warmth to the finished cordials and they're economical; in addition to being relatively inexpensive, a little goes a long way. In the last few years, Fireball, a sweetened, whiskey-based cinnamon cordial, has swept the United States. Popular at first among younger drinkers, bartenders in even swanky cocktail bars were soon downing shots of the fiery drink and slipping it into cocktails. It all seemed so new, so fresh, and maybe just a little bit of a joke to be downing something so seemingly lowbrow.

But cinnamon cordials are not new at all. Even when Victor Lyon wrote his recipe in the 1920s, the stuff was old, older than the United States even. In 1771, the Philadelphia merchants Bright and Pechin advertised such essentials as millstones, indigo, and beeswax along with cinnamon and aniseed cordials.[61] Nor were they popular in North America alone. In 1790, John Bamford offered ten dozen hogsheads of "exceeding fine" cinnamon cordials in London.[62] Such cordials, whether they were made from cinnamon or the stronger cassia, remained popular on both sides of the Atlantic well through the 19th century and regularly show up in merchants' advertisements in North and South Carolina, New York, Pennsylvania, Vermont, Illinois, Tennessee, Virginia, Ireland, England, and other places.

Let's take a look at a few versions.

Cinnamon and Cassia

First, be aware that in the United States, "cinnamon"—queen of the pantry in confectionery, baking, perfumery, and compounding—is often a pretender. Usually derived from the bark of cassia (*Cinnamomum cassia)*, it may also come from its buds, leaves, or twigs. This is the flavor we have come to think of as cinnamon and is what's usually used in cinnamon buns, candies, and other so-called cinnamon treats. Cassia has a more aggressive, distinctive aroma and flavor than its relative, Ceylon or "true" cinnamon (*Cinnamomum verum*).

Ceylon cinnamon is a softer, warmer spice than cassia, which is prized for its strong, almost biting taste and pungent aroma. Cassia oil (often labeled as cinnamon oil) is a particularly aggressive aromatic. Although we are familiar with its taste in countless products from toothpaste to cinnamon rolls, use cassia with caution; it easily takes over and unbalances syrups, cordials, and spirits, such as gins, if not treated with a light hand. Better to start with too little and add very small quantities until the desired taste and "hotness" is achieved. Dried cassia buds, which resemble cloves, were once widely used in confectionery and spirits but harder to find now.

CINNAMON CORDIAL

Lyon includes a straightforward cinnamon cordial on par with what we see in old household account books—little more than alcohol, cinnamon oil, and syrup. The giveaway that it's from a professional manual rather than a home recipe book is the inclusion of talcum powder. Its purpose in a recipe like this is to absorb the terpenes in essential oils that add little to the overall flavor but lead to cloudiness in compounded beverages. When the mixture is passed through filter paper, the talcum holding terpenes gets trapped.

Cinnamon Cordial

Prepare like Anise taking Oil Cinnamon and adding 2 drams caramel before filtering.

Anise Cordial

Oil Anise 1 1/2 drams
Alcohol 2 ounces
Talcum 1/2 ounce
Sugar 2 pounds
Water q. s to 4 pints

Mix oil and alcohol in mortar, stir in talcum and 1/2 pound sugar, add water slowly stirring constantly and finally add the remainder of the sugar when dissolved filter.

HELEN SAUNDERS WRIGHT'S CINNAMON CORDIAL

Among the more detestable Prohibition laws were those that forbade publication of recipes for making alcohol. Cocktail books were allowable (even if drys pursed their lips at the idea), but not books, pamphlets, or even newspaper articles that detailed how to make those cocktail ingredients. So, in 1922, when Helen Saunders Wright's publisher reprinted her 1908 handbook about doing just that, it was—in the words of Judas Priest's Rob Halford—breaking the law.

> This is seldom made with cinnamon, but with either the essential oil or bark of cassia. It is preferred colored, and therefore may be well prepared by simple fermentation. If the oil be used, one dram will be found enough for two or three gallons of spirit. The addition of two or three drops each of essence of lemon and orange peel, with about a spoonful of essence of cardamoms to each gallon, will improve it. Some persons add to the above quantity one dram of cardamom seeds and one ounce each of dried orange and lemon peel. One ounce of oil of cassia is considered to be equal to eight pounds of the buds or bark. If wanted dark, it may be colored with burnt sugar. The quantity of sugar is one and one-half pounds to the gallon. (Helen Saunders Wright, *Old-Time Recipes for Home Made Wines, Cordials, and Liqueurs from Fruits, Flowers, Vegetables, and Shrubs* [Boston: Page Company, 1922]

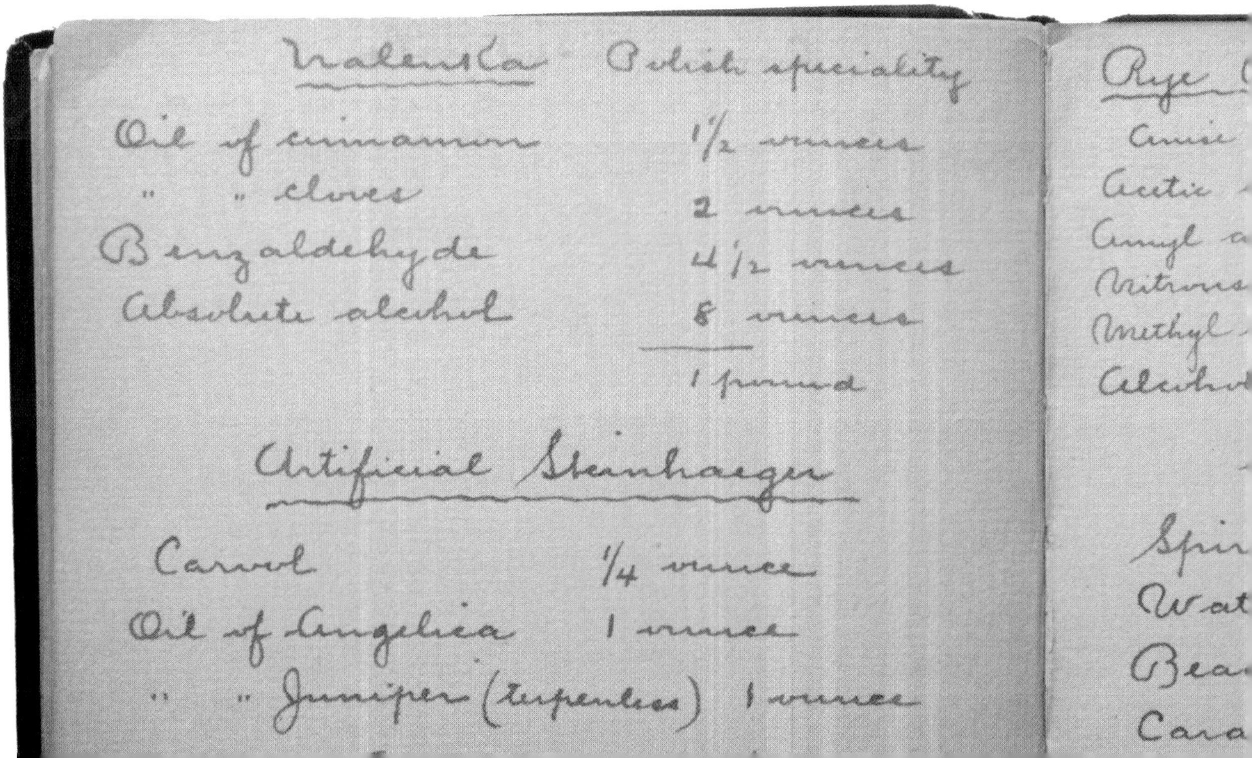

NALEWKA

Lyon dubs nalewka a Polish specialty. That's true as far as it goes, but his recipe is only one example of a broader type. Proper Polish *nalewkas* are sweetened infusions of fruits or botanicals in high-proof liquor. The finished products can be as high as 75 percent ethanol—tasty, but something that should be approached with caution. This version, made from oils and essence, is better in mixed drinks and pairs especially well with lemon and ginger.

Since straight benzaldehyde can be difficult for lay folk to get, I substituted almond extract and tweaked volumes accordingly.

NALEWKA ESSENCE

Cinnamon oil. . . . . 5 ml
Clove oil . . . . 7 ml
Almond extract . . . . 15–20 ml
90%-96% alcohol . . . . 30 ml

This makes about 2 ounces of nalewka concentrate, what would have been called *essence* or even *compound oil* in old manuscripts. Here's how to make a cordial with it:

NALEWKA

Nalewka essence (as above) . . . . . . 4 ml
40%–50% abv vodka . . . . 300 ml
Compounder's syrup (page 145) . . . 170 ml

Add the nalewka concentrate and alcohol to a 700 to 750 ml bottle or jar. Shake to dissolve it. Add the syrup, shake to mix thoroughly. Better when rested at least a week.

NALEWKA SOUR

The big clove note here makes this one I don't care to drink on its own, but judicious additions of nalewka to gin punches, lemonades, and sours are refreshing.

1 oz nalewka
1 oz fresh lemon juice
1 to 2 dashes of Angostura bitters
Club soda or ginger beer (optional)

Shake the nalewka, lemon, and bitters with ice. Strain onto fresh ice in a tumbler. Let it stand a bit to dilute. Or top off with a splash of club soda or ginger beer.

BALLS DEEP (HOT CINNAMON LIQUEUR)

Each summer Comic-Con pulls thousands of cosplayers, zombie enthusiasts, and Hollywood celebrity types to San Diego. In the city's East Village, a bar and restaurant named Neighborhood sees a lot of that traffic. The hidden cocktail bar Noble Experiment tucked away near the kitchen is surely part of the attraction. Another may well be the house-made cinnamon liqueur. Bar manager Ethan Ostrander makes almost 2 gallons at a time. I've scaled the recipe down for a more manageable yield of about 750 ml.

300 ml Evan Williams Bottled-in-Bond bourbon (100 proof)
300 ml Licor 43 (see note)
100 ml water
20 ml Bittermens Hellfire Habanero Shrub
70 grams crushed cinnamon sticks

Blend the liquids in a 2-quart nonreactive container. Add the crushed cinnamon sticks and steep for 20 minutes, stirring every five. Strain, filter, and bottle.

Licor 43 (*Cuarenta y Tres*) is a sweet Spanish cordial named for 43 herbs and spices that we're told go into its making. Vanilla, though, is the heavy hitter here. This liqueur provides all the sweetener in the recipe; no additional syrup is necessary.

PYROBLAST

Philadelphia bartender and author Katie Loeb makes a different hot cinnamon cordial that is as much of a blast as the name promises. Loeb calls for up to 2 teaspoons of cinnamon oil but I've tweaked her recipe to ease off the cinnamon.

1 liter 40% abv Canadian whisky, such as Canadian Hunter
1 cup Pyroblast Syrup (recipe follows)
About 1.5 to 2 ml cinnamon oil, depending how "hot" you like it

Combine the syrup and oil. Shake or stir until the mixture is homogenous. Stir this into the whisky and mix well before serving.

Katie notes that the finished cordial can be kept in a decorative decanter with cinnamon sticks, a whole star anise, and a few lemon or orange zests studded with cloves floating in it.

PYROBLAST SYRUP

3 cups water
12 cinnamon sticks, broken
16 whole cloves
4 star anise
12 allspice berries
12 black peppercorns
½ teaspoon red chile flakes
3 cups sugar

Bring the water to a boil in a small saucepan and add the spices. Allow to boil for 3 minutes. Add the sugar and stir to dissolve. Lower the heat and allow the syrup to simmer for 10 minutes, stirring occasionally.

Turn off the heat and allow the syrup to cool to room temperature. Strain out the spices before using and funnel into clean glass bottles for storage. Refrigerate for up to 1 month.

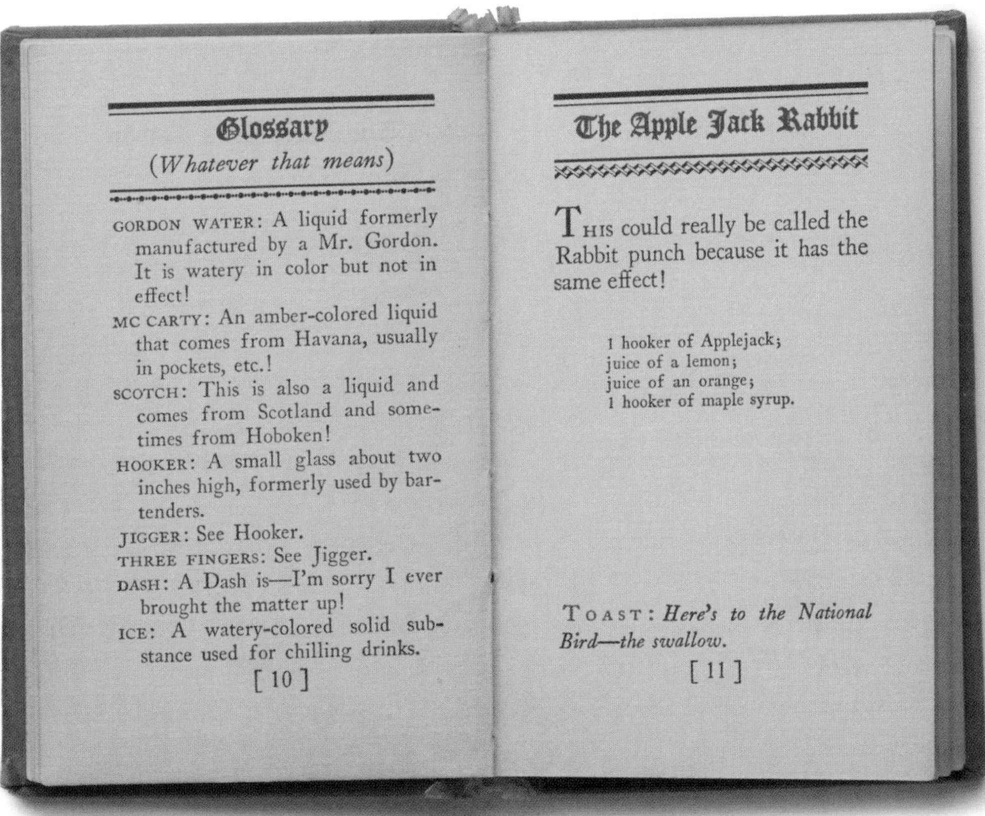

Glossary
(Whatever that means)

GORDON WATER: A liquid formerly manufactured by a Mr. Gordon. It is watery in color but not in effect!
MC CARTY: An amber-colored liquid that comes from Havana, usually in pockets, etc.!
SCOTCH: This is also a liquid and comes from Scotland and sometimes from Hoboken!
HOOKER: A small glass about two inches high, formerly used by bartenders.
JIGGER: See Hooker.
THREE FINGERS: See Jigger.
DASH: A Dash is—I'm sorry I ever brought the matter up!
ICE: A watery-colored solid substance used for chilling drinks.

[10]

The Apple Jack Rabbit

THIS could really be called the Rabbit punch because it has the same effect!

1 hooker of Applejack;
juice of a lemon;
juice of an orange;
1 hooker of maple syrup.

TOAST: *Here's to the National Bird—the swallow.*

[11]

Prohibition-era and collegiate slang combine in *Here's How!*, a 1927 pocket-sized cocktail booklet. In the circumlocution of the day, Gordon Water was gin, McCarty was (Bacardi) rum, and Scotch was . . . suspect.

Silesian corn whiskey spice

1 ounce to gallon concentrated spirit

Oil caraway	12 ounces
Oil Juniper	12 ounces
*Carob tincture	1½ pound
Corn spirit (proof)	7 pounds
	10 pounds

* St. John's bread

Wheat corn whiskey spice

Oil star anise	6 ounces
Oil caraway	10 ounces
Ethyl acetate	1 pound
Corn spirit (proof)	8 pounds
	10 pounds

1 ounce to gallon

Spice for whiskey

1 ounce per gallon maize brandy

Carob tincture	1 pound
Malt tincture (1-5)	2 pounds
Wine brandy	2 pounds
Black currant distillate	2 pounds
Corn spirit (proof)	3 pounds
	10 pounds

(For preparation of above see page 21)

CINNAMON FIZZ

I met Massachusetts biochemist, bartender, and blogger Frederic Yarm years ago at Tales of the Cocktail in New Orleans and have always liked his serious takes on drinks. He even plays it straight with Fireball, a cinnamon-flavored whiskey cordial that serious bartenders once avoided . . . but now many embrace as they do Fernet. Alternatively, try this one with cinnamon cordial, nalewka, Balls Deep, or Pyroblast.

2 oz cinnamon cordial
1.5 oz heavy cream
1 egg white
0.75 oz fresh lemon juice
0.25 to 0.5 oz 1:1 simple syrup (page 000)
Orange flower water

Dry shake all the ingredients except the orange flower water without ice to emulsify, and then with ice to chill. Strain into a Collins glass with 3 ounces of soda water. Add a straw; garnish with orange twist and finish with 3 drops orange flower water.

Anise

There's little middle ground with anise; people seem either to like it or hate its licorice taste. *Absintheurs* will recognize it as a big component of the favored drink while aficionados of sticky Chinese ribs may know star anise, an unrelated species that yields the same compounds. One or the other anise shows up in almost a dozen of the notebook's recipes, including absinthe, rye and "whiskey" ether, kümmel, and whiskey "spices" meant to be enhance whiskey or straight-up fake it.

Lyon's simple anise cordial (recipe follows) makes a perfectly respectable anisette that few would mistake for anything else. His Cordial Liquor of Danzig, named after the ancient coastal city now known as Gdańsk in Poland, has a heavy anise punch, but is rounded out with spices we're more accustomed to tasting in kümmel. The peppermint is a bracing touch. One ounce of this compound oil is used to flavor a gallon of spirit.

CORDIAL LIQUOR OF DANZIG COMP OIL

Roman chamomile oil. . . . . . . 1 drachm
Oil Mace . . . . 1 drachm
Oil Angelica. . . . . 14 drops
Oil Cloves . . . . 1 ounce
Oil Peppermint . . . . 1 ounce
Oil Caraway. . . . . 2½ ounces
Oil Fennel . . . . 3½ ounces
Oil Star Anise. . . . . 7 ounces
Total: . . . . 1 pound

Name Highest purity Course 3-A

Experiment No. No 28

Anise Oil	1 part
Acetic ether	10 parts
Amyl Alcohol	5 parts
Nitrous ether	10 parts
Alcohol	100 parts

Date 6/12/1924

Cordial Liquor of Danzig Comp Oil

Roman chammomile oil	1 drachm
Oil Mace	1 drachm
Oil Angelica	14 drops
Oil Cloves	1 ounce
Oil Peppermint	1 ounce
Oil Caraway	2½ ounces
Oil Fennel	3½ ounces
Oil Star Anise	7 ounces
	1 pound

ANISETTE DE HOLLANDE

Although many recipes use anise as the lone botanical, flavors in anisettes do get more complex. When star anise is added along with fennel, angelica, bitter almond, rose (and a few others, depending on whose formula is used), we get a more floral variety called *anisette de Hollande*, "Dutch" anisette. In their 1869 manual *De Schat der Likeuristen*, Henri Moens and Hubert Verburgt pinched Pierre Duplais's more robust formula that used a still, winnowing it down to six oils that a person could mix in the kitchen. Since pure bitter almond oil is troublesome to track down in the United States, I've adjusted their formula with almond extract.

- 9 drops star anise oil
- 8 drops anise oil
- 1 drop fennel oil
- 1 drop angelica oil
- ½ tsp pure almond extract
- 1 drop of rose otto or ½ to 1 tsp rose water
- 60 ml high-proof spirit (75%–96% abv)
- 550 ml 40% abv vodka
- 200 ml compounder's syrup (see page 145)

Dissolve the oils in the high-proof spirit. Add the vodka and almond extract (and rose water, if using). Stir thoroughly to blend. Add the syrup and blend again. Rest for 1 month before using.

No, not you: the bottle. Rest the bottle.

ANISETTE DE BORDEAUX

The fourth edition of *The Picayune's Creole Cook Book* from New Orleans from 1910 gives a simple recipe for making a different sort of anisette—well, simple as long as you own a small still and know how to operate it. Ah, if only that were allowed to American households these days. Alas, the feds forbid home distilling.

Anisette de Bordeaux, with its heavy dose of star anise, was once hugely popular. With slight variations, this particular recipe shows up in countless pre–World War I cookbooks and liqueur manuals, many of which seem to have pinched it from J. de Brevans, who was chief chemist of the municipal laboratory in Paris. *Anisette de Bordeaux* predates de Brevans, but it was his 1890 manual *La fabrication des liqueurs et des conserves* (issued in English translation in 1893 as *The Manufacture of Liquor and Preserves*) that got serious traction in America as the Golden Age of cocktails was in full swing. Even *Scientific American*[63] published the recipe. This version slightly tweaks metric measurements for an American audience.

If you can find full-bodied young Hyson, a green tea from China, by all means use it. If not, substitute another green tea such as gunpowder or *long jing* (sometimes called Dragonwell).

10 ounces of green aniseed
4 ounces of star aniseed
1 ounces of coriander
2 ounces of hyson tea
1 ounces of fennel
3½ gallons of alcohol
10 pounds of sugar
7 pints of water

The above ingredients may be purchased from first-class druggists and grocers. Take the aniseed, coriander, fennel, and Hyson tea, and pound well. Then macerate or steep for fifteen days in three and a half gallons of the finest rectified alcohol.

After this distill in a "bain-marie," or water bath. Then make a syrup with the ten pounds of sugar and seven pints of water. Mix well with the aniseed liquor and filter. Then bottle and keep in a cool, shady place. Several large bottles of anisette will be the result of the above quantities after distillation. The quantities may be reduced or increased in proportion to the amount it is desired to make.

LANIZÈT: SOUR MASH CAJUN ANISETTE

As is so often the case, not everyone wants or can afford store-bought wet goods . . . or has a still sitting around. Enter *lanizèt*, Cajun anisette, made with anise oil. You can find *lanizèt* year-round in Acadiana, though it is especially popular around Christmas. Maybe it's a nod to that season, maybe it's a hint of the potency lurking inside the bottle or jar, but south Louisiana anisette is often colored a vibrant, almost lurid, red. The recipe below is my own mashup of Ernest Matthew Mickler's higher-octane take on the classic in *White Trash Cooking* and Cajun chef Paul Prudhomme's more supple canned version in *The Prudhomme Family Cookbook*. Let it stand six weeks before using, Mickler says, "and you can't tell it from bought."

3 quarts/2.84 liters water
25 oz/700 g sugar
½ teaspoon anise oil
½ tablespoon vanilla extract
½ teaspoon red food coloring
3 cups/750 ml bourbon or Tennessee whiskey
5 to 7 lbs ice

Pour 1.5 liters of the water in a medium stockpot. Note the depth of the liquid. Later, you will boil the syrup to this height. For now, pour in the remaining water and all the sugar. Bring to a boil, stirring until sugar is dissolved. Lower the heat and simmer until the liquid reduces to 1.5 liters, 50 or 60 minutes, stirring occasionally. Remove from the heat.

While the syrup is simmering, sterilize five new or well-scrubbed 1-pint canning jars in a deep pot or canning pot. Leave the jars in the hot water until you're ready to use them. Wash and boil the lids and rings according to the manufacturer's directions.

When the syrup reaches that 1.5-liter mark, turn off the heat and remove the pot from the hob. Stir in the anise oil, vanilla, and food coloring until thoroughly mixed, then stir in the whiskey. Remove the jars from their hot water bath with tongs. Place the jars (don't touch with your bare hands) on a wooden surface or folded towels and immediately pour the crimson liquid into the jars up to ½ inch from the tops. Wipe any dribbles or spills from the rims with a clean, damp cloth and place hot lids on top with sealing compound down; screw on the metal rings firmly but not too tightly.

Line your sink with a damp dish towel; it will prevent the hot jars from breaking when they touch the cool surface. Immediately place the jars upright in the sink, then slowly fill it with cool tap water so it covers the jars. As the jars cool, you'll hear a series of metallic pops and pings; that's a vacuum forming in each jar. When the jars are cool to the touch, after 5 to 10 minutes, place them upright in a tub of ice, with ice to top off the jars, to cool the anisette as quickly as possible. Once contents of jars are well chilled, about 1 hour, remove the jars from the ice. Label and date the jars, then store upright in a cool, dark place.

Yield: 5 pints/2.4 liters

Ginger

Ginger, one of our very oldest spices, has been a staple in cooking and medicine for millennia. While many spices have notes of this or hints of that, the tan, knobby rhizome of a ginger plant tastes boldly, brightly of ginger; it *is* the reference note. There's ginger, though, and there's ginger. Fresh, dried, preserved, or powdered all have different characteristics. Fresh ginger holds promises of liveliness and sass, of exotic and ancient histories. There is a potency in a fat hand of fresh ginger that livens chutneys, marinades, sushi, soups, and all sorts of beverages, including ginger beer and ginger-flavored brandies, wines, and cordials.

Compounding pharmacists sometimes added essence of Jamaica ginger to simple syrup (1:25 ratio), the proverbial spoonful of sugar that helps medicine go down. Tasty ginger syrup readily jumped the drugstore counter to soda fountains. Such syrup, usually made from fresh ginger rather than dried or ginger oil, has become a standard in modern bars with robust cocktail programs.

LYON'S GINGER BRANDY NO. II

Of all the recipes in the notebook, Lyon's ginger brandy is among my favorites. Although it's made from brandy, the amount of syrup here makes a proper cordial. It's sweet, versatile, and packs a fiery punch. A scaled-down version follows but frankly, we've ended up using so much of this one that I'll double Lyon's recipe from here on.

Jamaica Ginger . . . . 8 ounces
Brandy . . . . 1 gallon

Bruise ginger thoroughly, macerate it in the brandy 2–3 weeks, strain. Then boil the marc gently in a gallon of water for 20 minutes, strain and dissolve 10 pounds of sugar in the aqueous liquid. Mix this one cold with the brandy maceration and finally clear with findings [*sic*].

Ginger Brandy No. 1

Finest essence of Jamaica Ginger (Finest Zing. Fort. B.P. 1885)	8 ounces
Oil of Lemon	10 drops
Brandy	1 gallon
Simple Syrup	½ gallon

Mix and store for several months.

No. II

Jamaica Ginger	8 ounces
Brandy	1 gallon

Bruise ginger thoroughly, macerate it in the brandy 2-3 weeks, strain. Then boil the marc gently in a gallon of water for 20 minutes, strain and dissolve 10 pounds of sugar in the aqueous liquid. Mix this when cold with the brandy maceration and finally clear with findings.

Non alcoholic ginger brandy

Essence of ginger with capsicum	2 ounces
Citric Acid	½ ounce
Burnt Sugar	¼ ounce
Syrup	1 gallon

VICTOR LYON'S GINGER BRANDY

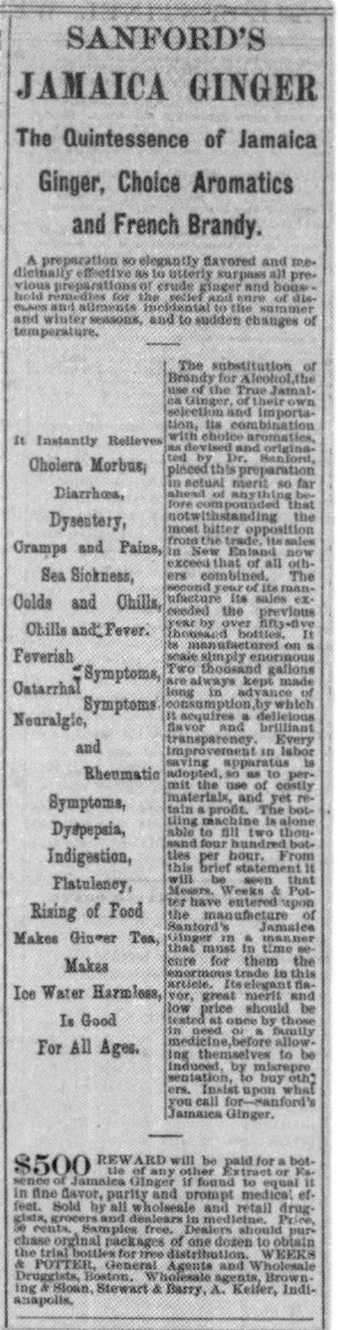

45 g dried, cracked ginger
750 ml Paul Mason VSOP brandy
2 lbs sugar
750 ml water

Macerate the ginger in the brandy for 2 to 3 weeks. When the ginger taste is strong, make a syrup by heating the sugar and water together, stirring until the sugar is completely dissolved. Allow to cool. Strain the ginger-flavored brandy into the cool syrup and bottle.

DR. FURNISH

Doctor Lyon's ginger brandy is a fiery concoction with a great ginger taste, but it's a bit sweet on its own. Dr. Tim Furnish, pain management specialist at the University of California San Diego, mixed Lyon's ginger brandy with citrus and dry gin for—well, not a painkiller exactly, but I will take two and call (a bit later) in the morning.

1 oz Victor Lyon's Ginger Brandy (see previous recipe)
1 oz London dry gin
0.75 oz fresh orange juice
0.5 oz fresh lemon juice
Dash of Angostura bitters

Shake with ice and strain into a chilled coupe.

STRONG TINCTURE OF GINGER

[*TINCTURA ZINGIBERIS FORTIOR*, TINCT. ZING. FORT., ESSENCE OF GINGER]

The 1885 BP formula Lyon specifies in his Ginger Brandy No. 1 comes from the 1885 edition of the *British Pharmacopoeia*:

> Take of Ginger, in fine powder, ten ounces; Rectified Spirit, a sufficiency. Pack the ginger tightly in a percolator, and pour over it carefully half a [British] pint of the spirit [e.g., 10 fluid ounces]. At the expiration of two hours add more spirit, and let it percolate slowly, until one pint of tincture has been collected.

Powdered ginger is a mess to filter, so use cracked dry ginger instead. Macerate 10 ounces of the ginger in 10 fluid ounces of high-proof spirits (90%–96% abv) in a glass jar or bottle. After 3 days, draw off the amount you need from the top and leave the rest to continue to steep in the spirits until needed.

For an extempore ginger syrup, add 15 to 20 ml (3–4 teaspoons) of this tincture to 500 ml of compounder's syrup (page 145).

ESSENCE OF JAMAICA GINGER

The "essence of Jamaica Ginger"—the infamous *jake* of Prohibition—is a separate recipe. Don't break the bank; a simple California brandy suffices. I use Paul Mason VSOP. The lemon oil is optional, but lemon and ginger are an old, comfortable couple; it's a nice touch here.

GINGER BRANDY NO. 1

Finest essence of Jamaica Ginger . . 8 ounces (see note)
Oil of Lemon . . . . 10 drops
Brandy . . . . 1 gallon
Simple syrup . . . . ½ gallon

For a more modest amount, try this scaled down version:

Jamaica Ginger (as above) . . . . . . 40 ml
Oil of lemon . . . . 2–3 drops
Brandy . . . . 750 ml
Compounder's syrup . . . . 375 ml

Mix and store for several months.

Ginger Wine

Best ginger root (bruised) ½ ounce
Capsicum 2½ grains
Tartaric acid ½ dram
Put into one pint 95% alcohol, let it remain one week and filter. Then add ½ gallon water which has been boiled with ½ pound crushed sugar. Mix when cold. To give color boil ¼ ounce cochineal ⅜ ounce cream tartar, ¼ ounce saleratus ¼ ounce alum in ½ PINT water.

GINGER WINE WITH COCHINEAL

Like caramel, cochineal is an old, old coloring. Since learning of its ability to create a strong, nearly permanent crimson dye from natives of Oaxaca, Europeans clamored for it to dye kings' robes, cardinals' vestments . . . and cordials. In some parts of the United States, red soft drinks are known tongue-in-cheek as "bug juice," not—as some would have you believe—because their high sugar content attracts bugs, but because their brilliant red may have been derived from the dried insects that make cochineal. The bugs in question are females of *Dactylopius coccus* which feed exclusively on *Opuntia ficus-indica*, a cactus which is now naturalized around the Mediterranean, parts of Latin America . . . and my neighborhood, where cochineal infestation is common.

Best ginger root bruised . . . . . ½ ounce
Capsicum . . . . 2½ grains
Tartaric acid . . . . ½ dram

Put into one pint 95% alcohol, let it remain one week and filter. Then add ½ gallon water which is been boiled with ½ pound crushed sugar. Mix when cold. To give color boil ¼ ounce cochineal[,] ⅜ ounce cream tartar, ¼ ounce saleratus[,] ¼ ounce alum in ½ PINT water.

note

The inclusion of saleratus dates this recipe from 1840 to the early 1860s. Saleratus was a chemical leavener used in baking that was eclipsed with the introduction of baking powder just before the American Civil War. Adding such alkalis to cochineal solutions helped turn them a deeper, richer red. Capsicum, on the other hand, is a classic pairing with ginger. Especially as ginger concoctions age, they may lose their bite. Chiles such as cayenne subtly bolster the fiery edge of ginger without drawing attention to themselves—unless we want to do just that by using large amounts or strongly flavored chiles, such as ancho, chipotle, or scorpion pepper.

Imitation crust on inside of wine bottles to resemble old age is a saturated solution of cream of tartar colored by Brazil wood or cochineal.

Mint

Since colonial times, Americans had settled rebellious bowels and kept chest colds at bay with doses of peppermint extract. They mixed it with water or alcohol or took the stuff—one shudders—straight. Mint-growing regions in New York and Michigan eventually rivaled the famed peppermint fields of Mitcham in England. By the beginning of the 20th century, some 90 percent of the world's oil of peppermint came from within a 90-mile radius of Kalamazoo, Michigan.

Where did all that peppermint oil go? Americans put a lot of it into crème de menthe. Newspapers and handwritten recipe books of the late 19th and early 20th centuries are stuffed with homemade crème de menthe recipes. And why not? It was a simple medicine—and pleasant cordial—that anyone could make with little trouble.

Lyon calls for mint in several recipes, sometimes as a component of more complex spirits such as Cordial Liquor of Danzig Comp Oil (page 165) or Absinthe Suissesse (page 134), sometimes for simple cordial. One I thought would be simple turned out a beautiful failure.

CRÈME DE MENTHE

Oil of peppermint. . . . . .2 drams
Fresh mint leaves . . . . 2 ounces
Alcohol (90) . . . . .5 pints
Sugar . . . . 2 pounds
Water to make . . . . .8 pints

Dissolve the oil in the alcohol, add the mint leaves, macerate for a few days, then add some water. Again macerate. Finally filter into the sugar and dissolve. If green mint leaves are not to be obtained, a little chlorophyll may be used.

This was the first recipe I tried from the notebook that just didn't work. It was all harsh angles and bracing menthol, altogether too overwhelming with both alcohol and mint. Then there was the sugar that misbehaved. When I blended the syrup with high-proof grain spirits, the dissolved sugar came out of solution. After about two days, fine crystals appeared on the inside of the bottle. Before long, they grew into large chunks of crystal-clear sugar that glistened as they caught the sunlight. Beautiful . . . and undrinkable. I keep it as a souvenir, a reminder that not everything in the book ought to be resurrected—and a prod to do things a little differently now and then.

That leads to Mint and Gum.

Crème de Menthe

Oil of peppermint 2 drams
Fresh mint leaves 2 ounces
Alcohol (90) 5 pints
Sugar 2 pounds
Water to make 8 pints

Dissolve the oil in the alcohol, add the mint leaves, macerate for a few days, then add some water. Again macerate. Finally filter into the sugar and dissolve.

If green mint leaves are not to be obtained, a little chlorophyll may be used.

MINT AND GUM

Bon vivant and world traveler Charles H. Baker Jr.'s opinionated, two-volume food and drink recipe-cum-travelogue *The Gentleman's Companion* (1939) unfairly languished for decades before modern booze slingers and drinkers rediscovered it. I turned to Baker for an alternate to Lyon's crème de menthe.

Baker calls for a ridiculously rich syrup he calls *gum* or *gomme* syrup (four parts sugar to one of water, clarified by heating with an egg white). That is one way to do it, but *gum* more properly refers to a powdered resin called gum arabic that helps stabilize syrup and lend an unbeatable smoothness to drinks. This version cuts Baker's volume and ditches his ersatz *gomme*, in favor of a more suave rendition using actual gum arabic. The resulting cordial carries the faintest taste of toasted marshmallow; actual gum syrup is not a good sweetener for every DIY cordial, but it's right at home with mint.

270 ml compounder's syrup or gum (pages 145 and 147)
475 ml filtered water
10–15 drops oil of peppermint
150 ml 96% alcohol
Green coloring, entirely optional, but a few drops will yield a muted emerald shade

Mix the gum syrup and water in a wide-mouthed 1- or 2-liter jar. Dissolve the peppermint oil in the alcohol, then add to the jar. Mix thoroughly. Cover tightly, let it stand for 5 days, then skim off all excess peppermint oil by laying a new white blotting paper, coffee filter, or paper towel on the surface and quickly wicking it away (a kitchen trick that helps degrease consommés of those last pesky bits of fat that keep them from being crystal clear). Adjust the color, if desired, with a few drops of green coloring.

Makes a bit less than a liter.

The gum has a tendency to make this cordial cloud in the bottle. Mixed in spirit-forward drinks, however, such as a Stinger (page 181), the cloudiness dissipates quickly.

SHAKER PEPPERMINT CORDIAL

The Shakers—more properly known as United Society of Believers—are a religious sect known for pacifism, communal lifestyle, celibacy, and simple, but powerfully compelling craftsmanship. Their foods likewise were uncluttered, their purpose laid bare. A manuscript at the Shaker Museum in Old Chatham, New York, contains a recipe for a "pleasant and wholesome" peppermint cordial.[64] It is simple, if a little one-note, but typical of homemade American mint cordials.

Take 60 drops of the oil of peppermint, 1 cup sugar, and one cup brandy. Put altogether into a marble mortar and work them well. Then add 8 quarts of water and add more brandy and sugar till it becomes a pleasant cordial. Observe that the oil of peppermint will not mix with water without some kind of spirits.

SNOWSHOE GROG

For a few short weeks in the winter of 2010, it seemed as if I might be moving to Appleton, Wisconsin. In the end, our family stayed in San Diego, which, as consolation prizes go, is not a bad one. While I was visiting to investigate the scene in snow-blanketed Wisconsin, locals introduced me to their own particular winter warmer: snowshoe grog or, simply, the *snowshoe*. A bumper of *snowshoe* did make braving the Baltic temperatures easier. Phillips Distilling Company bottles a version for the local market, but if you feel up to making your own, try this:

1 oz crème de menthe, peppermint schnapps, or Mint and Gum (page 177)

1 oz brandy

Stir with ice; strain into a shot glass.

Alternatively, if a few days fishing on the ice is your bag, do as some other hardy sportsmen do and whip up a bigger batch: pour equal parts of brandy and mint cordial in a thermos, seal it, and gently shake to mix. Here and there, some like it hot. If that's you, mix a batch as above, heat it in a saucepan gently (remember: alcohol is flammable) on a stove just so it's hot, but stop short of bringing it to an actual boil. Pour carefully into a warmed thermos.

Anise Cordial

Oil Anise	1½ drams
Alcohol	2 ounces
Talcum	½ ounce
Sugar	2 pounds
Water q. s to	4 pints

Mix oil and alcohol in mortar, stir in talcum and ½ pound sugar, add water slowly stirring constantly and finally add the remainder of the sugar when dissolved filter.

Cinnamon Cordial

Prepare like Anise taking Oil Cinnamon and adding 2 drams caramel before filtering.

Peppermint Cordial

Prepare like Anise taking 4 pounds of sugar and coloring with Chlorophyll

Cognac Essence

Cognacöl oder Oenanthether ℥ss	1 loth
Spiritus @ 90° T	6 loth

Auflösen

Stingers

Snowshoe Grog is a not a subtle drink; although it will help you get your swerve on, it's more of a way to fend off the cold. Its medicinal roots are clear in the wallop of mint packed into every shot. The Stinger, however . . . well, now, that's an altogether more refined drink I've happily downed even in sunny Southern California.

In 1891, William "the Only" Schmidt published *The Flowing Bowl,* a collection of drinks recipes with some gems and more than a few clunkers. His Après Souper is a sort of forerunner to the Stinger with the welcome addition of maraschino, a funky sweetened cherry distillate.

APRÈS SOUPER

Dash of gum syrup (page 147)
1 oz brandy
0.5 oz white crème de menthe
0.25 maraschino liqueur

Stir over ice and strain into a cocktail glass.

Schmidt gives another version he calls The Judge, which has an ounce of crème de menthe, two of brandy, and three dashes of gum syrup to round out the rough edges.

Crème Absinthe
Essence Wormwood 3/4 drams
" English Mint 3/4 drams
" Anise 1 ounce
" Sweet Fennel 4 1/2 drams
Distilled Essence Lemon 1 ounce

STINGER

By 1922, when Lyon was busily writing in his secret notebook, Robert Vermeire in London released *Cocktails—How to Mix Them*. Vermeire's Stinger is closer to what we're likely encounter today, even down to a dash of absinthe which, thankfully, is available again. It is my favorite of the Stinger-type drinks.

1.5 oz brandy
0.75 oz peppermint liqueur
Dash of absinthe
(optional, but give it a try)

Stir over ice and strain into a cocktail glass.

JEFF MORGENTHALER'S BLENDED GRASSHOPPER

Fernet-Branca is the not-so-secret "bartenders handshake" popular among staff in craft cocktail bars across the United States. The intense bitterness of this 78-proof amaro is muted in the tiny amount called for in this version of a grasshopper from Portland bartender and author Jeff Morgenthaler, but what a difference it makes. Its peppermint undertones double down on those mint oils from the grasshopper's traditional crème de menthe, while the fat from the ice cream covers the taste buds and is repeatedly melted away, layering and relayering flavors like Damascus steel.

1.5 oz green crème de menthe
1.5 oz white crème de cacao
1 oz half-and-half
1 tsp Fernet-Branca
Pinch of sea salt
4 oz vanilla ice cream
8 oz crushed ice, prepared with a Lewis bag and mallet or a food processor

Combine all the ingredients in a blender pitcher. Blend on low speed until smooth. Pour into an old-fashioned soda glass or a tall mug. Garnish with a mint sprig and serve with a straw.

Woodruff

ARTIFICIAL WOODRUFF ESSENCE

At Prater, one of my favorite beer gardens in Berlin, I sometimes order a big, low glass of the tart and cloudy local wheat beer, Berliner Weisse. If you are so inclined (some purists sniff at the practice), you may take yours *mit schuss*—with a shot. The shot in this case is a syrup of either red raspberry or green sweet woodruff. B. G. Reynolds makes an American version of woodruff syrup that lacks the lurid artificial green coloring so often found in German examples. Lyon's artificial woodruff essence leverages coumarin—the distinctive flavor of woodruff—derived from tonka beans. An essence such as this would be used to flavor syrups, light German wines, lemonades, and other cooling warm-weather drinks. Two ounces of Lyon's woodruff essence is enough to flavor a gallon of syrup.

Cumarin [*sic*]. . . . . 1 ounce
Hot Alcohol. . . . . 15 ounces

Dissolve then add

Alcohol. . . . . 2 pounds
Tincture Tonka Bean (1:5). . . . . 1 pound
Distilled Water. . . . . 6 pounds
Total: . . . . 10 pounds

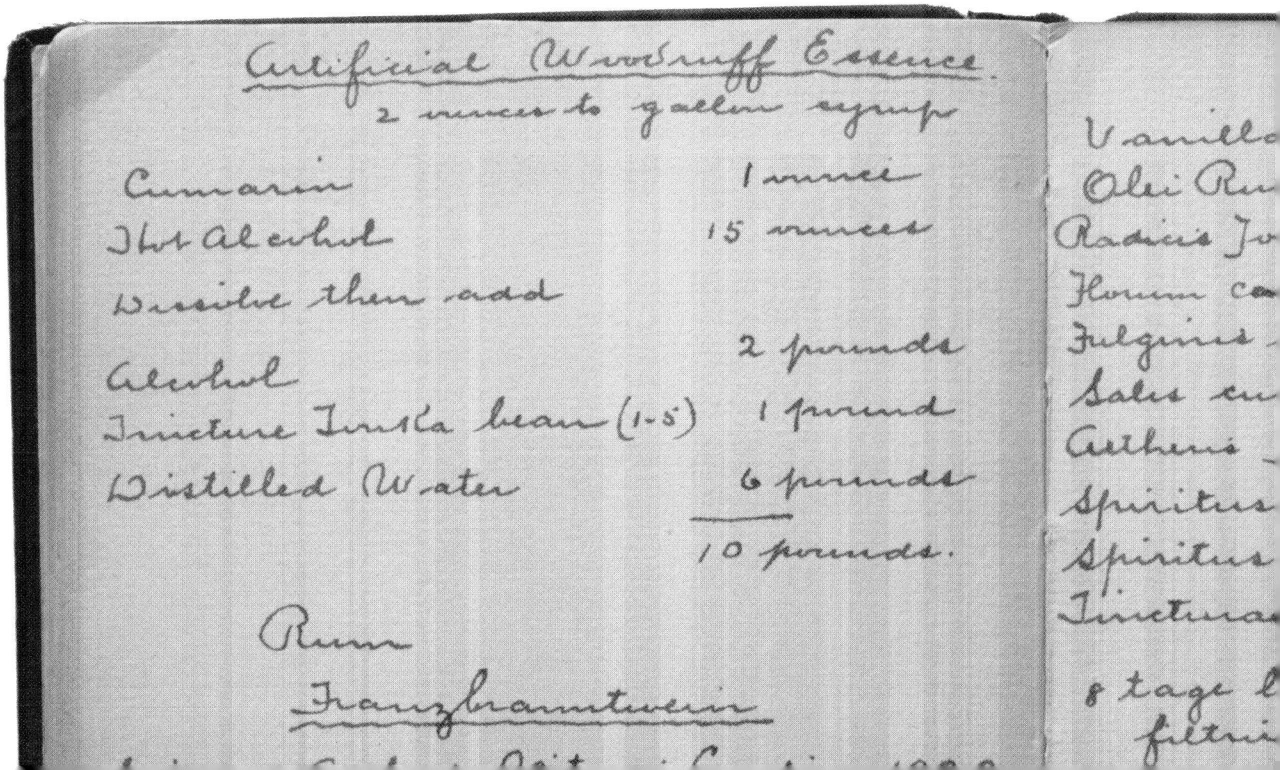

ACTUAL WOODRUFF ESSENCE

In *Das Getränkebuch,* a 1938 collection of drinks recipes, Hans Krönlein suggests stuffing slightly wilted woodruff leaves into a bottle (the new-mown hay aroma of coumarin in woodruff intensifies as the leaves lose moisture), filling it with wine, and corking it. It is then left in the sun to become strongly scented with coumarin. A few drops of this *Waldmeister-Bowlenessenz* in a glass of chilled white wine makes a quick *Maitrank* (recipe follows).

MAITRANK, OR MAY WINE

When we moved into our first place in Philadelphia some 20 years ago, friends brought a big Mason jar of May wine as a loft-warming present. *Maitrank,* as it's sometimes known, is a classic homemade German tonic with coumarin's unmistakable aroma of vanilla and new-mown hay. Like vermouth, Lillet, or Dubonnet, it is an aromatized wine, but with only one aromatic: sweet woodruff. Given Pennsylvania's centuries-old German presence and my taste for neglected drinks, it was a great fit. Here's how to make a small batch:

750 ml light white wine
100 ml brandy
A handful, about 50 grams, of fresh *Waldmeister* (sweet woodruff), including white flowers
1 Tbsp sugar or compounder's syrup (see page 145)

Stuff the sweet woodruff into a 1-liter hermetic jar. Add the remaining ingredients to cover the herb, seal, then give it a swirl and a shake to dissolve the sugar or syrup. Put it aside for 12 to 24 hours. A refrigerator or sunny window sill is fine; take your pick. Taste as you go; the coumarin taste can get quite strong. When it has the aroma and flavor you want, pull out the herbs. Serve chilled or top off with just enough chilled sparkling water to give it some lift.

HENLEY'S MAY WINE ESSENCE

Another version of May wine essence crops up in the fat handbook *Henley's Twentieth Century Formulas, Recipes and Processes*, a fascinating compendium of scientific knowledge of the early 20th century. Distiller Lance Winters of St. George Spirits in California was as enthusiastic about the old tome as I am. "If you were stranded on an island and the world has ended," he beamed, "you could restart civilization with that book."

Henley's uses high-proof spirit, double-infused with two batches of sweet woodruff.

> Fresh woodruff, in bloom or flower, is freed from the lower part of its stem and leaves, and also of all foreign or inert matter. The herb is then lightly stuck into a wide mouth bottle and covered with strong alcohol. After 30 minutes pour off the liquor on fresh woodruff. In another half hour the essence is ready though it should not be used immediately It should be kept at cellar heat (about 60°F) for a few days, or until the green color vanishes. Any addition to the essence of aromatics, such as orange peel, lemons, spices, etc., is to be avoided. To prepare the Maitrank, add the essence to any good white wine, tasting and testing, until the flavor suits. (Gardner D. Hiscox, *Henley's Twentieth Century Formulas, Recipes and Processes* [New York: Norman W. Henley Publishing Company, 1914], 770)

Orange

As popular as sweet and bitter oranges drinks have been for the last three centuries—nearly every compounder's formulary and rectifying manual printed has multiple versions of triple secs, curaçaos, and other orange-flavored spirits and cordials—it's a bit surprising that Dr. Lyon's notebook doesn't contain more recipes using it. Of the 300 and some-odd entries, fewer than 10 involve either orange peel, oil, or juice. Admittedly, those for rum shrubs make up for it. See scaled-down versions in the rum section (page 71).

Of the remainders, there's orange peel in the stomach bitters (page 139), sweet orange (and lemon) oil in the German absinthe (page 132)—and one handy little tincture that proves remarkably versatile around the bar: Orange Peel Flavoring. Lyon uses it in knockoffs of port wine and genever. It's a great orange extract for flavoring cakes, frostings, and like that, but compounders have used orange peel flavoring (or tincture or extract) to introduce additional layers of orange aroma and taste to cold compounded triple secs and curaçaos.

Curaçao at the Table

When brandy is used in connection with mandarin skins . . . it is there to make a cordial which may be sipped at leisure. The skin of the mandarin is deeply cut around the fruit's middle and each half then laid back until it is peeled off and appears like a small cup, the skin itself being turned inside out. Into this cup about 2 tablespoonfuls of brandy are poured and set on fire. As it burns it draws out the pungent oil in the mandarin skin and forms of cordial like curacao.

—Washington (DC) *Evening Star*, April 29, 1906

Aurantieae.
Citrus vulgaris Risso.

ORANGE PEEL FLAVORING

Steep 1 pound of orange peel in 1 gallon of 95% alcohol for 15 days. Filter.

MAKE-AT-HOME ORANGE PEEL FLAVORING

3 to 4 ounces dried orange peel
700 to 750 ml 90%–92% abv spirit

Combine the orange peel and alcohol in a 1-liter jar, seal, and let macerate for 2 weeks. Filter and jar.

QUICK AND DIRTY ORANGE FLOWER WATER

One night this past summer, a friend gathering ingredients for a Ramos Gin Fizz at my house asked if I'd like one. Bet your ass, I did. But I also knew we were out of orange flower water, a floral essence at the core of its taste. Going to the store was out of the question, so I did what any right-thinking DIYer would: I whipped up a batch right then and there with some essential oils, a spot of vodka, and a little water. Now, my quick and dirty orange flower water isn't made according to traditional methods. And, no, it doesn't have quite the same nose or taste as what squirts from little blue bottles of my preferred brand, A. Monteux, but once it's mixed into a creamy, heat-busting Ramos Gin Fizz, it's not a bad substitute. Not bad at all.

1 oz 100-proof vodka
1 to 2 drops neroli oil
1 drop bitter orange oil
2 oz distilled water

Pour the vodka into a 4-ounce bottle with a tight-fitting cap. Add the oils, stirring or swirling to dissolve. Add the water, seal tightly, and shake.

MIKE McCAW'S TRIPLE SEC

Seattle polymath Mike McCaw is an author, publisher, still builder, distillery consultant, globetrotting explorer, and distiller. Using just four ingredients, he makes triple sec with a highly concentrated flavor that 19th-century *liquouristes* would have called an essence. For a bottle of full-strength orange cordial, Mike adds a small amount of the concentrate to plain vodka and a bit of sugar. "If you use a mixture of sweet and bitter orange, and less sugar," Mike advises, "you can make a pretty nice Aurantii Amari clone. Use more bitter than sweet."

TRIPLE SEC CONCENTRATE

2 ml oil of lemon
2 ml oil of grapefruit
10 ml oil of sweet orange
500 ml neutral spirit (92–95% abv)

Dissolve the oils in neutral spirit. Pour the resulting concentrate into a dark, airtight jar and store in a cool place away from direct sunlight.

TO MAKE COLD-COMPOUNDED TRIPLE SEC

750 ml 40% abv vodka (divided)
1.5 ml concentrate (above)
140 g sugar

Pour 500 ml of the vodka into an empty 750 ml bottle. Add the concentrate and the sugar. Shake until the sugar dissolves and top off to 750 ml with the remaining vodka. Alternatively, put all ingredients into a 1- or 2-liter mixing flask and spin at 900 rpm until the sugar dissolves.

Usable at once, but better if left to marry for 1 to 2 weeks.

DIY ORANGE CORDIAL

From the stalwarts Grand Marnier and Cointreau to 19th-century-style Pierre Ferrand Dry Curaçao Ancienne Méthode and Solerno, a blood orange liqueur from Italy, we usually have several gallons of bittersweet orange cordials around the house. Yeah, okay, that's a bit much. Hush. The thing is, you can drink just fine without orange cordials, but you'll drink better with them. This simple DIY version makes a nice stand-in when you're on a budget.

- Zest from 2 to 3 navel oranges (about 10 grams)
- 7.5 g (about 1 tablespoon) dried bitter orange peel
- 2 cups brandy (see note)
- 4 whole cloves
- 600 ml (about 2.5 cups) of compounder's syrup (page 145)

Pour the brandy over the orange zest and peels in a resealable glass jar. Give it a swirl and let it rest for 20 to 21 days at cool room temperature out of direct sunlight. Add the cloves. Let rest for one more day. Strain the mixture into a large jar or mixing container. Add the syrup, stir to blend, and bottle. Let the cordial rest for another week before using. Best within 3 to 4 months.

Don't splurge on expensive brandy here. Paul Mason VSOP works just fine and comes in at less than the cost of a cocktail at many swanky bars.

Table of Signs and Abbreviations.

Sign	Latin	English	Abbrev.	Latin	English
℞	Recipe.	Take.	Collyr.	Collyrium.	An eye-water.
āā	Ana.	Of each.	Cong.	Congius vel Congii.	A gallon or gallons.
℔	Libra vel libræ.	A pound or pounds.	Decoct.	Decoctum.	A decoction.
℥	Uncia vel unciæ.	An ounce or ounces.	Ft.	Fiat.	Make.
ʒ	Drachma vel drachmæ.	A drachm or drachms.	Garg.	Gargarysma.	A gargle.
℈	Scrupulus vel scrupuli.	A scruple or scruples.	Gr.	Granum vel grana.	A grain or grains.
O	Octarius vel octarii.	A pint or pints.	Gtt.	Gutta vel guttæ.	A drop or drops.
f℥	Fluiduncia vel fluidunciæ.	A fluidounce or fluidounces.	Haust.	Haustus.	A draught.
fʒ	Fluidrachma vel fluidrachmæ.	A fluidrachm or fluidrachms.	Infus.	Infusum.	An infusion.
♏	Minimum vel minima.	A minim or minims.	M.	Misce.	Mix.
Chart.	Chartula vel Chartulæ.	A small paper or papers.	Mass.	Massa.	A mass.
Coch.	Cochlear vel cochlearia.	A spoonful or spoonfuls.	Mist.	Mistura.	A mixture.
			Pil.	Pilula vel pilulæ.	A pill or pills.
			Pulv.	Pulvis vel pulveres	A powder or powders.
			Q. S.	Quantum sufficit.	A sufficient quantity.
			S.	Signa.	Write.
			Ss.	Semis.	A half.

Examples of Common Extemporaneous Prescriptions.

Powders.

℞ Antimonii et Potassæ Tartratis gr. i.
Pulveris Ipecacuanhæ ℈i.
Fiat pulvis.
S. To be taken in a wineglassful of sweetened water.
An active emetic.

℞ Hydrargyri Chloridi Mitis,
Pulveris Jalapæ, āā gr. x.
Misce.
S. To be taken in syrup or molasses.
An excellent cathartic in the commencement of bilious fevers, and in hepatic congestion.

℞ Pulveris Jalapæ gr. x.
Potassæ Bitartratis ʒii.
Misce.
S. To be taken in syrup or molasses.
A hydragogue cathartic, used in dropsy and scrofulous inflammation of the joints.

℞ Sulphuris ʒi.
Potassæ Bitartratis ʒii.
Misce.
S. To be taken in syrup or molasses.
A laxative, used in piles and cutaneous diseases.

℞ Pulveris Rhei gr. x.
Magnesiæ ʒss.
Fiat pulvis.
S. To be taken in syrup or molasses.
A laxative and antacid, used in diarrhœa, dyspepsia, &c.

℞ Pulveris Scillæ gr. xii.
Potassæ Nitratis ʒi.
Fiat pulvis, in chartulas sex dividendus.
S. One to be taken twice or three times a day in syrup or molasses.
A diuretic employed in dropsy.

℞ Potassæ Nitratis ʒi.
Antimonii et Potassæ Tartratis gr. i.
Hydrarg. Chlorid. Mitis gr. vi.
Fiat pulvis, in chartulas sex dividendus.
S. One to be taken every two hours in syrup or molasses.
A refrigerant, diaphoretic, and alterative, used in bilious fevers; usually called *nitrous powders*.

℞ Pulveris Guaiaci Resinæ,
Potassæ Nitratis, āā ʒi
Pulveris Ipecacuanhæ gr. iii.
Opii gr. ii.
Fiat pulvis, in chartulas sex dividendus.
S. One to be taken every three hours in syrup or molasses.
A stimulant diaphoretic, used in rheumatism and gout after sufficient depletion.

WEIGHTS AND MEASURES ADOPTE[D] ... STATES PHARMACEUTICAL AS[SOCIATION]

534
WEIGHTS.

POUND.		OUNCES.		DRACHMS.		SCRUPL[ES].	
℔1	=	12	=	96	=	288	
		℥1	=	8	=	24	
				ʒ1	=	3	= 60
						℈1	= gr. 20

NOTE.—42½ grains added to the Avoirdupois ounce will make it equal to the above ounce.

Chapter six

Weights and Measures

A Pint's a Pint, Amirite? Or Amirite?

Whether we're talking about cocktails, brewing, compounding, or just mixing a bowl of punch, if you're going to read old booze recipes, you'll want to be up on the kinds of measurements likely to show up in primary sources. The hitch in that particular giddyup is that measuring systems vary over geography, time, and profession. Some measures fall out of use entirely or never were standardized in the first place. In this short chapter, we're going to look at some common ways to measure volume, weight, concentrations, alcohol content, and a few other odds and ends you may come across in old recipes.

Take the pint. Just about anyone who's raised an elbow at a pub can picture the size of one instantly. Perhaps you've even heard the old chestnut that the pint's a pound the world around. Of course, this holds only for an American pint and only if you wanted to measure pure water, not beer or gin. Even then, a pound of water isn't *quite* a full pint. But it's close enough for driving the basic relationship into schoolchildren's heads.

The problem, of course, is when one puts the saying to the test by actually going to places around the world where the British imperial pint reigns—20 ounces to America's 16—and suddenly recipes start to get wonky. That's just one example from hundreds of different measures. Every baker and home cook knows, for instance, that a tablespoon is 15 milliliters. Except when it's not. Australian tablespoons are 20 ml. So, too, were druggists' tablespoons. Some of them, anyway. In British Edwardian and Victorian recipes, a tablespoon could be closer to 25 ml. Fritz Blank, who gave me the notebook on which this book is based, ran a high-end French restaurant and had been a major in the Army Medical Corps. His tablespoon? Twelve millimeters. What about the capacity of gallons? Of barrels? Pfft. Pull up a chair and pour a drink; that could take all night to hammer out.

The kick is that, unless you're using calibrated lab equipment, your measuring devices may not be even close to accurate. Recently, for instance, I bought a set of commercial measuring cups that supposedly ran from 100 to 2,000 ml. There was a problem. The measurement marks weren't just off; they weren't even consistently off. An engineer would say that they were neither accurate nor precise. One thousand grams of room-temperature water—which should be 1 liter exactly—measured 960 ml in one container, 1,050 in another, and 890 in a third. Those cups are useful for mixing, blending, and scooping, but for precise measurements, I use a different set that I know is accurate. Likewise, don't just assume that your tablespoon holds 15 ml or that your 1-liter measuring cup really does measure a liter. Either buy from a reputable specialist or double-check yourself by pouring exact weights of room temperature water into the measuring cups (here's where your scale comes in handy). Since one gram of water equals one milliliter, the various volumes should weigh the same amount.

That Pint Might Not Be a Pint

The recipe for ginger wine on page 174 seems fairly straightforward. But hang on a tick before diving in. What's this *Tinct Zing. Fort BP 1885?* "BP 1885" refers to the 1885 edition of the *British Pharmacopoeia,* a massive tome that describes medicinal plants and drugs and gives formulas for their official preparation as prepared in the United Kingdom. It provides enforceable standards for pharmacists which, until its first 1864 edition, had not been aligned in the various London, Edinburgh, and Dublin pharmacopoeias. Similar volumes came at different times from the United States, Germany, Japan, and other countries, and continue to be updated. That—well, bolstered by mention of ounces, drops, and gallons—gives the recipe a firm British provenance and, in fact, it shows up in a 1907 book, *The Book of Receipts* published in London. The gallon, in other words, is not a US gallon; it's a larger imperial gallon. Likewise, the pint isn't the somewhat anemic American pint of 16 fluid ounces, but a full-on British 20-ounce pint.

Understanding Pharmacists' Weights and Measures

Physicians and pharmacists through the early 20th century relied on Latin for their notes, formulas, and prescriptions using alcohol (and everything else) because their tradition and training dictated it. As long as international colleagues could make out the handwriting, they could read and understand one another's work no matter what language each spoke at home. Perhaps just as important, writing entire bodies of work in Latin prevented lay readers from understanding material that dealt with potentially harmful, even deadly, ingredients.

It's not just their propensity to use Latin that may confound modern readers; the recipes can seem almost alien to those who are not accustomed to reading them. Weird characters that look like astrological signs and alchemical symbols litter the pages. Not to worry; once you get past scruples, grains, and drachms, the recipes are not so different from the cups and teaspoons used in cookbooks and blogs today.

Despite the alien look of the symbols, Western pharmacists followed a few conventional systems of measurement: **apothecaries' measures** for liquids used units such as gallons, dra(ch)ms, and fluid ounces. **Apothecaries'** or **troy weight** and **avoirdupois weight** dealt, not surprisingly, with mass using pounds, ounces, scruples, drachms, and grains.

Let's look briefly at the measures we're likely to find in old booze recipes.

Metric Measures

After some false starts at the end of the 18th century, the metric system of measurement with its meters, liters, and grams spread across Europe and eventually most of the world. The United States is a notable holdout; although our retail liquor and some food is sold in metric units, Americans still use pounds, teaspoons, cups, and other household measurements in our day-to-day interactions. As for liquor manuals and pharmacopoeias, the bulk of them published since about the middle of the 1800s call for grams, kilograms, liters, and millimeters in particular. Aside from minor spelling variations around the world, metric measurements are unchanged and remain

Take the Fifth

As an official measure, the "fifth" of booze is obsolete in America. Unofficially, it's another story. Doesn't matter if it's rye, bourbon, rum, or gin; the liquor bottle four-fifths the size of a quart is still known colloquially as a *fifth*. Just as a quart holds a fourth (i.e., a quarter) of a gallon, a fifth held a fifth of a gallon of spirits. Its replacement, the 750 ml standard, is only a smidge smaller (25.4 fluid ounces to the fifth's 25.6). Alcohol industry types may call the newer size a *seven-fifty* but just about everyone old enough to drink knows what bottle to grab when someone asks for a fifth. Call for a quart, though, and you'll get a liter.

easy to use. A kilo of sugar in 1923 weighed the same as a kilo does in 2015. Two rules of thumb, though, hold when interpreting old alcohol recipes with metric measures.

1. **Missing units are (probably) grams.** When a formula—say, for a cordial or gin—in a compounding manual does not specify units of ingredients, "gram" is almost always meant. "15 calamus, 35 juniper berry, 7.2 coriander," for example, should be read as "15 grams of calamus root, 35 grams of juniper berries, 7.2 grams of coriander seeds." Electronic scales that are accurate to within a hundredth of a gram can be had for less than the cost of a fast-food lunch. They're a better investment, anyway. If you don't already have one for your kitchen or bar, get one; they are particularly useful when precision is important.

> Es ist üblich, die Menge der ätherischen Öle in "Gramm" anzugeben, während man darunter "cc" versteht. Dies Kommt von der Einteilung der Meßzylinder her.
>
> It is common to specify the amount of essential oils in "grams" while it's understood to mean "cc." This comes from the division of the graduated cylinder.
>
> —Hans Göttler, *Rezeptbuch für Destillateure* (1909)

2. **Grams are (probably) milliliters**. Ethanol was weighed in old recipes that call for pounds or kilos of spirits—and a lot of them do. A stickler for details who tries out those old recipes might also weigh essential oils, because they usually called for grams of this or that oil. In practice, "grams" of essential oils and other aromatic compounds, such as fruit ethers, generally meant "milliliters." Although not technically correct, in many 19th-century liquor manufacturing books, "gram" became shorthand for "milliliter" because a milliliter of water weighs 1 gram. Extrapolating to liquids that were more or less dense than water would have led to some inconsistencies, but measuring the volume of multiple aromatic compounds in a graduated cylinder was more expedient than switching out counterweights on a small scale. Unless a text specifies that essential oils or other aromatic compounds truly should be weighed, read "grams" as "milliliters."

Celsius and Fahrenheit temperature measurements do affect proof readings of spirits, but the vagaries of alcohol at various temperatures is of interest primarily to manufacturers of spirits and those who collect taxes on them. Let's leave it to them. Formularies that use metric measures in the recipes themselves tend to use only two: volume and mass/weight.

Volume Measure

1,000 microliters (µl) =	1 milliliter (ml)	
10 milliliters (ml) =	1 centiliter (cl)	
10 centiliters =	1 deciliter (dl) =	100 milliliters
10 deciliters =	1 liter (l) =	1,000 milliliters
10 liters =	1 dekaliter or decaliter (dal)	
10 dekaliters =	1 hectoliter (hl) =	100 liters
10 hectoliters =	1 kiloliter (kl) =	1,000 liters

Mass/Weight Measure

10 milligrams (mg) =	1 centigram (cg)	
10 centigrams =	1 decigram (dg) =	100 milligrams
10 decigrams =	1 gram (gramme, gr., or g) =	1,000 milligrams
10 grams =	1 dekagram or decagram (dag)	
10 dekagrams =	1 hectogram (hg) =	100 grams
10 hectograms =	1 kilogram (kilo, kg, or k) =	1,000 grams
1,000 kilograms =	1 metric ton/tonne (t)	

Do Use Microliters, Don't Call Them Microns

A small but growing number of modern bartenders who incorporate essential oils and related aromatic compounds in their recipes have begun using a volume measurement they've dubbed a "micron." Their cordial or syrup recipes might call for 600 microns of black pepper oil, 175 microns of rose otto; that sort of thing. From California to Europe, I have tasted outstanding drinks these progressive and experimental bartenders throw down. *Micron*, though, is the wrong word.

A micron (µ) is a measurement of length. A thousand of them make a millimeter, a million form a meter. Brewers, distillers, and bottlers refer to them regularly when sizing filters to prepare products for market so their beers or vermouths or what have you do not cloud, throw sediment, or develop off-tastes in the bottle. The proper term for those tiny, tiny volumes bartenders have been squeezing into spirits and cordials, on the other hand, is *microliter*. How tiny? A single microliter (µl) measures one thousandth of a milliliter and a full liter has a million of them.

Automatic pipettes that measure microliters of highly concentrated aromas and flavors offer even more precision than the drops commonly called for in aromatherapy and most home/bar essential oil projects. One of those micropipettes can cost more than a decent mountain bike or a few years of gym membership. Plain ol' 3 ml plastic pipettes are far more affordable, even if they sacrifice precision. If you prefer punctilious cocktails to gym workouts and have the cash to splash, though, see the Resources (page 205) for a source.

Internal Rev. Chemist G.F. Beyer testing a batch of bootleg liquor. While government reports documented the near-universal horror of these bootleg liquors, it's worth keeping in mind that the seizures of such liquor generally came from sketchy places in the first place; country clubs and well-connected joints with well-heeled crowds who could afford protection money tended to not get raided nearly as often as places that catered to poorer, often immigrant, clientele.

Apothecaries' Weights and Measures

Throughout Europe and the United States, apothecaries used—and occasionally still do use—a system of measurements derived from Roman and Greek units. Unfortunately for those of us who want to understand the kinds of formulas for cordials, medicated wines, bitters, and compounded spirits found in old apothecary manuals, professionals from different medical traditions never quite managed to agree on how best to measure a Roman pound. Was it to be calculated using the weight of Roman coins? Was it perhaps somehow related to units of length? The weights of barley grains and carob seeds also came into play. The result is that over centuries and distance, such measurements as ounces and pounds rarely aligned. When dealing with concentrated substances such as essential oils or ethanol, even small variation might yield different results for those following formulas written in a distant lands.

So a 17th-century Spanish ounce may not quite align with a 19th-century German one. That doesn't mean we need to toss all the old measures overboard. Because most of the alcohol formulas we're likely to find come from 18th- through 20th-century manuals—with some, admittedly, from much earlier—pharmacy and medicine manuals of those eras do reveal the symbols and measurements we're likely to come across.

Removing Moles

Tartar emetic 15 grains in impalpable powder, soap ~~powder~~ plaster 1-dram and beat them to a paste. Apply this paste to nearly a line in thickness and cover the whole with strips of gummed paper. In 4 or 5 days the eruption or suppuration will set in and in a few days leave in place of the mole only a very slight scar.

Mary's Eye wash

Zinc Sulfat	gr i
Acid Boric	gr v
Aquae Destillat	℥ i

1 drop in each eye twice ~~three~~ times day

Rheumatism

Potassium Iodide		℥ ss
Vin Colchici		ʒ ii
Natr Salicylat		℥ ss
Kalii nitrat		ʒ i
Aquae distil	ad	℥ vi

Tablespoonful in tumblerful water every 2 hours. Later t-i-d p.c.

Weights

gr. Granum, -i =	grain(s)	
℈ Scupulus, -i =	scruple =	20 grains
ʒ Drachma, -ae =	drachm =	60 grains
℥ Uncia, -ae =	ounce (troy) =	480 grains
℔ Libra, -ae =	pound (troy) =	5760 grains
Lb. Libra, -ae =	pound (avoirdupois) =	7000 grains

Notice two different pounds. One, the **apothecaries'** or **troy** pound, weighs 12 ounces. It's still used in some settings such as weighing precious metals. I recall feeling distinctly cheated as a child after learning that a pound of gold only weighs 12 ounces. Never mind that a grade school child has, at best, scant gold reserves. An **avoirdupois** pound, on the other hand, is the familiar "pound of commerce" we use to measure oranges, chicken thighs, juniper berries, and husbands; it is 16 ounces.

Volume

♏ Minimum, -i =	minim	
gtt. Gutta, -ae =	drop	
fl ℈ or Fluidscupulus, -i =	fluid scruple =	20 minims
*f*ʒ or fl. dr. Fluidrachma, -ae =	fluid drachm =	60 minims
f℥ or fl. oz. Fluiduncia, -ae =	fluid ounce =	480 minims (8 drachms)
O. Octarius, -i =	pint =	16 fluid ounces (20 ounces in Imperial measures) or ⅛ gallon/congius
C. Congius, -i =	gallon =	8 pints

A half measure (ounce, drachm, scruple, whatever), may be noted as "ss" for *semis*. ℈ss thus is *semiscrupulus*, half a scruple, and ℥ss is semiuncia, half an ounce. Pre-1800 texts sometimes use a "long" or "descending" *s* as the first *s* in *semis* (the same letter that renders Milton's *Paradise Lost* as *Paradiſe Loſt*), so we also see *ſs* or ß, the German double *s*, to indicate halves.

Note that a lowercase *m* may be used for *minim* but may also indicate *manipulus* (a handful). Sorry. No rule of thumb here; context is the only thing that will reveal whether you're meant to use an itty-bitty amount of liquid or a big ol' fistful of dried herbs or spices.

II, IV, VI, VIII, This Is How We Calculate!

Roman Numerals

Our everyday Arabic numbers (0, 1, 2, 3, etc.) make even complex calculations straightforward, but that's not the only system around. The numeration we see in pharmacy texts even through Prohibition, for example, is usually adapted from Roman reckoning. For those not accustomed to the system that uses letters as numbers, those forgotten booze formulas in pharmacopoeias can be a bit bewildering. This is not surprising, considering that lay readers weren't meant to understand them; "bewildering" was partly the point. Tens of thousands of recipes for compounded spirits, bitters, tinctures, and medicinal wines from the 17th through early 20th centuries use this numbering system, though, so an understanding of the basics is in order. Today, although Roman numerals linger on in dating movies, publishing, denoting sequels, and telling time, their hash mark–looking method of counting has atrophied. The good news is that the ancient Roman numeral system is easy to pick up. Who, after all, is truly dumbfounded by the numerals in WW II, Superbowl XXX, or Henry VIII?

In conjunction with the apothecaries' weights and volumes, three main Roman numerals come into play in pharma-style alcohol recipes: I, V, and X. That is, 1, 5, and 10. Since, from time to time, other numerals do crop up, here's the whole set:

I, i, or j =	1
V or v =	5
X or x =	10
L =	50
C =	100
D =	500
M =	1,000

Make more complex numbers by combining these seven letters (note: there is no Roman zero). Two is noted as II (or more commonly in lowercase: ii). Three is iii. Often, the final or only *i* in a receipt can be noted as *j*—*ij* is read as "ii" (2) while *iij* is "iii" (3). One more point before we get lost in a quagmire of variants, inconsistencies, and idiosyncratic uses: writers tended not to use the same letter four times in a row. "Four," then, is not iiii (except on watch faces), but iv (one less than five). Likewise, 9 is ix (one less than ten) and, on the same principle, 400 is CD.

Prescription Julep

With the publication of his seminal book Imbibe! in 2007, drinks historian David Wondrich resurrected a 19th-century concoction dubbed the Prescription Julep that appeared in an 1857 issue of Harper's Monthly. Although it's a bit of a joke recipe (from "Quackenboss, MD"), the receipt is a good example of Latin and apothecaries' measures applied to a drink. Now, juleps are something of a house drink around here, so I cranked out a set of this version that blends rye whiskey with "strong" Cognac—and was very happy to find the drink itself is no joke.

SACCHA. ALB., ℥ij. (2 oz white sugar)

CUM AQUA FONTANA, QUANT. SUFF. (a sufficient quantity of spring water)

COGNIAC FORT., ℥iss. (1.5 oz strong Cognac)

SPIR. SECALICUS, ℥ss. (0.5 oz rye whiskey)

FOL. MENTHM VIRIDIS, AD LIB (mint leaves, as desired; 8–12 is good)

FIAT INFUSUM ET ADD. (make an infusion of these and then add)

GLACIES PULV.QUANT.SUFF. (a sufficient quantity of pulverized ice)

OMNIA MISCE. (mix everything)

A freehand translation: dissolve sugar in the water (2 ounces is a bit sweet; ratchet it back to about 1/2 ounce). Muddle the mint leaves in the resulting syrup (or simply use gomme or compounders' syrup). Just smoosh them a bit; don't beat them into submission. Add the rye and Cognac, give it all a stir, then top off with the finely crushed ice. The recipe doesn't say, but a freshly spanked mint sprig is traditional to stick in the ice. A short straw will force drinkers to bury their nose in the mint while drinking.

Overproof Cognac, "COGNIAC FORT.," stands up well to the inevitable dilution from fine ice melting into the drink. Two nice ones are Louis Royer Force 53 Fine VSOP and Selection Saint Sauvant XO Cognac from Merlet & Fils. Use what you've got.

Kitchen and Bar Measures

Finally, what pharmacists dub *household* or *domestic* measures have figured into compounded recipes for hundreds of years. Most of them are familiar in American homes and bars. Keep in mind that spoons, cups, and glasses have ranged widely in their capacities over the years. Whenever possible, it's best to verify their capacity in the same text in which the recipe appears.

When that's not possible, here are some of the more important measures you'll find in old booze recipes.

Teaspoon (tsp) =	4 to 5 ml
Dessertspoon =	8 ml
Tablespoon (Tb/Tbl/Tbsp) =	0.5 fluid ounce (the modern American standard is 15 ml, but it was 12–25 ml historically)
3 teaspoons =	1 tablespoon
2 tablespoons =	1 fluid ounce (fl oz)
1 cup =	8 fluid ounces
2 cups =	1 pint (pt)
2 pints =	1 quart (qt)
4 quarts =	1 gallon
Wineglass =	1.5 to 2 fluid ounces (45–60 ml) (drinks historian David Wondrich pegs a wineglass at 2 fluid ounces, but pharmacy texts[65] give a range)
Tea cup =	(about 150 ml)
Breakfast cup =	8 fluid ounces (about 240 ml)
Tumbler =	11 fluid ounces (about 330 ml)

Proof

Overproof rums, whiskeys, gin, and even some brandies have grown a lot more popular in recent years. They stand up particularly well in spirit-forward cocktails and are favorites with many drinkers, not just craft bartenders. Most folks have a sense that overproof spirits are somehow stronger than the regular offerings, but what is this "proof"? Simply, it's a measure of the alcohol content of a beverage.

As a measure of alcoholic strength, though, the term *proof* has been discarded by British and American governments, both of which now measure alcohol as a percentage of total beverage volume (% abv). The term gained popularity in Britain where tax officers—and navy sailors—used a crude sort of trial by fire to determine how strong a spirit was by mixing a bit of the spirit with gunpowder and then attempting to ignite the mix. If the wetted gunpowder burned briskly, it was said to be "over proof." Mixtures that failed to spark were "under proof." A low, steady burn indicated spirits actually at proof: 57.15 percent alcohol. By 1816, the term was retired in the UK in favor of measuring alcohol content with a floating hydrometer developed by excise agent Bartholomew Sikes.

When recipes call for brandy, whiskey, or other spirits so many degrees under proof (U.P.) or over proof (O.P.), check their provenance; British and American spirits will be slightly different.

Of course, the term still enjoys lively popular use. Throughout my travels interviewing moonshiners and folk distillers in the United States, 100-proof shine remains a touchstone of authenticity, the minimum strength at which one should drink it. Since both British and American proof are deployed in formularies and pharmacopoeias, let's look at both.

American Proof

In the United States, proof is simply twice the alcohol content at 60°F. One hundred proof is thus 50% abv. Eighty proof is 40% abv. Easy-peasy. Done. Next.

British Proof

The old British system is a bit trickier, but only a bit. Proof in the United Kingdom doesn't quite align with American usage. The chart on page 205 lists equivalents, but the British system boils down to this: proof spirit (e.g., 100°) is 57.15% abv which is very close to the fraction 4⁄7. To convert percentage abv to degrees proof, multiply by 7⁄4. For example, 100 percent (anhydrous or dehydrated) alcohol is 175° proof [100 × (7⁄4)]. What Americans call 80 proof (40% abv) is 70° proof in the British system [40 × (7⁄4)].

Sikes Hydrometers

Sikes hydrometers, named after their inventor, exciseman Bartholomew Sikes, were used officially in the United Kingdom from 1816 to 1907 to measure the strength of alcoholic beverages. Unofficially they remained in use even into the government of Margaret Thatcher. Antique specimens in their velvet-lined wooden cases can fetch hundreds and even thousand dollars from collectors. Find a whole vintage set, complete with original instructions, and you've found something rare indeed.

Two French Methods for Reckoning Proof

From the early 1800s until European standardization in the 1980s, France and Belgium used a particularly sensible method to reckon alcoholic strength. Their system, named after its inventor Joseph-Louis Gay-Lussac, was centesimal. That is, the entire range of possible alcoholic content was broken into hundredths. Each degree was one part per hundred parts of total volume; 0° held zero alcohol while 100° was pure, anhydrous spirit. It is essentially the modern *alcohol-by-volume* scale.

French methods weren't always so straightforward, though.

Cordial manufacturers and brandy blenders in the south of France once used a weight system, expressed in fractions, rather than volume to designate the strength of spirits. Ideally, such spirits were made from wine, but lesser grades from grains, beets, and marc (wine lees) did enter the market. Because French distilling and compounding manuals were so widely copied, terms such as "spirits at three in five" crept into books printed in other languages as well, sometimes without explanation. For the skinny on the system, let's dig into the granddaddy of French distilling texts, *A Treatise on the Manufacture and Distillation of Alcoholic Liquors* from Pierre Duplais. This is from an 1871 American edition:

> These numbers are not arbitrary; they indicate the weight, and not the volume, as some theorists have contended, of the quantity of water which it is necessary to add to any spirituous liquor to bring it to proof (Preuve de Hollande), or 19 degrees Cartier (50 degrees Centigrade).
>
> Thus the three-fifths is spirits at 29½ degrees, which mixed in the proportion of three parts of spirits with two parts of water, will give five parts in weight of brandy at 19 degrees.
>
> The trois-six is alcohol at 33 degrees, of which, if three parts are mixed with an equal weight of water, will produce six parts of brandy of the same degree, or 19 degrees Cartier. [Philadelphia: H. C. Baird & Company, 1871]

So, the first, or top, number indicates the weight of 85% abv spirit, while the second, or bottom, number is the total final weight of the blend. What's missing from the designation is the amount of water needed to bring the blend to proof. You could figure that quickly enough by subtracting the denominator from the numerator . . . or just refer to the chart (page 205) that compares American and British proof with the trois-six weights as well as degrees Cartier.

Cartier and Tralles Scales

The final two methods—at least for our purposes—for measuring alcoholic content in beverages are the Cartier and Tralles scales. The Cartier scale runs from 10 (0% alcohol) to 44⅛ (100% alcohol) and dates from the turn of the 19th century. We see it especially in Spanish, French, Portuguese, and Brazilian distilling and compounding texts. Equivalents are on the chart on page 205 .

German mathematician Johann Georg Tralles is the eponymous inventor of another scale, sometimes called the Prussian scale, based on volume. Degrees **Tralles** appear in American and German formulas and recipes for spiritous beverages. Because they are very close to the centesimal degrees of Gay-Lussac, we may regard them as equivalent.

Parts

Finally, we have **parts** (*Teile*, *Theilen*, or *Th.* in German which can look like Tb, tablespoon). Parts are simply ratios of ingredients to one another. Just as a classic Manhattan is made of one part vermouth to two of whiskey (plus bitters and, if you roll that way, a cherry, its attendant juice, and an orange twist), formulary recipes sometimes call for parts of essential oils or aromatic compounds. These are always volume measures, so each "part" may be a milliliter, a teaspoon, an ounce, or a big red bucket, for that matter—as long as the unit is the same. For kitchen and bar use, smaller units are more manageable. Cordial recipes in particular are often written in parts of each ingredient.

For example, a compounded orange curaçao flavor formula from *Fenaroli's Handbook of Flavor Ingredients*[66] uses a blend of sweet and bitter orange for the bulk of flavor, then rounds it out with smaller parts of lemon, rum ether, neroli, and warm spices. The result is more nuanced than a simple orange-flavored vodka:

Alcohol (96%) 418
Sweet Orange 350
Bitter Orange. 190
Lemon 22
Rum ether. .5
Neroli. 5
Cinnamon. .4
Clove 3
Nutmeg. 2
Coriander 1
Total. 1,000

Note that this is not curaçao . . . yet. For that, add 20 ml or so of this compounded flavor, along with fresh orange peel or tincture made from peels (page 187), to a bottle of vodka and 100 to 200 grams of sugar. See Mike McCaw's Triple Sec (page 188) for directions on how to proceed.

Proof Scales

volume				weight
Centesimal degrees (Gay-Lussac) (abv)	**American proof (at 60°F)**	**British proof (1816-1907)**	**Degrees Cartier**	**Trois-Six (Duplais) approx**
0	0	0.0	10″	
1	2	1.8	10 1⁄4	
2	4	3.5	10 3⁄8	
3	6	5.3	10 5⁄8	
4	8	7.0	10 3⁄4	
5	10	8.8	10 7⁄8	
6	12	10.5	11 1⁄8	
7	14	12.3	11 1⁄4	
8	16	14.0	11 1⁄2	
9	18	15.8	11 5⁄8	
10	20	17.5	11 3⁄4	
11	22	19.3	11 7⁄8	
12	24	21.0	12 1⁄8	
13	26	22.8	12 1⁄4	
14	28	24.5	12 3⁄8	
15	30	26.3	12 1⁄2	
16	32	28.0	12 5⁄8	
17	34	29.8	12 3⁄4	
18	36	31.5	12 7⁄8	
19	38	33.3	13″	
20	40	35.0	13 1⁄4	
21	42	36.8	13 3⁄8	
22	44	38.5	13 1⁄2	
23	46	40.3	13 5⁄8	
24	48	42.0	13 3⁄4	
25	50	43.8	13 7⁄8	
26	52	45.5	14 1⁄8	
27	54	47.3	14 1⁄4	
28	56	49.0	14 3⁄8	
29	58	50.8	14 1⁄2	
30	60	52.5	14 5⁄8	
31	62	54.3	14 7⁄8	
32	64	56.0	15″	
33	66	57.8	15 1⁄4	
34	68	59.5	15 3⁄8	
35	70	61.3	15 5⁄8	
36	72	63.0	15 3⁄4	
37	74	64.8	16″	
38	76	66.5	16 1⁄8	
39	78	68.3	16 3⁄8	

volume				weight
Centesimal degrees (Gay-Lussac) (abv)	**American proof (at 60°F)**	**British proof (1816-1907)**	**Degrees Cartier**	**Trois-Six (Duplais) approx**
40	80	70.0	16 5/8	
41	82	71.8	16 7/8	
42	84	73.5	17 1/8	
43	86	75.3	17 3/8	
44	88	77.0	17 5/8	
45	90	78.8	17 7/8	
46	92	80.5	18 1/8	
47	94	82.3	18 3/8	
48	96	84.0	18 5/8	
49	98	85.8	18 7/8	
50	100	87.5	19 1/4	
51	102	89.3	19 1/2	
52	104	91.0	19 3/4	
53	106	92.8	20 1/8	
54	108	94.5	20 3/8	
55	110	96.3	20 3/4	
56	112	98.0	21 ″	
57	114	99.8	21 3/8	
58	116	101.5	21 3/4	
59	118	103.3	22 ″	
60	120	105.0	22 3/8	
61	122	106.8	22 3/4	
62	124	108.5	23 1/8	2/3
63	126	110.3	23 1/2	
64	128	112.0	23 7/8	
65	130	113.8	24 1/4	3/4
66	132	115.5	24 5/8	
67	134	117.3	25 ″	
68	136	119.0	25 3/8	
69	138	120.8	25 3/4	
70	140	122.5	26 1/4	
71	142	124.3	26 5/8	
72	144	126.0	27 ″	
73	146	127.8	27 1/2	
74	148	129.5	27 7/8	
75	150	131.3	28 3/8	
76	152	133.0	28 7/8	
77	154	134.8	29 1/4	3/5
78	156	136.5	29 3/4	
79	158	138.3	30 1/4	4/7
80	160	140.0	30 3/4	

volume				weight
Centesimal degrees (Gay-Lussac) (abv)	**American proof (at 60°F)**	**British proof (1816-1907)**	**Degrees Cartier**	**Trois-Six (Duplais) approx**
81	162	141.8	31 ¼	5/9
82	164	143.5	31 ¾	
83	166	145.3	32 ¼	6/11
84	168	147.0	32 ¾	
85	170	148.8	33 ¼	
86	172	150.5	33 ⅞	
87	174	152.3	34 ⅜	
88	176	154.0	35 ″	3/7
89	178	155.8	35 ⅝	
90	180	157.5	36 ⅛	
91	182	159.3	36 ⅞	
92	184	161.0	37 ½	3/8
93	186	162.8	38 ¼	
94	188	164.5	38 ⅞	
95	190	166.3	39 ⅝	
96	192	168.0	40 ½	
97	194	169.8	41 ¼	8/9
98	196	171.5	42 ¼	
99	198	173.3	43 ⅛	
100	200	175.0	44 ⅛	

ABV in Typical Alcohols

ABV	**Typical alcohols: note that outliers push the limits in either direction, but most beverages below will fall into these ranges**
2–12	Most beers (though some outliers reach far into double digits)
9–18	Most wines and vermouth
18–22	Fortified and "dessert" wines
15–40	Cordials and liqueurs
30–60	Cocktail bitters
40–120	Distilled spirits such as whiskey, rum, gin, tequila, brandy, etc.
55–72	Absinthes
75.5	151 proof rums
80–95	Commercial spirits for blending and industrial use
95–96	Rectified "neutral" spirits (e.g., grain alcohol, spirytus)
96–100	Laboratory grade ethanol, rarely found in the retail market
99.2–100	Anhydrous or dehydrated alcohol

Resources

Essences, Oils, Flavors, and Compounds

Aftelier
aftelier.com
Oils, perfumes

Art of Drink
artofdrink.com
Acid phosphate and lactart

The Essential Oil Company
essentialoil.com
Essential oils and distillation equipment

The Good Scents Company
thegoodscentscompany.com
Flavor and aromatic compounds, oils, extracts, and essences

Healthy Village
healthyvillage.com
Medicinal herbs and cinchona

Herbiary
herbiary.com
Bulk herbs especially suited for making bitters and cordials

In Pursuit of Tea
inpursuitoftea.com
Specialty teas and infusions

Kalustyan's
kalustyans.com
Bulk spices and herbs

Lhasa Karnak Herb Company
http://www.herb-inc.com
Bulk spices and herbs

Liberty Natural
libertynatural.com
Bulk spices and herbs, oils

LorAnn Flavors and Oils
lorannoils.com
Oils, extracts

Modernist Pantry
modernistpantry.com
Acids, flavors, thickeners, and sweeteners

Monterey Bay Spice Company
herbco.com
Bulk spices and herbs, oils

Mountain Rose Herbs
mountainroseherbs.com
Bulk spices and herbs

Penzeys Spices
penzeys.com
Bulk spices and herbs, jars

Scents of Earth
scents-of-earth.com
Frankincense, myrrh, tonka beans, rose attars, oils.

Tenzing Momo
tenzingmomo.com
Bulk spices and herbs, some oils

Commercial Spirits, Bitters, and Syrups

Whether you work in the booze industry or are simply an enthusiast, you'll want a selection of whiskeys, brandies, gins, overproof rum, and other commercial spirits. Having lived in some out-of-the-way places, I know firsthand that it's not always easy laying your hands on the juniper juice and corn squeezin's bartenders and bloggers who live in big cities regularly use. Here are a few of my favorite firms that ship.

Remember: 40% abv spirits won't readily dissolve essential oils. It's worth checking these vendors' stock of high-proof neutral spirits such as Everclear, Golden Grain, or Polish *spirytus rektyfikowany* ("rectified spirit" that ranges from 92% to about 96% abv). Several brands are available; look for "*spirytus*" on the label and double-check the proof.

Astor Wines & Spirits
astorwines.com

B. G. Reynolds Syrups
bgreynolds.com

Binny's Beverage Depot
binnys.com

DrinkUpNY
drinkupny.com

Hi-Time Wine Cellars
hitimewine.net

K&L Wine Merchants
klwines.com

Master of Malt
masterofmalt.com

Shoppers Vineyard
shoppersvineyard.com

Small Hand Foods
smallhandfoods.com

Organizations and Useful Websites

Alcohol and Tobacco Tax and Trade Bureau (United States)
ttb.gov

The American Distilling Institute
distilling.com

Artisan Distiller
artisan-distiller.net

Craft Distillers' Alliance (UK)
thecda.co.uk

Flavor & Extract Manufacturers Association (the other FEMA)
femaflavor.org

Food Standards Agency
food.gov.uk

GRAS (Generally Recognized as Safe) Database United States Food and Drug Administration
fda.gov

Hobby Distiller's Association
hobbydistillersassociation.org

Home Distillation of Alcohol
homedistiller.org

International Fragrance Association
ifraorg.org

International Organization of the Flavor Industry
iofi.org

The IUCN Red List of Threatened Species
iucnredlist.org

Yahoo! Distillers
groups.yahoo.com/neo/groups/Distillers

Glossary

The first draft of this book's glossary was one of those times when my history as a museum curator got the better of me. That sprawling, 16,000-word chapter explained every ingredient in Victor Lyon's notebook: Latin, German, English, the lot. It was also way too much. At the gentle, but insistent, prodding of my patient editor, Ann Treistman, a new glossary emerged. What follows is a list of the more important or noteworthy ingredients from Lyon's old notebook. Forgive my omissions; there just isn't the space to cover everything.

Acetaldehyde has a distinct, pungent smell that can give the impression of fruitiness, juiciness, and, in wines, the "roundness" associated with older vintages.

Acetic Acid gives vinegar its pungent, savory, nose-wrinkling aroma. Its sharp taste can draw a mouth awry, but in small quantities it is a frequent adulterant of older compounded brandy and whiskey recipes.

Acetic Ether (more commonly known as ethyl acetate) has a pleasant, supple, brandy-like odor and is widely used to flavor modern foods and beverages.

Allspice has a warm, complex aroma and taste well suited to baking, sausages, jerk, and cordials. It appears in many old cordial recipes and is the primary botanical in a Caribbean cordial called Pimento (or Allspice) Dram that cocktail historian Ted Haigh once called "the most important liqueur in the world."

Almonds come in two broad types: sweet and bitter. The former are the common almond of baking, confectionery, and a singularly delicious syrup called orgeat that plays well in many rum and brandy drinks. Bitter almonds, on the other hand, are difficult, if not outright impossible, to find in American stores because they are toxic unless prepared with punctilious regard to safety. Natural almond oil—often called oil of bitter almond—is prepared from bitter almonds (or kernels of apricot, peach, or similar species) with high levels of pleasant-smelling benzaldehyde while "imitation" may be synthesized in labs—without risk of cyanide contamination.

Alum has been used to fine (that is, to clear) spirits of particulates or oily residue and to purify water. It was also sometimes used to fix, or make more durable, colors added to spirits.

Amyl Alcohol is any one of eight different molecules, or a combination of them, commonly found in fusel oil. By itself, amyl alcohol has a harsh, petrochemical odor, but in small amounts and with other compounds, it can lend pleasant apricot and banana aromas.

Amyl Butyrate is a common flavoring agent with a sweet taste naturally found in apples and with fruity overtones of pineapple and banana, giving drinks a sort of generic "tropical" taste. Many old rum formulas in particular call for it.

Angelica roots and sometimes seeds are used in vermouth, bitters, and gin, where they can lend peppery, bitter notes and hints of anise and juniper.

Anise is a cousin to fennel, caraway, and cumin. Anise is native to Greece and Asia Minor but has naturalized across Europe, North America, and Asia. Its seeds (actually little fruits) are a stalwart flavoring for spirits and cordials. Its licorice and fennel aroma is both sweet and warm. Anise oil may be from actual anise seeds, but is more commonly made from star anise.

Balsams, derived from a number of trees and shrubs around the world, are highly aromatic resins much used in perfumery, medicine, and some foodstuffs. Two types, balsam of Peru and balsam of Tolu, dissolve readily in alcohol and abound in pre-Prohibition formulas for cordials and flavored spirits. A third, benzoin, occasionally shows up in whiskey formulations and some mixed drinks. All three have notes of cinnamon and vanilla as well as an unctuous, soft, sweet, aromatic, and rich scent with bosky base notes, a quality perfumers call balsamic.

Benzaldehyde is one of the heavy hitters in the flavor industry. First isolated in the 19th century, it is derived from both artificial and natural sources, including the kernels of bitter almonds, apricots, peaches, and other *Prunus* species. Its classic flavor is the base of artificial almond extract and almond oil. Its sweet, woodsy aroma immediately brings to mind almonds, cherries, and fresh marzipan and is found in many essential oils.

Boise (pronounced bwaz-AY) is a wood extract, commonly made of oak, and occasionally of other woods. See page 95.

Butyric Ether, also called ethyl butyrate or pineapple oil, has a sweet, fruity, pleasant smell and is widely used in confectionery and beverages where its strong pineapple aroma shines through.

Cajeput tree leaves and young twigs are distilled to produce an essential oil similar to eucalyptus oil. In old ersatz spirits formulas, it serves to mimic age and impart faint bitterness. Uncommon in Western homemade drinks today, cajeput still enjoys some popularity in remedies for colds and throat complaints because of its penetrating and camphor-like odor.

Calamus see page 130

Capsicum: see page 89

Caramel see page 79

Caraway see page 147

Cardamom Beloved throughout Scandinavia in baked goods, warm, fragrant cardamom is common in older drinks manuals. It is used in gins, amari, some vermouths, and bitters. Cardamom-flavored syrup is a grateful addition to kitchens and bars.

Charcoal Because of its enormous surface area, carbon pulls impurities from spirits as they pass through. Distillers used it to "polish" spirits by removing unwanted compounds that cause off flavors and aroma.

Chiles see page 89

Cinchona, the bark of two species of South American trees, *Cinchona succirubra* and *C. calisaya,* is the source of quinine, used as an anti-malaria drug since the 16th century. In drinks, its bitter component provides the characteristic taste of tonic water in some vermouths, cordials, bitters, and aperitifs.

Beware: Ingesting too much quinine can bring on cinchonism, a condition caused by a buildup of cinchona in one's body. High doses can be fatal, but even low doses can bring on tinnitus, dizziness, nausea, blurred vision, hot flashes, and wrenching gut pains. Housemade tonic waters that leave visible cinchona floaties in the finished drink are best avoided.

Cinnamon and **Cassia** see page 158

Clove is a small evergreen whose unopened flowers are dried to make the spice familiar to westerners since Roman times. Clove is an aggressive flavor, easily overwhelming more delicate botanicals, and should be used with restraint.

Cognac Oil is one of the primary tools in the old rectifying manuals; its strong fruity aroma readily mixes with alcohol and gives a characteristic "brandy" taste with oily, fatty, and herbaceous notes. It is made from distilling wine lees, the sludgy dregs made of dead yeast and other precipitates left behind during the production of Cognac.

Colorants The proper color of a spirit or cordial makes the difference between an attractive product that commands a handsome price and one nobody wants. This was especially true during Prohibition when getting the color right (does that whiskey look yellow?) was often tricky. Counterfeiters of the era deployed a battery of woods, lichens, bugs, roots, and barks to get just the right tinge to their fake whiskey, wine, rum, and brandy. Many contributed flavors as well. Kino, for instance, is resin culled from different trees, especially eucalyptus and related varieties. It didn't just color spirits; it imparted astringency as well.

Among the more common colorants in older manuals were caramel (see page 79) and cochineal (page 174). Others included alkanet (roots of plants in the borage family), cudbear (various lichen species), and catechu (derived from the heartwood of a number of acacia species).

Brazil wood, logwood, and sandalwood, quite apart from their fragrant aromas, all lent a range of yellows and reds to cordials, wines, and spirits. Of roots, there were madder, rhatany, and tormentil, all of which yielded various reds for wines, especially faked port. Raspberry juice was used for the same purpose while its leaves lent astringency to country wines.

Cousin to ginger and sometimes called poor man's saffron, the dark yellow rhizome called turmeric has a pleasant, complex, peppery, and musty aroma with notes of citrus and ginger. It was used primarily as a yellow colorant for cordials and vermouths.

Coriander is one of the core gin botanicals, but is also used in bitters, pastis, vermouths, and Galliano liqueur. Its floral, spicy aroma complements a sweet, well-rounded flavor that smacks of orange. Pairs well with whiskey.

Coumarin see sweet woodruff recipes, page 182

Creosote has a range of meanings that vary over time and with local usage, but as it was used in 19th- and early 20-century beverage manuals, creosote was made from the heavy oil of wood tar. Another variety, made from coal tar, is toxic and should be avoided altogether. Small doses of bitter wood tar creosote give rich, smoky aromas to cured meats and beverages. Some versions of "liquid smoke" use creosote to simulate long, slow smoking.

Fennel Sweet, astringent, something like anise, something like licorice, fennel seeds are used widely in spirits and wines. Along with wormwood and anise, fennel is one of the three core ingredients of traditional absinthe and is often used to round out the flavor of kümmel.

Formic Ether, with its pungent, pineapple-like smell, was used to augment rums that had been cut with neutral spirits to enhance their rum-like aroma.

Fusel Oil More commonly called fusel alcohol in modern use, it is an oily-looking combination of amyl alcohols, acids, esters, and aldehydes that imparts characteristic flavor to spirits, especially whiskey. Though some recipes for compounded spirits call for it, fusel alcohol has a disagreeable odor and may contribute to hangovers; anything more than trace amounts can quickly ruin good liquor. In fact, distillers generally remove as much fusel alcohol as they can from most new spirits, leaving in just enough to break down and form new, pleasant-smelling compounds during barrel aging.

Galls are abnormal growths on plants caused by various species of parasites. Oak galls, formed by wasp larvae in growing oak trees, are often called for in old drinks formulas for the sharply bitter taste they give to vermouths, medicinal wines, and bitters.

Génépi see Wormwood

Gentian Two of the nearly 400 species of the mountainous plant gentian stand out for their use in beverages: yellow and spring gentians. It's one of the granddaddies of bittering elements in European tonics and liqueurs. Gentian root contributes bitterness to vermouths, cordials, bitters, amari, spirits, and even the soft drink Moxie.

Ginger see page 170

Glucose, also called dextrose or grape sugar, is not as sweet as table sugar, but is used like it to thicken and sweeten cordials, some bitters, and other alcoholic drinks. In syrups, it helps prevent crystallization.

Glycerine, also called glycerin and glycerol, is a colorless, nearly odorless, slightly sweet viscous liquid used to sweeten cordials and provide a rounder mouthfeel. Home distillers sometimes add as much as 15 ml to a liter of spirits, but it's quite delectable at even half that concentration. Its use in commercial spirits is frowned on and in some cases forbidden. It's not harmful, just a cheat that connoisseurs dislike.

Grains of Paradise see page 89

Hops extracts were sometimes added to quickly made Prohibition beers and whiskeys to simulate greater age and care in their making.

Horseradish see page 116

Hyssop is an ancient evergreen bush used in alcohol. In the 1st century AD, Pliny mentioned hyssopites, a wine impregnated with the bitter herb. Since then, the strong and minty leaves have been used in monastic liqueurs, vermouths, and absinthes.

Juniper see page 63

Licorice, a perennial shrub native to southeastern Europe and northwestern Asia, has a long taproot that adds sweetness, warmth, and a bit of earthiness to syrups, cordials, bitters, schnapps, vermouths, some porters, and spirits—most notably, gin.

Mace see Nutmeg and Mace

Mint, one of the world's most popular flavorings, is a protean herb prone to hybridizing, thus creating seemingly endless varieties. Broadly, though, the different types fall into two groups: peppermint and spearmint. Peppermint, and peppermint oil in particular, have a long history in medicine and drinks. More pungent than spearmint, peppermint tastes strongly of cooling menthol, but with a sweet aftertaste. Oil of peppermint is commonly used to make crème de menthe and it can be found in many cordials. Spearmint is the softer, more approachable variety. Mellow, with slight lemon notes and a cooling menthol effect when drinkers inhale after sipping some. Countless varieties exist, but this is the one for mint juleps, mojitos, mai tais, and other mixed drinks.

Nitrous Ether has a sweet, pleasant, fruity aroma with hints of vanilla and benzaldehyde and routinely shows up in old beverage compounding formulas. It is also known as ethyl nitrite. A 3.5-4.5% solution of nitrous ether was sold over the counter in the United States under the names sweet nitrite or sweet spirit of nitre as a cold remedy until the FDA ruled that was not generally recognized as safe (see GRAS, page 45). See Sweet Spirit of Nitre.

Nutmeg and Mace

Nutmeg and mace both come from the apricot-like fruit of *Myristica fragrans,* a tropical evergreen native to the Banda Islands of Indonesia, though now grown in several places. Nutmeg is the kernel of the fruit's seed while mace is the reddish-orange or amber colored aril (the lacy, web-like coving of each nutmeg). Usually sold separately. Buy whole and grate or ground as needed.

Nutmeg has a warm, rich, and pungent aroma. The flavor can be subtle and sweet, but it tapers off to a mildly bitter end. Rarely used as a primary note in spirits, it helps round out other flavors in some vermouths, absinthes, and gins. Often grated onto punches, some mixed drinks, and eggnogs just before serving.

Mace has an aroma similar to nutmeg's, though almost clove-like. The taste is both more subtle and more bitter than nutmeg.

Nuts A variety of nuts, including hazelnuts and walnuts, are used to impart bitterness, color, and astringency in spirits and in imitation of brandies.

Orris is the collective name for the bulbs of three iris species harvested after three to six years of growth and cured for another two or so. Generally sold as a powder, it has a fragrant, slightly earthy aroma. Its primary purpose, however, is to enhance or "fix" the aromas and flavors of other botanicals in gins, vermouths, absinthes, and some orange cordials.

Peppermint see Mint

Pyroligneous Acid is a complex mix of over 200 components, including acetic acid and methanol, created during the destructive distillation of wood. The dark yellow/reddish brown liquid is reminiscent of commercial liquid smoke. It was used in synthetic spirits—primarily whiskeys—to simulate barrel-aging.

Rose Forget insipid garden roses. Go for hugely flavored, intense red roses for rose drinks. Use the petals only and, if you've got a beef with bitterness, snip off the white base of each one. Rose is used in parfait amour, some vermouths, cordials, and flavored brandies. Rosewater is the aroma-saturated water left in the belly of a still after the essential oil (also called attar or otto of rose) is drawn off. Use a light touch; a little goes a long way.

Rosemary is a thick, woody evergreen shrub that can grow to the size of a small car (at least in our neighborhood). The leaves smell strongly of resin, pine, and camphor. Use a restrained hand; too much rosemary in a glass is like sucking pine needles.

Rum Ether, also known as ethyl oxyhydrate, is a wood distillate. Its aroma resembles that of rum and, despite lacking aromas important to real rum (such as isoamyl alcohol and β-damascenone), it has been used widely in spirits and the food industry overall.

Saffron see page 69

Salt Whole grains and flakes of salt are *de rigueur* for margaritas, salty dogs, and other cocktails. An old distiller's trick is adding non-iodized salt to stills during distillation to raise the boiling point of water, giving a greater ethanol percentage on a single run.

Spearmint see Mint

Star Anise is a particularly bold spice. Its aroma suggests licorice, anise, and fennel while the flavor is aggressive, slightly numbing, and lingering. The essential oil is widely used in anisettes, pastis, and cordials (see Anisette de Hollande and Anisette de Bordeaux, pages 167–168)

Sulfuric Acid Often called oil of vitriol in old texts, concentrated sulfuric acid is highly corrosive. It should be handled with the utmost care by people already familiar with its use. In Lyon's notebook, it is used to purify caramel, test the purity of spirits, create "beading oil" (see page 25), and as a barrel ager.

Sweet Oil Commonly pressed almond oil, but any neutral, edible oil. Often used to create "beading oil" for counterfeit spirits (see Sulfuric Acid).

Sweet Spirit of Nitre A once-common medicine in the United States, over the counter sales of pungent, sweet-tasting sweet spirit of nitre and its inclusion in any drug for any purpose were banned by the FDA in 1980. Used extensively in ersatz whiskey and brandy formulas. Since the mid-19th century, it has been known that inhaling it could cause cause dizziness, nausea, headache, heart irregularities, blueing of lips and nails, and even death.

Syrup see page 143

Tea Aside from its most excellent use as a beverage in and of itself, black tea adds astringency and color to punches, cocktails, and syrups. Teas pair well with fruits, flowers, and caramel. Green and "white" teas play well in punches and cocktails.

Tonka Beans Once hugely popular among distillers, liquor manufacturers, compounders, and bottlers (as well as tobacconists), tonka beans were banned as a food additive in 1954 because of their high coumarin content. The aroma is intense, sweet, and suggests new-mown hay, vanilla (for which it is often used as a substitute), cinnamon, and almonds. The dark, wrinkled beans may be purchased online or from well-stocked spice shops.

Vanilla and Vanillin One of our most beloved spices and second only to saffron in price, vanilla beans are the fermented and dried fruits of orchids native to Central America but now also grown in Madagascar, Indonesia, and elsewhere. The rich, intense aroma of fermented vanilla beans is unmistakable: creamy, balsamic, and sweet, with hints of soft leather and tobacco. Used in cocktails and products such as Kahlúa, Galliano, Tuaca, flavored vodkas, and numerous cordials. Vanillin seems as if it should be pronounced "va-NILL-in" but it's "VAN-ill-in." This phenolic aldehyde is the primary constituent of vanilla extract (other than alcohol). It is also found in wines, vinegars, and spirits that have been properly aged in toasted or charred oak barrels. It is sometimes added in small quantities to help rapidly "age" counterfeit spirits.

Vinegar is a mild solution (often 3-5%) of acetic acid. It is called for in some synthetic whiskeys and brandies, but reached wide popularity as a souring agent in drinks such as switchel and some shrubs.

Violet The ephemeral, transient aroma of *Viola odorata* is due to ionone, a chemical that temporarily blocks our ability to smell it once we've encountered the smell, despite the fact that the smell is still present—simply not for those who have just smelled it. The effect: the dry, floral scent and flavor comes on, then disappears. A few moments later, it comes rushing back, new attacks every few moments.

Wintergreen Oil of wintergreen, distilled from the leaves of low North American bushes, gives a bracing, minty, vaguely medicinal flavor to cordials and some counterfeit spirits. It may also be made from some species of birch trees and other unrelated species that produce methyl salicylate.

Woodruff, Sweet see page 182

Wormwood is a broad term that may refer to any species in the *Artemisia* genus, but *A. absinthium*—also called grand or common wormwood—is the definitive ingredient for making absinthe. *A. pontica* (Roman or petite wormwood), is often used as a colorant for absinthe as well. Several other species of these strongly bitter plants are used in spirits, absinthes, cordials, wines, and vermouths. Génépi, a related term, comprises several Artemisia species, including *A. genipi. A. rupestris,* and *A. umbelliformis.* Génépi grows in mountainous areas of Spain, France, Switzerland and Italy. The term may also refer to bitter liqueurs made from such species.

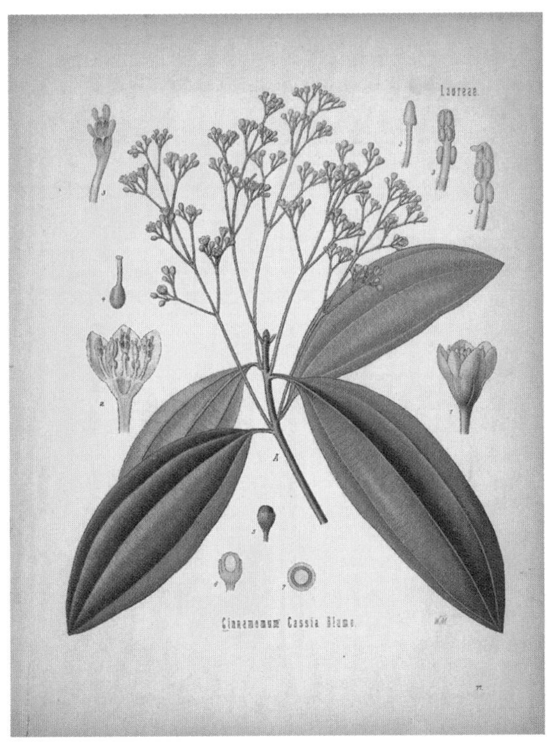

Bibliography

Baker, Charles H. Jr. *The Gentleman's Companion*. New York: Derrydale Press, 1939.

De Brevans, J. *The Manufacture of Liquor and Preserves*, translated from the 1890 French edition. New York: Munn & Co., 1893.

Brock, William H. *Justus von Liebig: The Chemical Gatekeeper*. Cambridge, UK: Cambridge University Press, 1997.

Burdock, George A. *Fenaroli's Handbook of Flavor Ingredients*, 6th ed. Boca Raton, FL: CRC Press, 2010.

Clarke, Paul. *The Cocktail Chronicles: Navigating the Cocktail Renaissance with Jigger, Shaker & Glass*. Nashville: Spring House Press, 2015.

Craddock, Harry. *The Savoy Cocktail Book*. New York: Richard R. Smith, 1930.

Cuming, Fortescue. *Sketches of a Tour to the Western Country*. Pittsburgh: Cramer, Spear, and Eichbaum, 1810.

Daly, Tim. *Daly's Bartenders' Encyclopedia*. Worcester, MA: Tim Daly, 1903.

Davis, Marni. *Jews and Booze: Becoming American in the Age of Prohibition*. New York: NYU Press, 2012.

Delahaye, Marie-Claude. *Pernod: Creator of Absinthe*. Auvers-sur-Oise, France: Musée de l'Absinthe Auvers-sur-Oise, 2008.

Duplais, Pierre. *A Treatise on the Manufacture and Distillation of Alcoholic Liquors*. Translated and edited from the French by M. McKennie, MD. Philadelphia: H. C. Baird & Company, 1871.

Embury, David. *The Fine Art of Mixing Drinks*. New York: Doubleday, 1948.

Fleischman, Joseph. *The Art of Blending and Compounding Liquors and Wines*. New York: Dick and Fitzgerald, 1885.

Furia, T. E., and N. Bellanca. *Fenaroli's Handbook of Flavour Ingredients*, vol. 2. Cleveland, OH: CRC Press, 1975.

Gardner, John. *The Brewer, Distiller, and Wine Manufacturer*. London: J. & A. Churchill, 1902.

Göttler, Hans. *Rezeptbuch für Destillateure*. Neustadt, Germany: Meininger, ca. 1908.

Hager, Hermann et al. *Hagers Handbuch der Pharmazeutischen Praxis: Für Apotheker, Ärzte, Drogisten und Medizenalbeamte*, vol. 1. Berlin: Springer, 1925.

Hahn, Eduard, and Johann Holfert. *Spezialitäten und Geheimmittel: Ihre Herkunft und Zusammensetzung*. Berlin: Springer, 1906.

Hassall, Arthur Hill. *Food and Its Adulterations: Comprising the Reports of the Analytical Sanitary Commission of The Lancet*. London: Longman, Brown, Green, and Longmans, 1855.

Herstein, Karl M., and Thomas C. Gregory. *Chemistry and Technology of Wines and Liquors*. New York: D. Van Nostrand Company, 1935.

Hiscox, Gardner D. *Henley's Twentieth Century Formulas, Recipes and Processes*. New York: Norman W. Henley Publishing Company, 1914.

Johnson, Eli. *Drinks from Drugs or the Magic Box: A Startling Exposure of the Tricks of the Liquor Traffic*. Chicago: The Revolution Temperance Publishing House, 1881.

Krönlein, Hans. *Das Getränkbuch*. Nordhausen am Harz, Germany: Heinrich Killinger Verlagsgesellschaft, 1938.

Lacour, Pierre. *The Manufacture of Liquors, Wines, and Cordials without the Aid of Distillation. Also the Manufacture of Effervescing Beverages and Syrups, Vinegar and Bitters*. New York: Dick and Fitzgerald, 1853.

Loftus, William R. *Loftus's New Mixing and Reducing Book for Publicans and Spirit Dealers and Retailers in General*. London, 1869.

Mahoney, Charles S. *The Hoffman House Bartender's Guide: How to Open a Saloon and Make It Pay*. New York: R. K. Fox, 1905.

McElhone, Harry. *Barflies and Cocktails*. Paris: Lecram Press, 1927.

M'Harry, Samuel. *The Practical Distiller*. Harrisburgh [sic], PA: John Wyeth, 1809.

Mickler, Ernest Matthew. *White Trash Cooking*. Berkeley, CA: Ten Speed Press: 1986.

Miller, Amy Bess, and Persis Fuller. *The Best of Shaker Cooking*. New York: Collier Books, 1985.

Moens, Henri, and Hubert Verburgt. *De Schat der Likeuristen: of Volledige Handleiding om Zonder Distilleerketels en Zonder Forneizen Alle Soorten van Uitmuntende Likeuren te Bereiden*. Ghent, Belgium: De Busscher en zoon, 1869.

Morgenthaler, Jeffrey. *The Bar Book: Elements of Cocktail Technique*. San Francisco: Chronicle Books, 2014.

Pereira, Jonathan. *The Physician's Prescription Book*. Philadelphia: Lindsay and Blakiston, 1852.

The Picayune. The Picayune's Creole Cook Book, 4th ed. New Orleans, 1910.

Prudhomme, Paul. *The Prudhomme Family Cookbook: Old-Time Louisiana Recipes by the Eleven Prudhomme Brothers and Sisters*. New York: William Morrow and Company, 1987.

Schmidt, William. *The Flowing Bowl: What and When to Drink*. New York: Charles L. Webster & Co., 1891.

Shannon, Richard. *A Practical Treatise on Brewing, Distilling, and Rectification*. London, 1805.

Simmonds, Charles. *Alcohol, Its Production, Properties, Chemistry, and Industrial Applications*. London: Macmillan and Co., 1919.

Smyth, William A. *The Publican's Guide Or Key to the Distill-House*. London, 1781.

Spinoza, Baruch. *Tractatus Politicus*, 1677.

Thomas, Jerry. *Bar-Tender's Guide*. New York: Dick & Fitzgerald, 1862.

Tolzmann, Don Heinrich. *Images of America: German Cincinnati*. Charleston, SC: Arcadia Publishing, 2005.

Tovey, Charles. *British & Foreign Spirits: Their History, Manufacture, Properties, Etc.* London: Whittaker & Company, 1864.

Turner, Jack. *Spice: The History of a Temptation*. New York: Alfred A. Knopf, 2004.

Tydings, Millard E. *Before and After Prohibition*. New York: Macmillan, 1930.

Ure, Andrew. *Dictionary of Arts, Manufactures, and Mines*. London: Longmans, Green, and Company, 1837.

Vasey, S. Archibald. *Guide to the Analysis of Potable Spirits*. London: Bailliere, Tindall & Cox, 1904.

Viereck, George Sylvester. *The Works of George Sylvester Viereck: The Candle and the Flame*. New York: Moffat, Yard and Company, 1912.

Walter, Eric. *Manual for the Essence Industry*. New York: John Wiley and Sons (1916).

Weiss, Harry B. *The History of Applejack or Apple Brandy in New Jersey from Colonial Times to the Present*. Trenton: New Jersey Agricultural Society, 1954.

Wilcox, R. W. *Materia Medica and Pharmacy*. Philadelphia: P. Blakiston's Son & Co., 1907.

Wiley, Harvey Washington. *Beverages and Their Adulteration*. Philadelphia: P. Blakiston's Son & Co., 1919.

Wondrich, David. *Imbibe!: From Absinthe Cocktail to Whiskey Smash, a Salute in Stories and Drinks to "Professor" Jerry Thomas, Pioneer of the American Bar Featuring the Original Formulae*. New York: Perigee, 2007.

———. *Punch: The Delights (and Dangers) of the Flowing Bowl: An Anecdotal History of the Original Monarch of Mixed Drinks, with More Than Forty Historic Recipes*. New York: Perigee, 2010.

Wright, Helen Saunders. *Old-Time Recipes for Home Made Wines, Cordials, and Liqueurs from Fruits, Flowers, Vegetables, and Shrubs*. Boston: Page Company, 1922.

Endnotes

1 Heywood Broun, "Books," *New York Tribune*, July 14, 1919, 8.

2 "Books: Self-Astounder," *Time*, May 11, 1931.

3 Otis Notman, "Viereck, Hohenzollern? Is New York's Romantic Poet a Grandson of Kaiser Wilhelm the Great?" *New York Times*, June 29, 1907.

4 *New-York Tribune*, July 17, 1918, 4.

5 "Viereck Expelled by Authors' League," *New York Times*, 26 July 26, 1918.

6 *New York Tribune*, August 16, 1918, 12.

7 Chronology: The Germans in America, accessed May 9, 2014, http://www.loc.gov/rr/european/imde/germchro.html.

8 Don Heinrich Tolzmann, *Images of America: German Cincinnati* (Charleston, SC: Arcadia Publishing, 2005), 111.

9 Nicholas J. C. Pistor, "Pershing or Berlin? A St. Louis Street Name Debate," *St. Louis Post-Dispatch*, February 3, 2014.

10 C. Wilcox, "World War I and the Attack on Professors of German at the University of Michigan," *History of Education Quarterly* 33, no. 1 (1993): 60–84.

11 "Negro Editor Arrested," *Washington Post*, January 17, 1920, 3.

12 "Treatises on Liquor Making Barred from Shelves of Libraries," *Pittsburgh Post-Gazette*, January 16, 1920, 4.

13 "Bootlegger's Patron Called Prize Freak: Flare-up in the Senate," *Alabama Anniston Star*, January 17, 1926, 1.

14 *Mass Moments* (blog), accessed February 1, 2015, http://www.massmoments.org/moment.cfm?mid=326, accessed February 1, 2015.

15 "Famous 'Booze' Sermon," Billy Sunday Online, accessed February 1, 2015, http://www.billysunday.org/sermons/booze.php3, accessed February 1, 2015.

16 "Dry Czar Favors Sale of Beer as Enforcement Aid," *Olean (NY) Times Herald*, April 14, 1926, 1.

17 Charles Norris, "Our Essay in Extermination," *The North American Review* 1928: 645-652.

18 "The New Alcohol Formula 39-B," *American Perfumer and Essential Oil Review*, October 1921: 328.

19 "Drinks for Drys," *Time*, April 8, 1929.

20 "Kings County Society," *Practical Druggist*, June 1922, 40.

21 "Enforcing the Prohibition Law," City Club Bulletin 13, no. 38, September 20, 1920.

22 Jonathan Pereira, *The Physician's Prescription Book* (Philadelphia: Lindsay and Blakiston, 1852), 86.

23 William A. Smyth, *The Publican's Guide or Key to the Distill-House* (London, 1781).

24 William R. Loftus, *Loftus's New Mixing and Reducing Book for Publicans and Spirit Dealers and Retailers in General* (London, 1869).

25 Wöhler und von Liebig, *"Untersuchungen über das Radikal der Benzoesäure," Annalen der Pharmacie* 3 (1832): 249–82.

26 B. B. Petrovska, "Historical Review of Medicinal Plants' Usage," *Pharmacognosy Reviews*, 6, no. 11 (2012): 1–5.

27 George A. Burdock, *Fenaroli's Handbook of Flavor Ingredients*, 6th edition, (Boca Raton, FL: CRC Press, 2010), 1566.

28 E. W. Bovill, "The Essential Oil Market," *Journal of the Royal African Society* 33, no. 132 (July 1934): 217–25.

29 Glenn Sonnedecker, "How to Adulterate Volatile Oils: A Pre-1906 Manuscript Formulary," *Pharmacy in History* 32, no. 4 (1990): 155–65.

30 "Repeal of Prohibition in Practical Effect in N.Y.," *San Bernardino (CA) County Sun*, October 14, 1933, 3.

31 "Customs Officers Hold Up Shipment of German Lamps," *Wilmington (OH) News-Journal*, May 12, 1922, 1.

32 John Gardner, *The Brewer, Distiller, and Wine Manufacturer* (London: J. & A. Churchill, 1902).

33 Mark H. Haller, "Philadelphia Bootlegging and the Report of the Special August Grand Jury," *Pennsylvania Magazine of History and Biography* April (1985), 215–32.

34 Harvey Washington Wiley, *Beverages and Their*

Adulteration (Philadelphia: P. Blakiston's Son & Co., 1919), 374.

35 "Quart of Whiskey, Gallon of Rum Equals Bootleg Havana Scotch," *Kansas Hutchinson News*, December 30, 1924.

36 William Kitchiner, *The Cook's Oracle; and Housekeeper's Manual*, 7th ed. (New York: J. & J. Harper, 1830).

37 A. Paine and A. D. Davan, "Defining a Tolerable Concentration of Methanol in Alcoholic Drinks," *Human & Experimental Toxicology* 20, no. 11 (November 2001): 563–68.

38 Charles Norris, "Our Essay in Extermination," *North American Review* 226, no. 6 (1928): 646.

39 See, for instance, A. Wood and F. Buller, "Poisoning by Wood Alcohol: Cases of Death and Blindness from Columbian Spirits and Other Methylated Preparations," *JAMA* 43 (1904): 972.

40 Charles Norris, "Our Essay in Extermination," *North American Review* 226, no. 6 (1928): 652.

41 Eduard Hahn and Johann Holfert, *Spezialitäten und Geheimmittel: Ihre Herkunft und Zusammensetzung* (Berlin, Germany: Springer, 1906).

42 Vice-Consul R.S. Warburton, "Reports on Frauds in the Brandy Trade, France," from bulletin issued by Victoria Department of Agriculture, 1888, 168–69.

43 National Prohibition Act, Title II, section 29.

44 "Gives Law on Cider," *Coffeyville (KS) Daily Journal*, December 4, 1920, 7.

45 "Take One with Me," *Pittsburgh Dispatch* [sic], July 28, 1889, 15.

46 "Raiders Steal 45 Barrels of Real Port Wine," *Carbondale (IL) Daily Free Press*, February 10, 1925.

47 Marni Davis, *Jews and Booze: Becoming American in the Age of Prohibition* (New York: NYU Press, 2012), 163.

48 "Cider Can Be Dealcoholized," *Practical Druggist*, December 1920, 39.

49 Stephan A. Padosch et al., (2006) "Absinthism: A Fictitious 19th Century Syndrome with Present Impact," *Substance Abuse Treatment, Prevention, and Policy* (2006): 1:14.

50 Marie-Claude Delahaye, *Pernod: Creator of Absinthe* (Musée de l'Absinthe Auvers-sur-Oise, 2008), 103.

51 Richard Shannon, *A Practical Treatise on Brewing, Distilling, and Rectification* (London, 1805).

52 Elke Scholten et al., "The Life of an Anise-Flavored Alcoholic Beverage: Does Its Stability Cloud or Confirm Theory?" *Langmuir* 24, no. 5 (2008), 1701–6.

53 See, for instance, Stanley Clisby Arthur, *Famous New Orleans Drinks and How to Mix 'Em* (New Orleans: Harmanson, 1937).

54 Jeffrey Morgenthaler, *The Bar Book: Elements of Cocktail Technique*, (Chronicle Books: San Francisco, 2014.

55 Charles S. Mahoney, *The Hoffman House Bartender's Guide How to Open a Saloon and Make It Pay*. (New York: RK Fox, New York (1905), 224.

56 Hans Göttler, Hans *Rezeptbuch für Destillateure*,. Neustadt, Germany: Meininger, (ca. 1908) Neustadt.

57 William Schmidt, *The Flowing Bowl: What and When to Drink* (New York: Charles L. Webster & Co., 1891), 196–97.

58 *The New Orleans Picayune, The Picayune's Creole Cook Book*, 4th ed. (New Orleans, 1910), 328.

59 Tim Daly, *Daly's Bartenders' Encyclopedia* (Worcester, MA: published by author, 1903), 113.

60 Paul Clarke, "60/30, #5&6: Epicurean and the Allies Cocktail," *The Cocktail Chronicles* (blog), November 25, 2010, http://www.cocktailchronicles.com/2010/11/25/6030-epicurean-and-the-allies-cocktail/.

61 *Pennsylvania Gazette*, January 10, 1771.

62 *Public Advertiser* (London), June 4, 1790, 4.

63 *Scientific American*: Supplement 35, no. 892 (1893): 14250.

64 Amy Bess Miller and Persis Fuller, *The Best of Shaker Cooking* (New York Collier Books, 1985), 413.

65 Such as R. W. Wilcox, *Materia Medica and Pharmacy* (Philadelphia: P. Blakiston's Son & Co., 1907), 19.

66 T. E. Furia and N. Bellanca, *Fenaroli's Handbook of Flavour Ingredients*, vol. 2 (Boca Raton, FL: CRC Press, 1975).

Index

Tables in the text are indicated in *italics*.

A

absinthe
  essence recipe, 125
  grades of, 142–43
  history of, xxi, 5, 8, 131
  as ingredient, 134–35
  louche form of, 129
  medicinal qualities of, 8, 124, 129
  overview of, 124, 126–28
  recipe for, 130
  serving method, 132
  styles of, 127
absinthe onion garnish, 135
Absinthe Onions, 135
Absinthe Suissesse, 134
"Absinthism: a Fictitious 19th Century Syndrome with Present Impact" (Padosch), 122
absinthium oil, 129
Acetic acid, 101
Acetic either, 86
Acetic ether, 113, 117
Actual Woodruff Essence, 183
adulteration, 30, 45–46, 67–68, 82, 127
aged syrups, 100, 146
Alamagoozlum, 65
allspice berries, 163
almond oil, 24–25, 46, 121, 167
American Journal of Pharmacy, 88
American proof measurement, 202
Amyl alcohol, 86
Anderson, Edwin P., 1
Andrews, Lincoln C., 111
añejo Havana Club rum, 76
angelica oil, 167
angelica root, 127, 130
Angostura bitters, 65–66, 104, 157, 161, 172
anise, 126–27, *127*, 165–69
  See also star anise
aniseed, Green, 168
anise oil, 86, 125, 130, 151, 167, 169
  See also star anise oil
anise seed, 42, 130, 139, 148
anisette cordials, 123, 142, 158, 165–69
Anisette de Bordeaux (1910), 168
Anisette de Hollande (1869), 167
apothecaries' weights and measures, 193–98
apple brandy, 109–11, 155
applejack, 107–10
Appleton rum, 74, 78
apple whiskey, 110
Après Souper (1891), 180
aromatherapy, 40, 43, 195
aromatic bitters, 60, 109
aromatic compounds, 21, 35, 39, 42, 48, 85, 145–46, 194–95
Around the World with Jigger, Beaker, and Flask (Baker), 65
arracks, 76–78
Arrakessenz formula, 77
Artificial Woodruff Essence, 182
The Art of Blending and Compounding Liquors and Wines (Fleischman), 2, 20, 71
astringency, 99, 121, 139
avoirdupois weight, 193, 198

B

"bain-marie" (waterbath), 168
Baker, Charles H., Jr., 65, 66, 110, 177
Balls Deep (Hot Cinnamon Liqueur), 162, 165
balsams, 35
Bamford, John, 158
The Bar Book (Morgenthaler), 36
Barclay, Armiger, 113
Barflies and Cocktails (McElhone), 104
Barleycorn, John, xxi
bar measures, 201
Bar-Tender's Guide (Thomas), 32
bartending manuals, 36

Batavia Arrack, 78
bathtub gin, 55–7
beading oil (The Doctor), xv, 24
beer, xxi, 13, 105
Bee's Knees, 61
benzaldehyde, 161
Berry, Jeff, 76
Beverages and Their Adulteration (Wiley), 82
Bittermens Hellfire Habanero Shrub, 162
bitters
  Angostura, 65–66, 104, 157, 161, 172
  aromatic, 60, 109
  Hostetter(ish) Bitters, 139
  overview of, 136–38
blackberry liqueur, 154
Black Ceylon Tea, 99
black market, 53, 59
Blank, Fritz, xii–xiv, 192
blender (gear), 36
blood orange, 84, 135
Boardwalk Empire (HBO), 118
boiled cider, 103
boise extract, 95, 99–100, 102, 121
The Book of Receipts (1907), 192
bootleggers, 2, 13–14, 39, 83, 88
"Bootleg Liquor" (Doran), 8
booze cherry, 76
The Bordeaux Wine and Liquor Dealers' Guide (1857), 92
bottle brush, 36
The Bottlers' Formulary (1910), 35
Bottoms Up! (Saucier), 59
Bovill, E.W., 45
brandied cherry, 75
brandy
  apple, 109–11, 155
  Brandy Fix, 104
  caraway flavored, 147–48
  cherry flavored, 104
  Cognac, 95, 103–4, 150, 155, 157
  essence of, 86–87
  ginger flavored, 170–73
  Harvard Cocktail, 104
  history of, 93–99, 120–21
  as ingredient, 74, 170, 172, 178, 180–81, 183, 189
  Sidecar, 103
  vinegar in, 101
Brandy Essence, 87
Brandy Fix, 104
brazil wood, 175
Brevans, J. de, 168
The Brewer, Distiller, and Wine Manufacturer (Gardner), 63
British & Foreign Spirits: Their History, Manufacture, Properties, Etc. (Tovey), 95
British Pharmacopoeia (1864), 33, 192
British proof measurement, 202
Brix refractometer, 38
Brock, William H., 28
Brooklyn College of Pharmacy, 16
Büchner filter, 38, 139
butyric ether, 69

C

cade oil, 40
calamus root, 45, 130
Campari, 60
The Candle and the Flame (Viereck), xiv, xix
capsicum, 89–91, 174–75
caramel, 30, 68–69, 79–82, 99–102, 117, 120–21
Caramel for Coloring, 79
Caraway Brandy, 148
caraway oil, 120, 153–54, 157, 165
caraway seeds, 8
Caraway Vodka, 150
carboys, 55
cardamom, 57, 78, 160
Cartier scale, 203–4
carvol/carvone, 154
cassia, 68–69, 129, 158–160
Cate, Martin, 118
Central Press (newspaper), 62
centrifuges, 42
Chartreuse, green or yellow, 59, 65, 155
cheat formulas, 24, 35
cherry brandy, 104
cherry garnish, 75–76
Chicago Defender (newspaper), 17
Chief Gowanus New Netherland Gin, 62
"chipped" whiskey, 83
cider
  boiled, 103
  Cider Champagne, 107, 109
  Cider Sherry Flip, 109
  Cider Without Apples, 107
  hard cider, 10, 51, 109, 114, 116
  history of, 105
  oil of, 50–51, 107
  The Stone Fence, 109
Cider Champagne, 107, 109
cider oil, 50–51, 107
Cider Sherry Flip, 109
Cider Without Apples, 107
cinchona, 136, 139
cinnamon
  Balls Deep (Hot Cinnamon Liqueur), 162, 165
  Cinnamon Fizz, 165
  cordials, 82, 138, 158–165
  Helen Saunders Wright's Cinnamon Cordial, 160

cinnamon (*continued*)
oil of, 43, 129
sticks, 84, 109, 163
Cinnamon Fizz, 165
citrus oils, 40–42
citrus zest garnish, 103
City Club (Chicago), 17–18
Claret Wine, 114
Clarke, Paul, 32, 157
clove oil, 82, 129, 161, 165
cloves, 84, 109, 114, 148, 162–63, 189
club soda, 104, 161
The Cocktail Chronicles (Clarke), 32, 157
cocktail guides, 1, 30, 32
cocktails
absinthe, 126–27
brandy, 102–4
egg based, 144
foam for, 24
gin, 59–61
and overproof alcohol, 201
rum, 75, 78–79
and syrups, 147
Zeeland, 119
Cocktails—How to Mix Them (Vermeire), 181
Cognac brandy, 95, 103–4, 150, 155, 157
Cognac Charente Type, 99
cognac oil, 30, 81, 82, 121
Cognac syrups, 100
Cointreau, 60, 103
Cointreau Noir, 74
Cold-Compounded Triple Sec, 188
cold pressing, of oils, 42
The Collins, 66
colorants, 69, 80, 145, 175
Comic Con, 162
compounded gin, 55–57
compounder's syrup, 103, 145, 161, 167, 173, 177, 183, 189
compounding formularies, 30, 34–35
compounding manuals, 19, 38, 71, 82, 89, 157, 194
Compound Liqueur Oil French Absinthe, 129
condensers, distillery, 28
The Cook's Oracle (Kitchiner), 78
Copper Distilled Bourbon, 81
Cordial Liquor of Danzig Comp Oil, 165–66
cordials
caraway flavored, 147–157
chile flavored, 156
cinnamon flavored, 82, 138, 158–165
coloring of, 174
Cordial Liquor of Danzig Comp Oil, 165–66
Crème de Menthe, 176–77
DIY Orange Cordial, 189
ginger flavored, 170
history of, 141
iced, 153
Mike McCaw's Triple Sec, 188
Mint and Gum, 177
mint flavored, 175–78
nalewka essence, 161
orange flavored, 184–89
production method, 142–43
Shaker Peppermint Cordial, 178
syrups for, 144–45
Cordus, Valerius, 33
coriander, 127, 129, 139, 168
counterfeit alcohol, 2, 8, 11–13, 55, 67–68, 83, 95, 114, 121, 123
counterfeit prescriptions, 16–17
Craddock, Harry, 32
The Craft of Gin (Smith), 64
Crème de Menthe, 176–77
crème de menthe
and essential oils, 35, 123, 175
as ingredient, 134, 178, 180, 181
medicinal qualities of, 8
smuggling of, 14
Cuba Libre, 66
Cuming, Fortescue, 107
curaçao, 65, 71, 76, 118, 141, 184, 185
curiosities, 25
Cymar (lab supply firm), 38
daiquiris, 75

D

Dalrymple, Alfred V., 17–18
Daly, Tim, 155
Davis, Marni, 112
Death in the Gulf Stream, 66
Death's Door White Whiskey, 80
Delahaye, Marie-Claude, 126
De Materia Medica (Dioscorides), 32
Demerara, 80, 143
denatured industrial alcohol, 13, 88
De Schat der Likeuristen (Moens and Verburgt), 167
Detroit Athletic Club, 59
Dietsch, Michael, 71
Dioscorides, 32
Dispensatorium Pharmacopolarum (Cordus), 33
distilling
and absinthe, 126
of apple spirits, 110
of essential oils, 22, 39, 41–42
of gin, 57
history of, 34–35, 69, 93
home, 4–5, 9, 13, 38, 48, 168

and industry standards, 142
manuals, 6, 93, 127, 143, 203
in prisons, 6
of rum, 67
DIY Orange Cordial, 189
DIY Summer Cup, 118
The Doctor (beading oil), xv, 24
doctored drinks, 2, 24
Dolin Vermouth de Chambéry, 76
Doran, J.M., 8
Dr. Furnish, 172
dried sour cherries, 84
druggists, 15–18, 30, 33–34, 193–95
The Druggists' Circular (1913), 151
druggists' manuals, 8, 125
drugstore whiskey
See medicinal alcohol
Dubonnet Cocktail, 59
Duplais, Pierre, 127, 143, 167, 203
"Dutch" anisette, 167
Dutch gin
See genever

E

egg drinks, 24, 65, 134, 144–45, 165
18th Amendment, 3–5, 9–10
Einstein, Izzy, 112
El Dorado rum, 74, 78
electromagnetic stirrer, 37
Ellestad, Erik, 78
El Presidente, 75, 76
Embury, David, 111, 157
enfleurage, 42
Epicurean, 157
Erlenmeyer flasks, 37
essence
of absinthe, 125
brandy, 86–87
of cordials, 161
defined, 48
formulas, 68–69
Jamaican Ginger, 170, 173
rum, 48, 67–68, 158
violet, 125
of wine, 117, 184
woodruff, 182–83
essential oils
and absinthe, 125, 129
adulteration of, 45–47
affecting spirit grades, 142
buying and storing of, 48–49
and cordials, 151, 153–54, 158–160, 167
and crème de menthe, 35, 123, 175
defined, 39–41
distilling of, 22, 39, 41–42
and flavor, 21
fragrant taint, 47
and gin, 55, 57, 64
history of, 29
medicinal qualities of, 8
and necessary gear, 36–38
and orange flavored recipes, 187
and poisoned liquor, 85
and rum, 67, 74
safety of, 43–45
and syrups, 144–46
weights and measures, 194–96
Evan Williams bourbon, 162
Expatriate (bar), 154

F

fake alcohol
See counterfeit alcohol
Farber, Dan, 100
Fatherland (ed. Viereck), xx
FDA (Food and Drug Administration), 44–45
Fenaroli's Handbook fo Flavor Ingredients, 204
fennel oil, 125–27, 127, 129, 150–51, 165–68
Fernet Branca, 181
Ferrand dry orange curaçao, 74
filtering medium, 37
The Fine Art of Mixing Drinks (Embury), 111, 157
flasks, 37
flavor, defined, 27
Flavor & Extract Manufacturers Association, 45
flavored whiskey, 82
Fleischman, Joseph, 2, 20, 71
flips, 109
flower waters, 42
The Flowing Bowl (Schmidt), 155, 180
foamy spirits, 24
Fogarty, Frank, 59
folk distilling
See moonshine
"Food Flavors: Benefits and Problems" (Hall), 27
formic ether, 68–69, 77
formula, defined, 22
Formula 39-B, 14
fragrant taint, 47
French 75, 66
French Absinthe, 129
French proof measurement, 202–3
fresh fruit garnish, 104, 118
Fritzsche Bros., 81–82
Front Porch Lemonade, 80
funnels, 37
Furnish, Tim, 172

G

galangal oil, 74
galls, 99, 121
garnishes
absinthe onions, 135
cherry, 75–76
citrus zest, 103
fresh fruit, 104, 118
lemon twist, 59, 74, 104
lime, 74, 154

garnishes (*continued*)
- mint, 74, 80, 118, 181
- orange, 60, 165
- sunflower petal, 74

Gaudin, Lucien, 60
Gay-Lussac, Joseph-Louis, 202
gear, 36–38
genever, 63–66
gentian, 136, 139
The Gentleman's Companion (Baker), 66, 110, 177
Germain-Robin, Hubert, 95, 99, 100
German-Americans, xx–xxii, 147
Das Getränkbuch (Krönlein), 183
Gettler, Alexander, 88
gin
- Bee's Knees, 61
- Chief Gowanus New Netherland Gin, 62
- compounded, 55–57
- Dubonnet Cocktail, 59
- and essential oils, 55, 57, 64
- "Holland" gin, 19, 62–63, 66
- homemade (bathtub), 55
- as ingredient, 59–61, 118, 135
- The Last Word Cocktail, 59
- London dry, 62, 66
- Lucien Gaudin, 60
- medicinal qualities of, 8
- Old Tom, 57, 66
- Southside, 60
- specific types of, 57

ginger beer, 118, 161, 170
ginger brandy, 170–73
ginger oil, 42–43
Ginger Wine with Cochineal, 174–75
Givaudan, 82
glass bottles, 36
gomme syrup, 65, 177
Göttler, H., 194
graduated cylinder, 38
grain schnapps, 91
grains of paradise, 89–91
grams, 194
grapefruit oil, 188
GRAS: Generally Recognized as Safe, 44–45
grenadine, 74–76, 85, 111, 135
Grier, Jacob, 154
grinders, spice or coffee, 36
Guide to the Analysis of Potable Spirits (Vasey), 39
Gum kino, 139
gum syrup, 147, 177, 180

H

Hagers Handbuch der Pharmazeutischen Praxis (Hager), 125
Haigh, Ted "Dr. Cocktail," 47
half-and-half, 134, 181
Hall, R.L., 27
hard cider, 10, 51, 109
Harry's Bar, 104
Harvard Cocktail, 104
Havana, Cuba, 75
Helen Saunders Wright's Cinnamon Cordial, 160
Hemingway, Ernest, 66
Henley's May Wine Essence, 184
Henley's Twentieth Century Formulas, Recipes and Processes (Hiscox), 184
Here's How! (cocktail booklet), 163
Herrengedeck, 89
high-proof alcohol, 39, 41, 167
Hiscox, Garner D., 184
The History of Applejack (Weiss), 109–10
The Hoffmann House Bartender's Guide (Mahoney), 160
Holcomb, Wynn, 104
Holland gin, 19, 62, 63, 66
Hollands
- *See* genever

home brewing, 13, 105
home distilling, 4–5, 9, 13, 38, 48, 168
honey syrup, 61
hops, 107
horehound candy, 84
horseradish, 116
Hostetter, Jacob, 136
Hostetter(ish) Bitters, 139
Hotel Nacional Special, 75
hydrosals, 42
hyper critical carbon dioxide extraction, 42
Hyson Tea, 168
hyssop, 127

I

Ice Caraway/Kümmel/Liquor, 147, 152–53
illegal sources of alcohol, 13–14
Imbibe! (Wondrich), 200
Imbibe magazine, 157
imported spirits, 5
Industrial Alcohol and Chemical Division of the Prohibition Unit, 8
International Fragrance Association, 44
International Organization of the Flavor Industry, 45
intoxicating beverages, 9, 13–14
Italian vermouth, 76, 104
Italian Vineyard Company, 112

J

The Jack Rose, 111
Jamaica Ginger essence, 170, 173
Jamaican rum, 65, 119
Jeff Morgenthaler's Blended Grasshopper, 181

jenever
See genever
Jersey Lightning, 110
Johnson, Eli, 28–29
Journal of the National Medical Association, 8
The Judge, 180
juniper berries, 21, 42, 46, 55, 57, 63–64
juniper oil, 8, 30, 59
Justus von Liebig: The Chemical Gatekeeper (Brock), 28

K

Kings County Pharmaceutical Society, 16
kirschwasser, 104, 150
kitchen measures equivalents, 201
kitchen scale, 37, 194
Kitchiner, William, 78
Klus, Tommy, 156
Korn, 89–90
Kornschärfe, 90–91
Kramer, John, 105
Krönlein, Hans, 183
kümmel, 119, 142, 147–157
The Kümmel Fizz, 154
Kümmel formula, 151
Kümmellikör, 120, 157

L

Lacour, Pierre, 103, 145
Laird & Company, 110
Laird's 100-proof apple brandy, 155
Lanizèt: Sour Mash Cajun Anisette, 169
The Last Word Cocktail, 59
Latin names, 18–19, 33–34, 193
Lazar, Michael, 74
legal sources of alcohol, 9–13
lemon juice, 60–61, 66, 71, 74, 80, 85, 103, 161, 165, 172
lemon oil, 188
lemon twist garnish, 59, 74, 104
Leopold Bros., 141
Licor 43 cordial, 162
Liebig, Justus von, 28–29
lime garnish, 74, 154
lime juice, 59, 71, 74, 111, 154, 180
lime oil, 66, 75
Lime Simple Syrup, 74–75
lime wheel, 74
liqueur ratios for cordials, 143
"local options" laws, 119
Loeb, Katie, 162
Loftus, William, 24, 101
Loftus's New Mixing and Reducing Book (Loftus), 101
loopholes, legal, 2, 4, 9, 10, 15–16, 112
Los Angeles Times (newspaper), 85
Lost Spirits Cuban-style rum, 71
louche form, in absinthe, 129
Louisville Courier-Journal, xviii
lower-proof alcohol, 13, 21, 39, 41
Low Grade Artificial Rum, 69
Lucien Gaudin, 60
Lyon, Victor A.
absinthe recipes, 123–25
anise cordial recipe, 165
Arrakessenz, 77
background of, xv–xx, 8
and beading recipes, 24
brandy essence, 86
brandy recipes, 102
cider recipes, 105–7
cinnamon flavored cordials, 159
Crème de Menthe recipe, 176–77
and garnishes, 135
Ginger Brandy recipes, 170–73
gin recipes, 57
and ingredient safety, 44
Kornschärfe, 90
kümmel, 148
and methyl alcohol, 85
mint flavored cordials, 175–76
and moonshine, 53
nalewka cordials, 161
notebook of, 1, 6, 21–22, 30, 53
oak in recipes, 99
orange flavored recipes, 184
and poisoned liquor, 85–88
Port Wine Essence, 117
Port Wine recipe, 114
Rumessenz, 68
rum recipes, 67
shrub recipes, 71, 118
syrup recipes, 100
whiskey recipes, 81
woodruff essence, 182

M

mace oil, 165
maceration
of absinthe, 130
and anisettes, 168
and arrack, 77–78
of ginger flavored drinks, 170–73
of mint flavored drinks, 176
and moonshine, 81
of orange flavored drinks, 187
and rum, 68, 71
and vodka, 150
and whiskey, 84
Machado, Gerado, 76
mag bar, 37–38
"Magic Box" (Eli Johnson), 28
mai tai, 66
Maitrank, or May Wine, 183
Make at Home Orange Peel Flavoring, 187

malt syrup, 13
Manual for the Essence Industry (Walter), 48
manuals
- bartending, 36
- and cocktail recipes, 167–68
- compounding, 19, 38, 71, 82, 89, 157, 194
- distilling, 6, 93, 127, 143, 203
- and doctored drinks, 2
- druggists,' 8, 125
- and essential oils, 39, 48
- rectifiers,' 34–35, 184
- weights and measures, 22, 142, 193–94, 196, 203

The Manufacture of Liquor and Preserves (de Brevans), 168
The Manufacture of Liquors, Wines, and Cordials without the Aid of Distillation (Lacour), 103, 145
maple syrup, 103
maraschino liqueur, 59, 75, 180
margaritas, 71, 156
Mary Pickford cocktail, 22, 75
mason jars, 36
materia medica, 32
McCaw, Mike, 188
McElhone, Harry, 104
measures and weights, 193–96, 201
measuring cups/spoons, 36–37, 192
measuring devices, 192
medicinal alcohol, 8, 10, 15–18, 32–33, 84, 124, 129, 136–38, 180, 196
melissa (lemon balm), 127
methanol (wood alcohol), 45, 86, 89
Methyl alcohol, 85, 86
metric measures, 193–94
M'Harry, Samuel, 20, 62, 93–95
Michael Lazar's Mai Tai, 74
Michaelson, M. Alfred, 14
Mickler, Ernest Matthew, 169
microliters, 195
microplanes, 37
Mike McCaw's Triple Sec, 188, 204
milk washing, 105
milliliters, 194
mint
- in absinthe, 127
- cordials, 175–78
- as essential oil, 42–43
- as flavoring, 27
- garnish, 74, 80, 118, 181
- as ingredient, 175–181
- leaves of, 60, 176
- Mint and Gum, 177–78
- Shaker Peppermint Cordial, 178
- "spanking" the mint, 40

Mint and Gum, 177–78
missing units, 194
Mission Bell, 156
Mitchell, John, 1
Moens, Henri, 167
mojito, 60
Monkey Gland, 135
moonshine
- and authenticity, 202
- and counterfeit alcohol, 81
- and home distilling, 13, 93
- and Lyon's notebook, 53
- and prisoners, 6
- and spirit foam, 24
- syndicates, 4

Moonshine! (Rowley), xii
Morgan, J. Pierpont, 65
Morgan, William M., 14
Morgenthaler, Jeffrey, 36, 181
morphine, 34
mortar and pestle, 38
Murray, George, 109

N

Nalewka, 161, 165
Nalewka Sour, 161
nanosmuggling, 14
National Bottlers' Gazette, 116
National Medical Association, 15
National Prohibition Act, 3–4, 10, 11–12, 17, 105, 112
- *See also* prohibition; Volstead Act

near beer, 13
Negroni, 60
neutral spirits, 39, 43, 55, 57, 68, 77, 83, 95, 142, 188
New York Distilling Company, 62
New York Public Library, xvii, 1
Nitrous ether, 86, 117
"noble experiment"
- *See* prohibition

Noble Experiment (bar), 162
"non-intoxicating" alcohol, 13
Norris, Charles, 14, 88
notes, in flavor, 27

O

oak barrel whiskey, 83
Oak wood, 99
Old Peach, 103
Old-Time Recipes for Home Made Wines, Cordials, and Liqueurs from Fruits, Flowers, Vegetables, and Shrubs (Wright), 160
Old Tom gin, 57, 66
onions, as garnish, 135
Orange cordial, 189
orange curaçao, 76, 119, 204
Orange Flower Water, 187
orange garnish, 60, 165
orange juice, 71, 85, 135, 172
orange oil, 41
orange peel, 60, 76, 139, 160, 187, 189

Orange Peel Flavoring, 141, 184, 187
orgeat, 74, 134
Ostrander, Ethan, 162
overproof (O.P.) spirits, 43, 201–2

P

Padosch, Stephan A., 122
pale sherry, 109
"parts" ratios, 204
Pearson Square, 50–51
peelers, 37
Pekoe tea, 77
Pelican Saloon, 65
peppercorns, 163
peppermint liqueur, 181
peppermint oil, 8, 35, 45, 153, 165, 175–78
Pharmaceutical Journal and Transactions, 33–34, 148
pharmacists, 15–18, 30, 33–34, 193–95
Pharmacopoeia Londinensis (1611), 82
pharmacopoeias, 30–34, 45
Philadelphia Union Club, 119
Phillips Distilling Company, 178
Picayune Kümmel, 151
Picayune's Creole Cook Book (1910), 151, 168
Pickford, Mary, 22, 75
Pimm's Cup, 118
pineapple juice, 24, 75
pint measurement, 191–92
pipettes/micropipettes, 36, 195
Plain spirits, 67–69
plastics, 36
poisoned liquor, 29, 85–88
pomegranate grenadine, 111
port wine, 114, 184
Port Wine Essence, 117
Potions of the Caribbean (Berry), 76
The Practical Distiller (M'Harry), 20, 62, 93–95
Prater (beer garden), 182
pre-prohibition, xx, 2, 5, 8–9, 33, 110, 147
Prescription Julep, 200
prisons, 6
production method, 86–88, 142
prohibition
  and ciders, 105, 110
  criminality of, 5–6
  geographic borders of, 74–75
  and illegal sources alcohol, 13–14
  and legal sources of alcohol, 9–13
  and Lyon's notebook, 6–8
  and medicinal alcohol, 15–18
  overview of, xxi–xxii, 1–5
  pre-prohibition, xx, 2, 5, 8–9, 33, 110, 147
  and wines, 112
proofs, measurements of, 201–2
The Prudhomme Family Cookbook (Pruhomme), 169
Pruhomme, Paul, 169
prune juice, 69
Puerto Rican 151, 71
Pumpenheimer, 19
Punch (Wondrich), 146
Pure Cognac of 17 Underproof, 100
purity, of alcohol, 30
Pyroblast/Pyroblast syrup, 162–63
pyroligneous acid, 67, 77

Q

Quick and Dirty Orange Flower Water, 187
quintessential oils
  See essential oils

R

raisins, 30, 105, 107
Ramos Gin Fizz, 42, 134, 187
"rectified wood spirit," 86
rectifiers' manuals, 34–35
red chile flakes, 163
redistilled gin, 57
red vermouth, 119
religious exemptions, 4, 10
Remsberg, Stephen, 67
Repeal Day, 3
"Repeal of Prohibition in Practical Effect in N.Y.," San Bernardino County Sun, 52
"Report on the Supply of Spirit of Wine Free of Duty for Use in the Arts and Manufactures" (1855), 148
Reynolds, B.G., 182
Rezeptbuch für Destillateure (Göttler), 194
Richmond Planet (newspaper), 1
rich syrup, 145, 177
Rock & Rye, 84
rock candy, 84
roman numerals, 199
rose liqueur, 155
rose oil, 45, 151, 167
rose water, 42, 155, 167
rum
  añejo Havana Club rum, 76
  Appleton rum, 74
  distilling of, 67
  El Dorado rum, 74, 78
  El Presidente, 76
  essences, 48, 67, 68, 158
  Jamaican rum, 65, 119
  Lost Spirits Cuban-style rum, 71
  Low Grade Artificial Rum, 69
  maceration of, 68, 71

rum (*continued*)
Michael Lazar's Mai Tai, 74
roman numerals, Appleton rum
Rumessenz, 68
shrubs, 71, 135
Swedish Punch, 78
Twelve Mile Limit, 74
white rum, 74, 153
William Kitchiner's Mock Arrack, 78
Rumessenz, 68
rum ether
See formic ether
"rum row," 74
Rum Shrub recipe, 71
Russian Caraway, 153–54
Rye Ether, 86
rye whiskey, 74, 84–85, 110

S

sacramental wine, 4, 10, 112
saffron, 67, 69, 82, 145
saloon culture, 2, 5–6
salt, 68, 153, 181
Salt Lake Herald (newspaper), 113
Sam Ward's Recipe, 155
Sanford's Jamaica Ginger advertisement, 172
Saucier, Ted, 59
"Save the Boy!" propaganda, 132
The Savoy Cocktail Book (Craddock), 32
Schiedam
See genever
Schmidt, William, 155, 180
Schweizer Absinthöl (Swiss Absinthe Oil), 125
Scientific American (periodical), 168
Seed, Eric, 76
separatory funnel, 38
Shaker Peppermint Cordial, 178
The Shakers (United Society of Believers), 178
Shannon, Richard, 129
Sheridan Rye, 12
Shrubs (Dietsch), 71
Sidecar, 103
Sikes hydrometers, 202
Simple Caraway Vodka, 150
simple syrup, 36, 60, 66, 74–75, 103–4, 109, 143–45, 165, 170, 173
Sketches of a Tour to the Western Country (Cuming), 107
sloe gin, 57
Smith, C.P., 14
Smith, David T., 64
Smuggler's Cove, 118
smuggling, 4–5, 74
Smyth, William, 24
Snowshoe Grog, 178, 180
soda water, 66, 165
Sonnentanz, 119
Southside, 60
Spezialitäten und Geheimmittel (1906), 90
spiced tea, 78
Spice: The History of a Temptation (Turner), 28
Spinoza, Baruch, xxii
Spirit Beading, 25
spirit hydrometer, 38
spoons, 36
star anise, 143, 147, 150, 162–63, 168
star anise oil, 125, 129, 151, 165, 167
state laws on alcohol, 5
Stauch restaurant, 152
steam distillation, 42
Steele, Richard, 30
Stenson, Murray, 59
St. George Spirits, 184
still (equipment), 21, 38, 111
Stinger (1922), 181
stingers, 180–81
stomach bitters advertisement, 138
Stone, Gwydion, 129, 131, 132
Stoned dry plums, 99
The Stone Fence, 109
Stonewall Jackson, 109
strainers, 37
stretching the spirit technique, 95
Strong Tincture of Ginger, 173
sugar
and absinthe, 126–27, 130, 132
in anisettes, 168–69
in arracks, 78
and bitters, 139
and caramel, 79–80
in ciders, 107, 109–11
in cordials, 120, 141–43, 148–160, 177–78, 183, 188
and crème de menthe, 176
in ginger flavored drinks, 170–74
laws regarding, 105
and necessary gear, 36–38
in shrubs, 71
and spirit beading, 25
and syrups, 99–100, 104, 114, 143–47, 163, 189
sulfuric acid, 24–25, 45, 67
Summer cup, 118
Sunday, William "Billy," 6
sunflower petal garnish, 74
supplies, 36–38
Swedish Punch, 78
Sweet Caramel Syrup, 80
sweet spirit of nitre, 67
sweet vermouth, 118

sweet woodruff, 182–84
Syrup Charentais, 99–100
syrups
  aged, 100, 146
  Charentais, 99, 100
  and cocktails, 147
  compounder's syrup, 103, 145, 161, 167, 173, 177, 183, 189
  for cordials, 144–45
  defined, 143
  and essential oils, 144–46
  flavoring of, 146
  gomme syrup, 65, 177
  gum syrup, 147
  honey syrup, 61
  Lime Simple Syrup, 74–75
  malt syrup, 13
  measuring of, 144
  Pyroblast syrup, 162–63
  rich syrup, 145, 177
  simple syrup
  See simple syrup
  Sweet Caramel Syrup, 80

T

talcum powder, 159
taste, 27
The Tatler (newspaper), 30
tea, 27, 67, 69, 77–78, 99, 119, 121, 139, 168
temperance
  See prohibition
terpeneless oils, 41
Thomas, Jerry, 32
Tiki Oasis, 80
tonka beans, 182
Tovey, Charles, 95
Tractatus Politicus (Spinoza), xxii
Trader Vic (restaurant), 74
Traité de la Fabrication des Liqueurs et de la Distillation des Alcools (Duplais), 143
Tralles, Johann Georg, 204
Tralles scale, 203–4
travel exemption, 10–12
A Treatise on the Manufacture and Distillation of Alcoholic Liquors (Duplais), 127, 203
"Tricks of the Wine Doctor" (Barclay), 113
triple sec, 188
troy weight, 193, 198
TTB (US Alcohol and Tobacco Tax and Trade Bureau), 57
Turner, Jack, 28
Turner, John, 15
turpentine, 30, 45, 46, 47
Twain, Mark, 85
Twelve Mile Limit, 74
21st amendment, 5, 55

U

underproof (U.P.) spirits, 202
The United States Dispensatory (1845), 33
Untersuchungen über das Radikal der Benzoesäure (von Liebig and Wöhler), 28
Upshaw, William, 3
Ure, Andrew, 92
US Alcohol and Tobacco Tax and Trade Bureau (TTB), 57

V

vanilla, 68–69, 77, 151
Vanilla beans, 99
vanilla extract, 169
vanilla ice cream, 181
Vasey, S. Archibald, 39
"Vauxhall nectar," 78
Verburgt, Hubert, 167
Vermeire, Robert, 181
vermouth, dry, 60, 76, 157
Victor Lyon's Ginger Brandy recipes, 170–73
Viereck, George Sylvester, xiv, xviii–xx
vinegar, 71, 81, 101, 105, 121
violet essence, 125
vitriol oil, 24, 25
vodka, 150, 161, 167, 187–88
volatile oils
  See essential oils
Volstead, Andrew, 4, 81
Volstead Act, xx, 4, 6, 9, 17, 112, 119
  See also National Prohibition Act
volume measurement equivalents, *195*, *198*
Voronoff, Serge Abrahamovitch, 135

W

Waldmeister-Bowlenessenz (sweet woodruff), 183
Walter, Eric, 48
Ward 8, 85
Washington (DC) Evening Star (newspaper), 185
Washington, George, 107
waterbath ("bain-marie)," 168
Watterson, Henry, xviii
weight measurement equivalents, *195*, *198*
Weiss, Harry B., 109–10
whiskey
  apple, 110
  "chipped," 83
  Death's Door White Whiskey, 80
  flavored, 82
  oak barrel, 83
  Rock & Rye, 84
  rye, 74, 84–85, 110
  Ward 8, 85
white rum, 74, 153

White Trash Cooking (Mickler), 169
wholesale compounding, 22
Wiley, Harvey W., 67, 82
William Kitchiner's Mock Arrack, 78
Wilson, Woodrow, 4–5
wine distillate, 99–100
wines
  coloring of, 114
  DIY Summer Cup, 114
  history of, 112–13
  Port Wine Essence, 117
  preventing bad taste and sourness, 116
  Sonnentanz, 119
wintergreen oil, 46, 82
Winters, Lance, 184
Wöhler, Friedrich, 28
Wondrich, David, 146, 200, 201
wood alcohol poisoning, 85–88
woodruff essences, 182–84
Wormwood Society, 132
wormwood/wormwood oil, 46, 125, 127, 129, 131
Wright, Helen Saunders, 160

Y

Yankee antifreeze, 110
Yarm, Frederic, 165

Z

Zeeland cocktails, 119
zest, of citrus, 84, 103, 150, 157, 162, 189

Acknowledgments

Deaths, dying, suicide, and heartbreaking disappointment: the last year has been brutal. Friends both dear and casual lost or took their lives, marriages crumbled, and loved ones endured stomach-churning setbacks. As spring slides into summer, fresh insults continue. Working on this book through this cruel year has been a reminder that I am surrounded by kind, generous, and smart people who have shared their time, expertise, recipes, and insights with me.

Here are a few of them. If I have forgotten anyone, forgive the oversight.

Thanks first to my editor at Countryman Press, Ann Treistman. When Ann asked if I wanted to write another moonshine book, I deflected the question. She was game enough to take on this one instead. For their most excellent photography, I am indebted to John Schulz and Daniel Fishel of StudioSchulz in San Diego. And to designer Nick Caruso who turned my meandering discussion of the nadir of beverage arts in American history to the gorgeous book in your hands. My agent Lisa Ekus advised, guided, and arranged so much while Sally Ekus and everyone else at the Lisa Ekus Group pitched in to make this manuscript happen.

Rare books expert Charles Keller offered advice on Lyon's original handwritten notebook while Will Elsbury, Military History Specialist at the United States Library of Congress, tracked down esoteric historic information. Sushan Chin, archivist at The New York University School of Medicine, provided some background material on der unsichtbare Mann, Victor Lyon, while librarian Nancy Kervin helped with materials in the US Senate collections and Rebecca Johnson Melvin uncovered Viereck material at the University of Delaware. At the University of California, Davis Axel Borg, special collections archivist Liz Phillips, Thomas Collins, and Lynne Kimsey, director of the Bohart Entomological Museum, all shared the time and expertise.

Distillers and fermenters Gwydion Stone, Dave Smith, Lance Winters, Dan Farber, Hubert Germain-Robin, Maggie Campbell, Chip Tate, Michael Skubic, Mike McCaw, Carl Sutton, and Robert Birnecker graciously offered various technical, historical, and translation assistance. Bartenders and servers Scott Beattie, Jacob Grier, Bobby Heugel, Tommy Klus, Katie Loeb, Jeff Morgenthaler, Ethan Ostrander, Stephen Shellenberger, Matt Van Wagner, Audrey Saunders, Gaz Regan, Michael Lazar, Vipop Jinaphan, and Frederic Yarm provided recipes and directions for various concoctions. Amy Stewart (*The Drunken Botanist*), who knows her way around a poisonous plant or two, lent a hand flagging some of the more problematic botanicals in the old notebook.

Melinda Huff at Cynmar Corporation provided lab equipment that made much of this work faster and more efficient. Canadian chemist, author, and bartender Darcy O'Neil generously provided samples of some of the more esoteric compounds I used to test these and other compounding formulas. Thanks also to cocktail historian Ted Haigh for insight into liquor adulteration, Greg Boehm for sharing scans from his collection, and Dave Arnold for liquor manipulation ideas.

Otto von Stroheim at Tiki Oasis and the staff of Denver's Museum of Contemporary Art invited me to use their audiences as guinea pigs for some initial vetting of the topics in this book; thank you all. In Berkeley, perfumer Mandy Aftel vetted my ideas on essential oils while "Professor" Steve Remsberg, Jeff "Beachbum" Berry, and Luis Ayala gave insight into historic and contemporary rum fakery. Blair Reynolds of BG Reynolds Syrups provided samples of his woodruff syrup — and inspired me to plant a load of Waldmeister in our California garden. In Emeryville over mezcal and hops, Adam Rogers of *Wired* magazine humored me while I teased apart ideas. Back in San Diego, Ryan Morris organized my notes, transcriptions, and translations, a project that had stymied others.

Above all, there was the man who has been at my side for more than twenty years, Tim Furnish. Without his unwavering encouragement, Victor Lyon's old notebook might still be tucked away in my library seeming for all the world like a dreary old book of questionable poetry.